CATHOLIC
ROOTS
MORMON
HARVEST

CATHOLIC
R O O T S
MORMON
H A R V E S T

A STORY OF CONVERSION AND 40 COMPARATIVE DOCTRINES

ERIC SHUSTER

CFI
Springville, Utah

ISBN 13: 978-1-59955-257-6

Published by CFI, an imprint of Cedar Fort, Inc., 2373 W. 700 S., Springville, UT 84663
Distributed by Cedar Fort, Inc., www.cedarfort.com

LIBRARY OF CONGRESS CATALOGING-IN-PUBLICATION DATA

Shuster, Eric, 1962-
  Catholic roots, Mormon harvest / Eric Shuster.
    p. cm.
  ISBN 978-1-59955-257-6
  1. Church of Jesus Christ of Latter-day Saints--Doctrines. 2. Catholic
Church--Doctrines. 3. Shuster, Eric, 1962- 4. Shuster, Marilyn, 1954- 5.
Mormon converts--Biography. 6. Ex-church members--Catholic
Church--Biography. 7. Conversion--Church of Jesus Christ of Latter-day
Saints. I. Title.

  BX8635.3.S58 2009
  230'.93--dc22

2009002827

Cover design by Jen Boss
Cover design © 2009 by Lyle Mortimer
Edited and typeset by Melissa J. Caldwell

Printed in the United States of America

10 9 8 7 6 5 4 3 2 1

Printed on acid-free paper

Dedicated to my beautiful wife and eternal companion, Marilyn—whose love, devotion, and inspiration have been a constant source of strength and happiness in my life.

Contents

Foreword

C*ATHOLIC Roots, Mormon Harvest* is the story of sincerity in search of religious truth. In this book, Marilyn and Eric Shuster give a compelling and personal account of their quest for spiritual fulfillment. They tell of the hard work required to challenge their own scripting. They tell of the difficulties they encountered in confronting a lifetime of tradition and warm family and cultural ties as they moved forward in their quest. In the end, they tell of a great discovery: the discovery that their Catholic roots contained much that is good, wholesome, and enduring, and which at the same time prepared them for the rich Mormon harvest.

The Shusters make it clear that their roots are Catholic. The two were devoted and knowledgeable Catholics, not casual church-goers. Their Catholicism was woven joyfully into the fabric of their lives. They were reluctant to be introduced to The Church of Jesus Christ of Latter-day Saints, but this reluctance faded as they learned step-by-step that all the Catholic threads in their spiritual lives did not have to be pulled out before the Mormon threads could be woven in. Having made this discovery, they built upon the foundation of their Catholicism and moved forward in their quest. They carried with them the goodness acquired in their Catholic upbringing into their conversion into Mormonism. In short, they added to their existing faith in order to acquire greater faith.

Catholic Roots, Mormon Harvest is about change with all its grinding inconsistencies and inconveniences. It is the story of a pilgrimage, and the joy and fulfillment found along the way. Most of all, it is an account of faith and struggle, growth and inquiry, intellectual courage and challenge.

Among the most basic and universal of human predispositions is the desire—nay, the need!—to believe, to identify, and to establish our relationship with God, and therefore, to infuse meaning into our mortal existence. Finding meaning in life constitutes one of life's greatest struggles, and as wayfarers on the road to meaning, we walk many different paths: some cling to philosophy, others to varied personal belief systems, still others to "organized religion," which so often (almost always?) documents its beliefs structures and wisdom literature in print. Thus have been born holy books such as the Koran, the Bhagavad Gita, and the Bible, for example.

In the Christian community, the Bible generally claims a sacred position, though opinions vary as to its true meaning. The Shusters, for their part, make it clear that it was through their deep affection for the Bible that they came to embrace the Book of Mormon. The Bible filled them with a love for truth—"Rock-solid-diamond truth," as Mr. Shuster puts it. The Bible taught them about the mission, ministry, and sacrifice of the foreordained Christ; it gave them a love for the teachings of the apostles and prophets; and it enhanced their understanding of the great good that institutions can do by mobilizing around biblical teachings. Eric says the Bible provided him with a "vocabulary for interacting with deity." The Holy Bible was in these and other ways the foundation, the launching pad that instilled hope; the Book of Mormon became, in the Shusters' experience, the upright structure, the powerful ballistic, that stood upon that foundation and conferred ultimate confidence.

Mr. Shuster's book is a serious history of search and struggle, of comparing and contrasting doctrine with doctrine. Therefore, it is to some degree a scholarly work. The author proceeds logically and carefully. The narrative is well-documented and clearly argued. However, Mr. Shuster does not revisit the arcane disputes "resolved" at the Council of Nicaea, the quarrel over homoousios, the Donatist Controversy, and other matters of interest to the writers of religious histories. Nor does he stir the muddy waters downstream from these events. Instead, he goes directly to the Source, the Living Waters of the Spirit, to frame his questions and offer his answers. Mr. Shuster argues that God speaks directly to our souls through that same "still small voice" that guided and comforted Elijah. Having learned from the teachings of his Catholic beginnings—teachings that told of prophets and angels, of visions and miracles, of men and women made holy by internalizing doctrines and receiving ordinances—Shuster tells us of his discovery of the fulfillment of those teachings in the doctrines and practices of The Church of Jesus Christ of Latter-day Saints.

The skeptical reader might ask with some alarm, "Angels in this day? Visions, revelations, and miracles anew? Spiritual experiences such as those enjoyed by the ancient Saints—now, in our own time? Gold plates, the Urim and Thummim, and the inspired translation of ancient texts into modern scripture? John the Baptist, Peter, James, John, Moses, Elias, Elijah, Michael, Gabriel and others, all appearing and empowering men in this day? The actual appearance of God the Father and His Son to a young truth-seeking boy in Palmyra, Ontario County, in the state of New York?"

Many despair and turn away when they are told of such things. Others chuckle smugly at such "childish imaginings."

Mr. Shuster's humble response runs as a sustaining theme throughout his book: Truth is Truth, however much it may shock and offend when first presented. This shock and offense are softened when one remembers that with God all things are possible. For the Deity who created viruses and galaxies and all things in between, such manifestations would be trivial. It is the faith of men that limits, not the powers of the Almighty.

This is a safe book. People of all faiths—or of no faith at all—can read it and be enriched. It is not polemical. It is not a grand argument. The Shusters bare their souls and tell us of their search for plain and precious truths. In a world bloated with a confusion of choices, their search is everyone's search.

Mark L. McConkie
Professor, University of Colorado

Preface

Born into strong Catholic families, Marilyn and I were raised in the beauty and wonderment of the Catholic Church. We attended Catholic schools, rarely missed liturgical celebrations, and led passionately Catholic lives.

Marilyn chose the path of becoming a Franciscan nun, obtaining a degree in Catholic theology, working for a parish and then a diocese, making scripture reading and prayer a key part of her life.

I chose the path of being active in the Catholic music ministry, being director of the Big Brothers and Big Sisters organization for my parish, considering seriously the Catholic priesthood, participating in youth and young adult Catholic ministries, and enjoying regular prayer.

Marilyn and I met at a Catholic young adult retreat where we were both leaders trying to help our brothers and sisters find a greater depth of spirituality. We later married in the Catholic Church, raised our family in an active Catholic lifestyle, had our first son baptized Catholic, and maintained an active role in our parish ministries.

While we harbored concerns for our beloved Catholicism, we never considered leaving the Catholic faith, a faith in which we had grown up and had dedicated our lives to. The Catholic Church was our home, our identity, and the center of our lives. We had no thought that this would ever change.

But change it did, beginning with our move next door to a Latter-day Saint family who showed us a level of Christianity we had never before seen. Their examples of service, faith in the Lord Jesus Christ, and family unity touched our hearts and motivated us to learn more. After many months of study, prayer, and inspiration from the Holy Ghost, we entered into the waters of baptism and became members of The Church of Jesus Christ of Latter-day Saints.

This is our story, in our own words, of our conversion to the Latter-day Saint faith. Here we share with you the highs and the lows, the joys and the tribulations. This story includes our comparison of the doctrines of the Catholic Church and The Church of Jesus Christ of Latter-day Saints—many of which we compared before we were baptized, and others we have done since that time.

Our story is not one of disillusionment with Catholicism that drove us away from the faith, but rather one of having found something more that prompted us to change. We did not come to our decision because we had been failed by the Catholic Church, or because we had failed as Catholics. Rather, our taking the path we did was an extension of our Catholic upbringing and experience, and this extension became a marvelous transformation. It is this transformation—not any negative feelings toward the Catholic Church—that we wish to share with you.

We have lost nothing and gained everything in this transformation. All that is good, uplifting, pure, and beautiful in Catholicism we have brought with us. Our journey, like yours, will continue into the eternities. As Latter-day Saints, our knowledge of where we came from, why we are here, and where we are going is continually growing. We are maximizing our faith in the Lord Jesus Christ, while offering our family the fulness of the gospel as a map in mortality to help us return to our Heavenly Father. This is the meaning and purpose of The Church of Jesus Christ of Latter-day Saints.

Wherever you may be in your spiritual journey, we pray that the inspiration of the Holy Ghost will be yours as you read about our journey and the unspeakable joy that it has brought to us and to our family. May this joy also be yours.

Acknowledgments

Many people contributed to this book in many ways. It is not possible for me to name them all here. A few, I am sure, have drifted from memory. Others contributed in ways not easily expressed, and so must go unnamed. You know who you are; please accept my sincere thanks. A few stand out. To them I send these special thanks:

To Marilyn, my wife, my eternal companion. She supported me, stood by me, and made significant contributions to the content of this book. She was my companion throughout our religious journey and throughout the sometimes grinding work of reporting it here. Without her, this book could not have been written.

To my children Jason, Dee Dee, and Ryan for believing in their dad and bringing me the love, joy, and challenges I need to grow and have happiness in mortality.

To my extended family—especially my mother and father—for their love, dedication, and involvement in my life, helping to mold and shape the person I am today.

To Charles Sale, my dear friend and editor. He tested my thoughts, challenged my assertions, and edited my writing. He helped me say what I intended to say, and he dedicated himself to my completion of this book. Without his skillful editing, the outcome of this work would have been uncertain. He made it certain.

To Dr. Ken Knapp, the most devout and dedicated Catholic I know— for his direction, encouragement, suggestions, and friendship.

To Hartmut Woerrlein, my best friend and a prolific author, who believes in me and was an inspiration from the very start.

To Alex Kalamarides, my business partner and close friend, who constantly challenges me intellectually and motivates me to a greater level of excellence.

How to Use This Book

THIS book is meant to be both a story about our journey in conversion, as well as a reference text on the doctrinal comparisons between the Catholic Church and The Church of Jesus Christ of Latter-day Saints—which I will often refer to as "both churches." This book is meant to speak to Catholics and Latter-day Saints alike, attempting to bridge understanding and respectfully share facts and commentary.

As a Catholic Reader

You may be of the Catholic faith, perhaps given this book by a Latter-day Saint friend who desires for you to know more about the their religion. Or perchance you may be curious as to why someone would leave the rich traditions of the Catholic Church to join a religion that seems to you to be elusive, obscure, and out of the mainstream. Or it's possible you simply want to know about some of the doctrinal differences and similarities between both churches for your own edification. In all cases this book can satisfy your endeavor.

As a non-Catholic Reader

You may be a Latter-day Saint, or someone from another religion, who desires to know more about the Catholic Church or The Church of Jesus Christ of Latter-day Saints. You may wonder how someone might convert from one to the other. Perhaps you desire to know the differences in beliefs between the two churches in order to broaden your own understanding. No matter the case, this book will illuminate these subjects for you.

Reading This as a Storybook

You may elect to read this book as a story from cover to cover just as you would a novel. If you choose to do so, you will be guided through our backgrounds from our early childhoods, to the time of our marriage, and how we came in contact with The Church of Jesus Christ of Latter-day Saints. The book then chronicles the details of our eighteen-month expedition from a newly married couple, active in the Catholic religion, to our baptism into the Latter-day Saint faith. We provide details into the events of the investigation and intimate insights in the ups and downs we experienced along the way.

Following our conversion story, and a word or two about doctrinal preparation, I'll walk you through a comparison of a selection of key doctrines of the Catholic Church and how those compare to those of The Church of Jesus Christ of Latter-day Saints. These comparisons follow a fairly logical order and flow, which will allow for a story-like sequence for you as the reader.

Reading This as a Reference Text

You may elect to treat this book as a reference text by skipping around from one section to another, diving into selected comparisons on an ad hoc basis. We've done our best to order each section into a logical flow, with one section often building upon the understanding from one or more of the previous sections. As such, there are a few times when the doctrines presented in one section assume the reader has read a previous section and comprehended the content accordingly.

In order to enhance your flexibility in ad hoc navigation of the book I'll attempt to highlight when previous sections are being leveraged so as to make it easy for you to locate the required content for review.

1

Our Conversion Story

WE begin with a story of religious conversion—a particular and very personal religious conversion. It is an account of the journey I took with my wife, Marilyn Williams Shuster, from our deep roots in the Catholic Church to our ultimate fulfillment and harvest in The Church of Jesus Christ of Latter-day Saints.

I have sought to give this account in a way that might inspire others to take a similar journey—if not from the same place as ours began or to the same destination, then at least to a deeper understanding of who they are, why they are here, and where they are going.

Eric's Background

I was born in 1962 in San Jose, California, as the second youngest of four boys and two girls. My mother was raised Catholic, and my father converted to Catholicism shortly before they were married in 1950. My parents were devout Catholics during my early years, with my dad being an active member of the Knights of Columbus, and my mom and dad both frequently volunteering in the parishes we attended. I was fortunate to have an excellent example of Catholicism growing up.

My father worked as a systems engineer for two different defense contractors, while maintaining active-duty status in the United States Air Force reserve, retiring as a lieutenant colonel. Dad flew both single-engine fighters and multi-engine cargo planes and fit the typical profile of a commander who believed in strict discipline and hard work.

My father was a pioneer in the field of computers, an intellectually brilliant man who always provided well for our material needs. Although

1

he struggled with alcoholism for many years, creating strife for our family, my dad finally overcame his regular drinking shortly before my wife and I were married in November 1987.

Despite his struggles with alcoholism, there was never a question as to my dad's love for me and our family. He was always doing something for someone else, was involved in many activities in the community, and served as a solid example of service for my family and me. There isn't a man alive that I love more than my father.

My mother is an identical twin. She was raised during World War II and lived for a time in Korea when her father was stationed there as an officer in the military. My mother had, and still has, a keen sense of business and a strong financial mind. Once my siblings and I were old enough to fend for ourselves at home, she went to work as a bookkeeper in the private sector before settling on a job with a local Catholic Church during my teenage years.

Our parish at that time had a Catholic college preparatory school that I attended my junior and senior years of high school. Mother tended to the bookkeeping of the parish and worked regularly with finance officials of the San Francisco Diocese. Mother worked for the Catholic Church long enough to earn a full retirement for a job well done. My mother is a remarkable lady, whose intelligence, patience, and ability to endure left a deep impression on me.

My brothers and sisters all followed very different paths in their lives, each making choices that led them all away from the Catholic Church to one degree or another.

The journey I chose was somewhat different than that of my siblings. In my early youth, sports became my primary outlet. I enjoyed the activity, but particularly the feeling of happiness I felt when my parents attended my games. In addition to sports, I was deeply interested in spiritual matters, and regularly attended church and catechism in my early years. There was a comfort for me in being in church.

I vividly remember riding my bike to Mass at the nearby Catholic church on a Sunday morning when I was in the seventh grade. I made it a priority to attend Mass each Sunday and pray that our football team would win our games. That season our football team won only one of eleven games. I took this as a sign that God did not concern himself with football, or at least pee-wee football!

I also had an interest in playing guitar. My eldest sister was a professional musician, who also toured as a leader of a folk music group early in her career. My sister taught me the basics of guitar, and I learned the rest on my own. Regrettably, I never pursued formal musical training.

Despite my commitment to sports and music, I had my first experience with alcohol at age fifteen, and I continued to drink throughout out my high school and young adult years. Despite the choices I made, I never turned my back on attending the Catholic Church. In my own way, I always felt cleansed of any sins committed during the week when I walked into church on Sunday.

Concerned for my well-being, my parents took me out of the public school system in my junior year of high school and placed me in the Catholic college preparatory school where my mother worked. Although I at first thought I had died and gone to hell (or at least purgatory) with all of the added homework, I soon discovered the kids were not that different and I found a new comfort zone.

During my junior and senior year of high school, I fell in love with a young woman and experienced the ups and downs of teenage romance. During this time I was counseled by a parish priest during monthly confessions to consider the well-being of my girlfriend and try to refrain from inappropriate activity. I was left with the impression that I needed to try my best, but not necessarily that I was committing a grave sin that needed to be stopped immediately. The counsel was confusing.

Despite any challenges I had with my social life, I earned the Saint Joseph's award for community service and was a member of the local Big Brothers and Big Sisters organization. During this period I yearned for spiritual happiness, but was also drawn into a life of fun and games, including playing in rock bands and the life that went along with it. I didn't see a need to reconcile the two; it was far easier to just keep moving forward and hope the two would never clash.

I graduated from high school in 1980 and attended San Jose State University to pursue a degree in industrial management engineering. I worked full time for a high-tech company in the Silicon Valley and went to school at night while living at home.

The switch to college brought about several changes in my life: My focus on a career in the high-tech industry took center stage; my girlfriend and I split up; I left the band and formed a Christian folk group at the Catholic Church; my father and I built a recording studio in my parents garage; and my involvement with the Big Brothers and Big Sisters increased to the point where I was appointed director of the organization.

I also taught myself the drums and piano and began writing and recording music on a regular basis. In short, I was growing up.

In 1986 I graduated from college with an engineering degree and accepted a job with Compaq Computer Corporation, then a small computer company in Houston, Texas. Eventually, Compaq became the largest PC manufacturer in the world, and I rode the wave of the computer industry as a young professional. The move from the Silicon Valley of California to Houston, Texas, allowed me to grow outside the shadow of my family, while tempering my exposure to the active drug and alcohol scene of the Silicon Valley. Moving away from California to Houston would prove to be one of the best decisions of my life.

My new-found freedom allowed me to focus more fully on my professional career and a budding interest in Catholic youth and young adult ministry. In March 1987, while on a Catholic young adult retreat in Madisonville, Texas, I met my wife, Marilyn, who was the Associate Director of Youth and Young Adult Ministry for the Houston-Galveston Diocese of Texas. In addition to being an attractive woman, I was fascinated by the fact that Marilyn was a former Franciscan nun, and held a degree in Catholic theology from a prestigious Catholic university in Houston. Although attracted to me as well (as I found out later), Marilyn felt I was too young for her and chose not to date me, despite my frequent invitations.

In what became a relentless pursuit of her affection, I requested her help on a regular basis with the young adult events going on in our parish. I admitted to her later that I made up a few of those events in order to spend time with her. During the two months or so that I was finding excuses to get Marilyn involved with our parish, she consistently refused to meet with me over dinner, or do anything with me that might be considered a date. I learned later that she was secretly pondering a more serious relationship with me.

One evening Marilyn and I met at her office to discuss a possible liturgical ceremony for the young adults of my parish. It was just us two and a Domino's pizza. We never talked much about the young adult event. I formulated a strategy for the end of the evening that would help me understand where our relationship was going. Determined to bring an end to the mystery, I decided it was time for a kiss.

If she refused, I might receive a slap in the face, but I would at least have confirmation of it being time to move on; if she accepted, I would have validation of it being time to pursue a more serious relationship.

We kissed, I did not get slapped, and on our first official date a week later—she having just returned from a retreat in Arkansas—I asked Marilyn to marry me. Her answer was a simple, "What took you so long?"

Having to wait at least six months to get married in the Catholic Church, we began taking pre-marriage classes designed to help us get to know one another. A former priest of over twenty-five years and a former nun of over twenty years were the couple assigned to be our sponsors. They had met in New Mexico during a church-sponsored event and decided to leave their vocations and get married. It was extremely enlightening to have such a couple teach us about marriage. Both were extremely devoted to the Catholic faith and found deep meaning in their decades of service as a priest and nun. They were also excited to be husband and wife in this new chapter of their lives.

Shortly before Marilyn and I were married, we purchased a home in Magnolia, Texas. The home was more like a mini-ranch, with nearly three acres of land and a barn for Marilyn's horse, a mare that was expected to foal a few months later. In November of 1987 we were married at Christ the Good Shepherd Catholic Church in Spring, Texas.

We were excited about our fixer-upper home in the country and about the new life we were starting together. Little did we know that living next door was a family that would change our lives forever.

Marilyn's Background
as told by Marilyn Shuster

I was born on October 24, 1954 in Tulsa, Oklahoma, into a Catholic family of eight children (five boys and three girls). My father was raised Catholic, while my mother was raised Baptist and then converted to Catholicism at the time of her marriage. My family growing up can easily be described as staunchly Catholic, from our unwavering commitment to attending church each week, to the involvement of my parents and siblings in a variety of church-related activities, including Catholic school attendance.

As a youngster I attended Saint Pius the Tenth Catholic School through sixth grade, and then, for family economic reasons, I transferred to and attended public schools for the remainder of my grade-school education in Tulsa. From my earliest recollections, I can remember being drawn to and having a great love for the religious traditions of the

Catholic Church, including midnight Mass at Christmas, stations of the cross at Lent, Ash Wednesday and Palm Sunday, the May Crowning of the Virgin Mary, Easter egg hunts at the church, and many other religious celebrations. This was both a psychological and spiritual staple for me growing up.

Although my family and I always seemed to have an inclination toward religion, that inclination took a backseat to the everyday challenges of life during my high school years. It was the late 1960s and early 1970s where war protests, flower power, and the hippie movement were in force all around us. Although I experimented with elements of the movement, I stayed clear of the more serious issues that plagued many during this tumultuous period.

Out of economic necessity, at age fifteen I began working at a local retail store in Tulsa. Keeping a regular work schedule injected an added element of responsibility in me, and when combined with my general religious inclination and conservative nature, helped me to remain honest and not delve too far into the societal trappings of the day. I can remember feeling the pangs of consciousness from time to time during these teenage years, having been taught sufficiently the difference between right and wrong, and being pricked in my soul when choosing to make unwise decisions.

At one point I moved into a house with my sister Therese, who had always been a good person, never having smoked, drank alcohol, or experimented with drugs. Living with Therese was positive—it provided me motivation to move away from these destructive things in my life.

One night when I was feeling the weight of my life's choices, I knelt down alone in my room and pleaded with the Lord that I would do anything he asked if he would just help me overcome my guilt. It was the most sincere prayer of my life to that time, offered in desperation by one desiring freedom from the bondage of sin. After beseeching my Savior for divine intervention, I can remember feeling what appeared to be a blanket of peace wash over me, filling my whole being with great joy. The feeling was so overwhelming that it brought me to tears and caused me to sob for what seemed like hours.

With this spark of spiritual motivation, I found a small pocket-sized King James New Testament Bible that someone had given me long ago that I hung onto (not knowing why). Holding the small book in the palm of my hand, I opened it and began to read. I found myself feasting from the words of the Bible as if I had emerged from a famine that lasted for many years. I couldn't get enough of the words that flowed from the pages of the book into my soul. Reading consumed all of my waking hours as I experienced the peace and joy I so longed and pleaded for from the Lord, which came minute by minute through each and every verse.

One might say that on that night, and the ensuing time shortly afterwards, I was born again. My soul had been awakened by the word of the Lord and I felt like a changed person. I felt true and sincere joy for the first time in my life. My sister Therese noticed the change and one night questioned me on the subject. I can remember turning to her and telling her that all the answers to life's questions could be found in the scriptures and that I had found a buried treasure. In bearing my testimony of this discovery, I realized that I was indeed a changed person from a spiritual standpoint.

I started going back to the Catholic Church on a regular basis. My love of singing motivated me to join the choir, where the choir director and his wife, Pat and Cheryl Teague, took me in and became my spiritual directors. Pat and I would spend many hours talking about spiritual matters and how they related to me in my own life. My heart and soul needed so much healing, and I came to realize that only the Lord could provide the healing that I so desperately needed. This was an extremely tender time for me and the Lord provided me the necessary support to find rest from the world.

Through these spiritual experiences I found the strength to rid myself of all of the physical issues facing me, except smoking. At the time it seemed to be the least of my worries, having gone through so much change in a short period of time. One day I was reading from Paul's first letter to the Corinthians, chapter six verse nineteen, which states: "Know ye not that your body is the temple of the Holy Ghost which is in you, which ye have of God, and ye are not your own?" Upon reading this scripture I was pierced in the heart with the sharpness of this wonderful truth! From that very moment, I never picked up another cigarette again, nor did I ever experience a craving for nicotine from that time forward. This was truly a miracle, as several times before I had tried to quit and was never able to overcome the physical and psychological cravings associated with cigarettes. The difference this time around was that I was relying on the Lord and He was blessing me in this righteous endeavor.

As a Catholic having rid myself of bodily addictions, and having developed a fervent desire to read the scriptures and spend considerable time in prayer, I felt a compelling need to give back to the Lord and serve Him in some greater way. The answer, I felt, was the Lord calling me to the religious life as a nun. Perhaps it was what I needed at the time, or perhaps I was trying to escape the world. For whatever reason, I felt compelled to follow the prompting and began looking into different sister communities and religious orders to learn more about the religious life.

I visited several orders, one being the Sisters of the Sorrowful Mother, a community of nuns who followed a Franciscan rule. I was particularly partial to this order, having developed a great love for Saint Francis of Assisi, the patron saint of animals and the ecology, who lived and ministered during the thirteenth century. During one of my visits with the leaders of this sisterhood, while listening to an overview of the community, I heard a man's voice tell me "go with them." I immediately turned around to see who it was, but there were no men in the room, only sisters. I accepted this experience as a clear manifestation from the Lord to join the Sisters of Sorrowful Mother. And so, at twenty-three years old I made all of the necessary arrangements to commit my life as a servant of the Lord as a Franciscan nun in the Catholic religious life. My mother and father were both delighted, while other members of my family were somewhat indifferent to my decision.

My four years in the convent as a postulant, and then as a novice nun, was a time of reflection, study, healing, and spiritual growth. During this period I was given ample time for scripture study, prayer, and service in a variety of capacities. Our order was dedicated to rendering medical service in the greater Tulsa community by operating Saint John's Hospital among other things. I found myself volunteering at the hospital as a nurse's aid, something which I had been interested in for quite some time. Later on I realized that nursing was not my gift, so I turned my attention toward teaching. On the surface it appeared that I found exactly what I was looking for in the Franciscan order.

In 1980 I moved to Texas as part of the order to study at the University of Saint Thomas, a well-known and respected Catholic university in Houston. My goal was to receive a Bachelor of Arts in Catholic Theology, which I intended to use to teach Catholic school and to be a spiritual director at some point in my religious career. While pursuing my studies, I continued as a nun living in Houston. At this time I also began to pursue more seriously my love of art, not only studying art in college, but also doing an occasional contract painting or a painting for friends or family.

In spite of my zeal for the life that I was living, over time the utopian religious world that I had created began to show signs of strain and imperfection as I experienced a number of things that slowly led me away from the thought of a religious life as a nun. Some of the very things that I was trying to escape from were quite prevalent within the convent—mainly alcohol and off-color jokes. To add to my encroaching anxieties, I observed some of the sisters being closer with one another than I felt comfortable with. Although I wasn't familiar with homosexual behaviors at that point of my life, the possibilities made me uncomfortable and caused me to further question my vocation. Amidst these worries, I had ever increasing thoughts of future marriage which I knew could never happen if I was to remain a nun. Despite the anxieties I was feeling over the possibilities of life in a religious order, my love for the Savior and the Catholic faith never wavered during this tender time of my life

After four years in the convent as "Sister Marilyn," I was granted a dispensation to leave the convent, putting an to my pursuit of final vows as a nun. However, I remained committed to my studies of Catholic Theology and the pursuit of service within the Catholic Church. In 1983 I graduated Magna Cum Lade with a Bachelor of Arts in Catholic Theology, with a minor in Art.

Shortly after graduation I accepted a job as the youth minister for the Prince of Peace Catholic Church in Spring, Texas. This thanks to a glowing recommendation letter from the bishop to the parishes of the Diocese of Galveston-Houston on my behalf. It was at Prince of Peace, at the tender age of twenty-nine, that I started my career in Catholic Youth Ministry, with the vision of making a difference in the lives of youth and young adults within the Catholic Church.

My experience at Prince of Peace was mixed. I quickly grew to love the youth of the parish and was excited about the opportunity to work with them and their parents on spiritual growth and education. With the zeal of a convert I tackled my new job with enthusiasm and energy. Tempering my wonderful experiences at this parish was a pastor struggled with alcoholism, and his eventual successor who later abruptly departed to marry the rectory's secretary. These were eye-opening experiences for me that left a lasting impression, although not serious enough for me to consider leaving the Church that I loved and was dedicating my life of service to.

Although I was proud of the work we accomplished with the youth of the parish, a key frustration of mine was the lack of involvement of parents in the ministry and in the spiritual lives of their youth. So much of what we taught the youth as part of our youth ministry program was rarely reinforced in the home. Looking back twenty years later, it is easy to me to understand the dismal results reported on Catholic youth in the book *Soul Searching, The Religious and Spiritual Lives of American Teenagers*, which highlights findings of the National Study of Youth and Religion conducted from 2001 to 2005.

Following my parish experience, desiring to minister at the diocese level, I left Prince of Peace and accepted a job working as the Associate Director of Youth Ministry for the Diocese of Galveston-Houston. The office was under the direction of Sister Carol Wagner, a Dominican nun and bundle of energy who was strongly committed to youth ministry. Our group was commissioned to serve the youth leaders of the surrounding parishes, including the training of youth ministers, organizing youth conferences, and facilitating a variety of events within the diocese. To keep pace we traveled the globe to be trained in youth ministry techniques, acquire foreign language skills, and to interact with other Catholic youth leaders. During this period I was able to earn the coveted *Certificate in Youth Ministry Studies* from the Diocese of Galveston-Houston, the University of Saint Thomas, and the Center for Youth Ministry Development.

My work with the diocese was far more enjoyable and rewarding than what I had experienced at the parish level. Besides the opportunity to be involved in a broader ministry, I no longer had to worry about the parents of the youth and the constant frustration of their absence in the spiritual lives of their children. However, although I could escape dealing directly with that subject at the diocese level, I spent a good amount of time listening to parish youth ministers talk about the same issue.

Another challenge among the parishes at the time was lack of priesthood involvement in youth ministry. Priests were often too busy with other parish duties to get involved in youth activities and frequently delegated such involvement to salaried youth ministers, who were normally overworked and underpaid.

In addition to youth ministry, our office was also chartered with organizing and facilitating a formal young adult ministry in each of the parishes. Young adults were considered those Catholics who were single and over eighteen years of age. This ministry was particularly challenging, but one that I strongly related to given the earlier experiences of my life, the radical conversion I had in my early twenties, and the fact that I was a single adult myself.

Although one might read of my experiences in Catholic Church leadership and think I had every right to be disenchanted, the fact was that my disappointment was met with an equal or greater desire to strive for change within the Church. I worked with exceptionally dedicated individuals, and associated with other Catholic lay people, who were passionately committed to driving out the bad and highlighting the good. We were united by a union of faith to move forward because we loved the Catholic Church and felt God was present in the work we were doing.

The journey from my conversion and the dedicating of my life to the Lord at twenty-three years old, to working for the Catholic diocese as the Associate Director of Youth Ministry at age thirty was one of ups and downs. The exhilaration of feeling the Spirit of the Lord, breaking the bondage of sin, and finding spiritual direction were some of the greatest and most significant events of my life. This joy was mixed with disappointment, false expectations, and grief over the state of the Church that I had dedicated my life to. Not knowing anything better, I chose to press on.

In March 1987, while on a Catholic young adult retreat in Madison-ville, Texas, I met my eternal companion, Eric. Despite Eric was serving as a leader in the young adult group at the time, we didn't have an opportunity to meet during the retreat planning meetings and therefore, met on the retreat. Eric spoke to the group on faith and friendship, sharing with the group his bout with substance abuse. I was impressed by his strength and character and wanted to know more about him. It was a great weekend, sharing lots of time with Eric, while ministering to the other young adults in our group.

Shortly after the retreat Eric called me, asking if we could go out on a date. I was already working hard (perhaps too hard) on an existing relationship and didn't feel it was appropriate for me to see Eric. In addition to that, being eight years older than Eric I felt he was too young and that I was ready for a more serious relationship and didn't think that a relationship with such a large age difference would work out. Because of that, I turned Eric's date invitations down, but kept in touch with him.

Undaunted, Eric continued to call and chat, throwing in an occasional invitation to lunch, dinner, or something else that he could think up. I enjoyed my time on the phone with Eric, as he always made me laugh and seemed to bring out the best in me. Although I wouldn't go out on a date with him, Eric would arrange times for us to meet to discuss young adult activities within his parish.

One evening Eric and I met at my office to discuss "another young adult activity" for his parish. Eric brought a pizza with him and we passed the time talking about everything but the activity. We had fun as the time passed quickly, and before we knew it, it was time to go home. Much to my surprise, at the end of the evening and before getting into my car, Eric kissed me. It may sound cliché, but that moment seemed to literally stand still. I wanted him to kiss me, but when it happened, I still wasn't prepared for it. I knew then that I had some decisions to make and would use a retreat I was going on the next week in Arkansas to do that.

An hour later that same evening, Eric called and asked if he could come by and give me something before my departure on the retreat. He drove the fifty miles to my home from his home in Spring, Texas, to give me seven self-addressed and stamped post cards, saying: "Perhaps you can write me every day during your retreat." I came to know that this was vintage Eric, coming up with something creative and out-of-the-blue to surprise even the most suspecting of people. We parted and I made my way up to Arkansas.

During the retreat I prayed about Eric and what that the Lord wanted me to do about our relationship. It was a peaceful time for me and one in which I felt the Lord directing me to see more of Eric. The relationship I was currently involved in was going nowhere, and it was clear to me that I was developing strong feelings for Eric. I diligently wrote Eric each day by using the post cards he gave to me, sketching pictures on each one to convey some of my thoughts I had each day of the retreat. I couldn't wait to get back and talk to him.

On the night of our first date, Eric asked me to marry him, to which I replied: "What took you so long?" I knew that I wanted to be with Eric, and that the Lord wanted us to be together. About eight months later, we were married at Christ the Good Shepherd Catholic Church in Spring, Texas, with Sister Carol Wagner as my maid of honor. During the ceremony Eric and I exchanged the vows that we wrote to one another, both proclaiming that we would be together forever in heaven, even after our death, and would never part as a couple. Although we accepted our ceremony would be "until death do you part," our writing into our vows a more eternal perspective made us feel a greater happiness and hope. We had no idea at the time that being together for all eternity as man and wife was possible—not through the priesthood that married us in the Catholic Church, but through the sealing powers of the priesthood in the holy temple. It was sometime later that we learned about this glorious gospel truth and realized our desire of being together forever was possible.

Shortly before Eric and I were married we purchased a home in Magnolia, Texas. The home was cute, needed a lot of work, and most important had a barn for my Arabian horse, who was pregnant at the time.

We were excited about our new marriage, new home in the country, and about the new life that we were starting together. We had no idea what was about to take place over the next year or so that would have an impact on us for all eternity.

Our Conversion

Becoming Aware

In the first two months of our marriage, two key events took place which had a profound impact on our lives. These two events, although we didn't know it at the time, began a conversion story that lasted eighteen months, culminating in our baptism and testimony of the restored gospel of Jesus Christ.

On the morning of January 1, 1988, Marilyn and I made the decision to cease drinking alcohol completely. It was a decision that was a long time coming for me, and one that Marilyn very wisely confronted me on before things got out of hand. The final catalyst came after a New Year's Eve party where I had a little too much to drink. That morning Marilyn offered to quit drinking if that would make it easier on me. It wasn't as difficult of a decision as it had been in the past, as Marilyn meant more to me than anything in the world. If my drinking could even remotely cause unhappiness with Marilyn, it had to go. Thus began the first alcohol-free Shuster home in history (as far as we know it). We never chided nor felt uncomfortable around those who chose to drink alcohol in our presence—we would politely refuse and enjoy ourselves, knowing we were doing what was right for us.

The second significant event was our becoming pregnant with our first son, Jason. We were excited beyond comprehension and looking forward to bringing new life into the world. As happy as we were, this event also caused us both to immediately become sensitive to many aspects of our environment, including church. We began to consider if we had all of the tools necessary within our spiritual home to raise our family in the gospel of Jesus Christ. We started thinking about role models and those who might be in our circle of friends—especially those we attended church with.

As we experienced this new focus on family and spirituality, we experienced a number of unsettling things about the Catholic Church that concerned us as a married couple. It is not appropriate, nor necessary, for us to go into the details of the many issues and instances with the Catholic Church that disappointed us and caused trepidation as we started our family. There were priestly indiscretions and a lack of leadership in addressing these indiscretions. There were chronic shortages of priests for the ministry activities we were involved in and on-going parental involvement concerns for the Catholic youth. The Church that we grew up with and loved as children and young adults was now showing signs of strain as we entered our parental years and our perspectives evolved. Despite our anxiety we pressed on and continued our lives as Catholics, choosing to strengthen ourselves individually and as a family by reading the scriptures, singing spiritual songs together, serving in our Catholic ministries, and doing what we could to strengthen (and be strengthened by) our fellow Catholics.

As the year 1988 rolled on, before our son Jason was born, Marilyn continued her work with the diocese, while we both remained active in young adult ministry and took the time to sing in a quartet that performed at Church Masses on a weekly basis. Some of our fondest memories of Church revolve around our involvement with music and the joy it brought to our lives.

Not the Episcopal Church

Given our concerns, we started passively thinking about investigating other churches to simply learn more and see if there was something outside of Catholicism that might work for our family. I'm not sure how strong our intentions were in looking into other faiths, but it felt like the right thing to do at the time. Our thought was to start with those churches closest to the Catholic faith, beginning with the Episcopal Church. Could the Episcopal Church be what we felt the Catholic Church was meant to be? We thought it might be worth investigating.

Each Sunday on our way to the Catholic Church, we would pass an

Episcopal Church on the outskirts of Tomball, Texas. It caught our eye each Sunday, although neither one of us knew much about the Episcopal faith except that it was very similar to Catholicism.

One Sunday morning, not having a singing commitment to attend to, we decided to go to the Episcopal Church and see what it was like. Excitedly we got dressed and started towards the church. Since we had passed the church building what seemed like a million times before, we didn't need any directions. We knew there was a service at 9:45 AM and therefore left with plenty of time to spare.

Driving down that same road we had been on numerous times we looked for the church and couldn't find it! We drove up, down, and back again several times and still couldn't locate that Episcopal Church that we passed every Sunday for months. We went into the city of Tomball and stopped at a phone booth to look up the address. In doing so I couldn't find the Episcopal Church in the phone book anywhere. Being at a loss for an explanation, we returned home confused and worn out.

A few days later, Marilyn awoke to tell me of a dream she had. The dream included our being a part of the Episcopal Church, and the entire church being in chaos and disarray. She recalled feeling concerned and confused in the dream. Marilyn strongly believes the Lord talks to individuals in dreams and took this as a sign that the Episcopal Church was not the one for us.

The next Sunday on our way to sing at church, we saw that same Episcopal Church we passed very Sunday. There it was in plain view—that same Church we couldn't find the Sunday before.

Case closed, the Episcopal Church was not for us. The whole event was a shadow of things to come, although we didn't know that at the time.

The Mormon Neighbors Next Door

Settling in our new home, we took notice of our neighbors next door—the Torgesens. They were a family with ten children, all of whom were polite, well-mannered, and extremely helpful. Marilyn and I being somewhat "city folks" and often unable to understand the rigors of country living, quickly learned our neighbors were a wealth of information and willing souls to help us. In doing so, they would occasionally share a phrase or two that let us clearly know they were Christian.

As we came to know the Torgesens better, it was obvious to us that they had something special, from the feeling we had inside their home, to the unmistakable attitude of service and love that they showed for us. Their Christian example generated a great deal of curiosity within us as to what religion they might be.

One day while working outside, I noticed one of their children wearing a shirt with the words *Brigham Young University* across the front. I seemed to remember that BYU was some type of Mormon institution. I asked if someone in their family went to BYU, to which they answered yes—several members of their family. I then boldly asked what religion their family was, to which the child proudly answered, "We're Latter-day Saints . . . you probably know us as Mormons."

Upon hearing these words a chill ran down my spine. Mormons! That chilling feeling was followed by a great sense of disappointment. I had secretly hoped that this wonderful family was some type of mainstream Christian religion that we might begin to look into. I was hoping for Methodist, Lutheran, or even Baptist. I was totally unprepared for them being *Mormons*. At the time it was a devastating piece of news.

I ran inside and boldly proclaimed to Marilyn, "Our neighbors are weirdos." I explained that the family next door was Mormon and that surely meant a multitude of things: there was definitely more than one wife—how else could one family have ten kids? There was certain to be a horse-drawn buggy in the garage somewhere, and that black hats with gold buckles were likely worn by the crew on holidays and special occasions. Those were my thoughts about the Mormon religion.

How ignorant I was at the time of the Latter-day Saint faith! Of course, I came to find out later that although my thoughts on Mormonism were strange indeed, that others had ideas and opinions of Mormons that were far worse and distorted from a spiritual and doctrinal point of view than mine.

Marilyn calmed me down and said she really didn't know anything about the Mormon faith and that we shouldn't judge the family just yet on the merits of religion alone. I realized she was right and in the ensuing months, we cautiously socialized with the Torgesens, careful not to get drawn into what might be a religious trap. After all, we knew that Catholicism was the true Church on earth and that all other religions were just off-shoots of the real thing.

Much to our surprise, the Torgesens continued to be kind, helpful, generous with their time, and always there when we needed them. The mother, Allene Torgesen, would have short conversations with Marilyn, always sharing a short spiritual thought that would provide Marilyn a glimpse into the doctrine of their faith. There wasn't any pressure on joining their church, just helpful and kind gestures that spoke volumes in faith.

During this time, while Marilyn was pregnant with Jason, we had an outbreak of pine bark beetle in our area, which systematically began killing many of the large pine trees on our property. In all, we lost seventeen trees that season, all of which were in the 40 to 60 foot height range. Faced with a crisis that could have led to spending thousands of dollars cutting down trees, our neighbor Gerry Torgesen (the father) pulled out a chain saw, grabbed his older sons and some rope, and came over to offer help in cutting down the trees. One by one he and his sons would come over, tie off the infected tree, and fall the tree with near-expert precision. We would then burn the tree and hope that the beetle wouldn't spread.

The very last tree we took down has made for a rather humorous story line for the last several years. If we were to have let this particular tree fall naturally, it would have taken out a power line and damaged a portion of the horse fence. Believing we could maneuver the tree into a much better fall position, we tied off the tree and Gerry began cutting. In a matter of minutes it was clear that we were over our heads with this one. The massive tree swayed back and forth and it was anyone's guess where it was now going to fall. We all kept pulling the tree in the direction we wanted it to fall, but to no avail. That tree fell in a totally different spot. Instead of falling where we had hoped, or even where it would have gone naturally, we managed to pull the tree to fall in such a way that it took out the power line to the water well, took out the phone line, demolished a large section of fence, barely missed one of our cars, and ripped the electrical box clean off of our home with sparks flying.

It was quite a spectacle to observe.

Gerry and his boys just stood there in shock, with the chain saw still sputtering. Moments later Gerry began apologizing profusely. The whole scene was so incredible, I actually started laughing uncontrollably. Here was a guy who saved us thousands of dollars by helping us cut down trees, only to have the final tree cause a mess, leaving him feeling horrible in its wake. We all had a good laugh, and called out an electrician.

Enter Alan, the Mormon Craftsman

Halfway through Marilyn's pregnancy, despite not knowing anything about home improvement or construction, I decided to create a master bathroom out of an existing downstairs bathroom adjacent to the master bedroom. I was never one to shy away from a challenge so it seemed perfectly natural to take on such a daunting home improvement project. After gutting the bathroom in grand fashion, we were forced to begin using the upstairs bathroom for the time being.

One evening, after Marilyn took a bath upstairs, she came down to sit awhile with me on the couch. As I put my arm around her I noticed the couch backrest was wet. I smelled the cushion and it smelled like peach bubble bath. I looked up and saw water trickling through the ceiling. We had a problem with the plumbing upstairs that, over time, had caused water damage to the downstairs bathroom. After inspecting the damage, the insurance company gave us a check to pursue repairs and we began a search for a skilled carpenter to help us replace rotted base plates in the bathroom I was remodeling.

Gerry and Allene from next door suggested we call a friend of theirs, Alan Blankenship, who built houses for a living. We called Alan and he came over to assess the damage. Upon seeing the gutted downstairs bathroom, with a big smile on his face he asked, "Have you ever done this before," obviously skeptical of my ambitious project. I told him that I had never done anything like it before. With an even bigger smile on his face, he gently mentioned, "You may not know what you are doing, but you sure have a lot of guts."

After methodically looking over the damage, Alan began creating a list of materials that would be required. I asked him how much he would be charging for the project. Without directly answering the question, he told me to obtain the materials on the list and he would be over on Saturday. I asked him again how much he was going to charge us and he said, "Nothing—I'll come over and we'll do it together." Still in disbelief I asked how much he would charge, to which he replied, "Nothing—you need some help and I'm going to give it to you."

I was suspicious of his offer, but such suspicion was offset by the dwindling confidence I had in my ability to tackle the bathroom. I had someone willing to help, and I was going to jump all over that.

When Saturday came Alan arrived with his tools and a small ice chest. Marilyn offered him a cup of coffee, which he politely refused. I immediately suspected we might have another Mormon on our hands. After all, didn't the whole world drink coffee except Mormons?

Alan and I worked on the bathroom all day, with him teaching me a number of construction insights that I never would have known otherwise and would likely have never stumbled on myself. It was a pleasant day, with not one word spoken about religion. Later on as we were discussing the events of the day, Marilyn and I agreed we were blessed by the presence of a very kind and generous person.

A few days later we came to learn that Alan was between homes while moving his family to another town in Texas, and he was in need of a place to stay temporarily. We immediately called Alan and offered him one of our upstairs bedrooms, feeling we could repay his generosity in helping us with our bathroom. Alan reluctantly took us up on our offer, but on the condition that we allow him to finish our bathroom. Feeling humbled, we reluctantly agreed. It felt a little strange that we were repaying his kindness and he was repaying our kindness with more kindness.

"What are these Mormons made of?" I wondered.

Alan's Bold Testimony from the Bathroom

During the day I went to work, leaving Alan to work on the bathroom and Marilyn at home to tend to a number of different things in preparation for our newborn. At this time Marilyn's pregnancy was in the third trimester, and she had left her job at the diocese to be at home.

While working on the bathroom, Alan and Marilyn began regularly engaging in conversations regarding religion and gospel doctrines. Armed with a degree in Catholic theology, Marilyn was game to discuss, even debate, religion with anyone. The discussions were often very lively. I would frequently receive calls at work during this time from a flustered Marilyn, who couldn't believe that anyone could be so sure about their religious beliefs as Alan was. They discussed the Trinity, the premortal life, the Book of Mormon, prophets, and several other subjects relating to the restored gospel. Although frustrated at times, Marilyn enjoyed the stimulating conversation.

At night Alan would come downstairs with his Book of Mormon to read and talk to us about our day. Alan was as sincere as anyone could ever be, with a heart of pure gold. We weren't sure what to make of the Book of Mormon, but one thing was for sure, it clearly wasn't hurting

Alan's spirituality one bit. Alan's Christian witness to us was powerful and left a strong impression.

After finishing the bathroom and before leaving to join his family, Alan gave each of us a copy of The Book of Mormon. Alan shared with us its sacred nature as another testament of Jesus Christ. We were both somewhat excited about having a copy of The Book of Mormon, although not sure what to make of its place from a spiritual standpoint. Alan planted a lot of seeds before his departure to join his family, and he would return later to enjoy the harvesting of those seeds.

The Investigation Begins

We were finally blessed with the arrival of our son Jason Francis Shuster on October 4, 1988. We gave him the middle name Francis because October 4 was the date we celebrated the Feast of Saint Francis as Catholics, and because Marilyn always had a special place in her heart for Saint Francis of Assisi. As nervous first-time parents, we were glad to have a wealth of experience next door in Gerry and Allene. Marilyn often took advantage of Allene's experience from helping calm a crying baby, to dealing with minor ailments and other baby-related situations.

In late 1988 we took a trip to California to visit my family in the San Jose area. Before going to California, Gerry and Allene suggested that we visit the Oakland Temple, which was not far from San Jose. I could vaguely remember seeing the temple from the highway when I lived there years before. Although their making such a suggestion appeared somewhat unusual, we were intrigued when they showed us a picture of the temple.

While in California we decided we had time one day and would make the trip to the Oakland Temple. It was about an hour away, so we bundled up Jason and took off down the highway. When we arrived at the temple we were immediately struck with the feeling that we were on holy ground. There was a peace and tranquility that was all around the temple grounds. We entered the visitor's center and were greeted by two young women missionaries, along with an older couple serving a mission.

Their countenance was bright, and they were obviously happy to be there and to see us. We accepted their offer to watch a movie on the history of The Church of Jesus Christ of Latter-day Saints and did so with great interest. The movie was interesting, but it was the feeling we had from the missionaries that was perhaps more memorable. The feeling we had at the time was much the same we were experiencing from our neighbors the Torgesens. These missionaries, much like the Torgesens, were polite, gentle, and kind, giving us a positive and good feeling in our hearts. Like Alan, they left a very strong impression on us and was the brightest spot of our trip.

After our return to Texas, Jason contracted viral meningitis and became seriously ill. In our second day at the hospital in Houston we received a call from Gerry Torgesen, asking if they could come to the hospital to give Jason a blessing. We weren't sure what a blessing was, but were glad to have them come to see us, as no one from our Catholic parish had come to visit us during the crisis, despite having identified ourselves as Catholic on the incoming hospital paperwork.

Gerry and Allene arrived that evening with two young men missionaries. Gerry and the missionaries administered to Jason, laying hands on him in the name of Jesus Christ, and calling on the authority of the Melchizedek Priesthood with a blessing of healing. Marilyn and I had never seen this done before, and felt a spiritual power in the room, along with the sweet presence of peace. Gerry and Allene then offered to keep an eye on Jason as we took a long walk around the hospital grounds. In a matter of three hours, Jason's fever broke and we left the hospital the next day.

The hospital experience was one that left us pondering what it all meant. We were being served by this wonderful family, witnessed to by a man who built houses, and given the gift of healing and spiritual peace during a time of crisis. It was clear to us that these Mormons were Christians, but it was unclear to us how such spiritual people, who lived the gospel so fully, could be a religion that was so vague and unknown to us as Mormonism was at the time. Our lack of knowledge of the religion caused us to have great suspicion, despite the wonderful things we were witnessing.

We were afraid of the unknown and weren't sure how to proceed.

Later that month we received a call from the Torgesens, who invited us to attend a "family home evening" at their home. They told us there would be singing, a movie, a game, and a treat. We felt it was harmless enough, and I loved treats, so we accepted the invitation and joined them.

After they sang the song "Families Can Be Together Forever," we watched the video *Together Forever*. The video looked in to the lives of different people, expounding on the simple truth of families being together forever in the gospel of Jesus Christ. The movie was extremely touching, and we felt this enormous wonderful feeling in the room. Tears welled up in Marilyn's and my eyes, as we desired deeply what the movie was offering—the opportunity for our family to be together forever. We were immediately reminded of the marriage vows we wrote to one another, which explicitly said we would be together forever, as opposed to the traditional "till death do us part."

Following the movie Gerry and the older kids shared their testimony of the gospel of Jesus Christ, their love for us, and expressed how much they desired our happiness in life. Gerry, then pointing to two young missionaries in the room, with a gentle voice said, "Perhaps you could meet with the missionaries to learn more about this." I didn't recall even seeing the missionaries in the room when we arrived. The two sharply dressed young men smiled and asked if we were available the coming Tuesday. I hesitated, feeling for a moment we were being somehow set up. I told the missionaries we were busy that evening, not wanting to get involved. The young man then said, "How about Wednesday?" I told him again that we were tied up. The missionary smiled widely and asked about our availability on Thursday. I realized that he was not going to give up, and I told him that Thursday would be fine.

Our Investigation Goes to the Next Level

Our first few meetings with the missionaries were very interesting indeed. The young men were extremely polite, well-versed in scripture, and had a very specific process of teaching that they followed with great precision. Whereas starting in 2005 the missionaries were counseled to be more flexible and follow the spirit in teaching by using the *Preach My Gospel* manual, in 1989 there were six discussions and the missionaries didn't stray too far from those discussions, except to resolve concerns and answer specific questions.

And did we have a lot of questions—especially Marilyn!

I found myself quite interested in what the missionaries were teaching, since in my life up to that time, I felt I had received very little formal religious education, despite going to a Catholic high school and completing many years of catechism; therefore, the opportunity to learn the gospel of Jesus Christ from the ground up was very stimulating and spiritually rewarding.

Marilyn, on the other hand, had accumulated many years of formal religious education in obtaining her degree in Catholic theology and other related certifications, was well-versed in the scriptures, and had very definite ideas and thoughts on the doctrines of Christianity. As such, each night we met with the missionaries Marilyn was on the edge of her seat, ready to challenge what the missionaries were saying and ask pointed questions on a variety of principles and doctrines.

On many occasions Marilyn was frustrated with the structured nature of the missionary's teaching, telling the missionaries that what they were teaching she was already familiar with and to move onto the next subject. Patiently, the missionaries would go through their routine, often using props, flip charts, and other teaching aids to illustrate certain points. Although the teachings appeared somewhat juvenile to Marilyn or myself on occasion, at the time we didn't realize that the Lord was trying to help us "become as little children" and learn key gospel principles in their native form. Later on, this would become much clearer to us. For the time being it made some of our nights with the missionaries painfully slow.

I could feel myself progressing in gospel knowledge, while Marilyn wanted to get into deeper theological discussions and begin understanding each and every doctrine of The Church of Jesus Christ of Latter-day Saints.

When the missionaries would come over, they carefully listened to what Marilyn had to say and would confidently answer what they could based upon their knowledge, while promising to return the next session to answer that which they were not familiar with. It was quite surprising how much the missionaries were able to answer using their knowledge of the Bible and the gospel of Jesus Christ.

After several weeks I remember the missionaries challenging us to pray about being baptized. I recall having a great feeling of excitement in wanting to be baptized. I had learned so much about the gospel of Jesus Christ in meeting with the missionaries, and felt strongly the great example of our neighbors was a true testament of what The Church of Jesus Christ of Latter-day Saints can do for a family.

Marilyn on the other hand was not ready to consider baptism. She strongly felt that she had already been baptized as an infant and was not in need of another baptism. Furthermore, Marilyn wasn't 100 percent sure about the Mormon religion, let alone leaving the Catholic faith she loved and was committed to. Marilyn felt a sense of loyalty and comfort in the tradition of the Catholic Church, despite the many disappointments she had experienced in the past.

I was not going to be baptized without Marilyn. Thus, we continued our investigation. Even if I wanted to pressure Marilyn, which I didn't, you have to know she is the last person to be pressured on matters of religion and faith. I decided to be patient and allow things run their course.

On certain occasions the missionaries would teach about a specific principle or doctrine that was contrary, either vastly or only slightly, to the mainline theological teaching of the Catholic Church. There were many times that Marilyn would comment "that isn't what the Catholic Church teaches, but what you have taught is what I have always believed."

Like so many Catholics, what is taught by the Catholic Church is not necessarily what is believed from a faith perspective by its members and vice versa. The Latter-day Saint doctrines of the premortal life, the organization of the Church, the existence of prophets, modern-day revelation, and even the nature of the Trinity were a few that Marilyn found comfort in, even though the Catholic teaching was contrary. The doctrine of The Church of Jesus Christ of Latter-day Saints taught by the missionaries was for the most part in perfect harmony with what Marilyn believed to be true.

Marilyn had labored earnestly as a nun and as a student of Catholic doctrine; however, her sensitivity to the Holy Spirit allowed her to recognize truth in religious doctrine, even when that doctrine was in opposition to that which she intellectually learned, studied, or was taught in Catholicism. This became a true gift to us both as we earnestly sought the truth during our investigation.

During this time Allene from next door and Marilyn would have short spiritual conversations over the fence in the yard or during brief visits to each other's homes. One day Allene told Marilyn, "You'll be baptized into the Church; it's just a matter of time." Marilyn gave her a polite response, but inside she was seething that Allene could be so sure of such a thing! The rebellious youth in Marilyn came out. She said softly to herself, "No, I'm not—you just wait and see."

When Marilyn told members of her family that she was investigating The Church of Jesus Christ of Latter-day Saints, there were a variety of reactions, spanning from those that didn't care to those who criticized Marilyn sharply for such an investigation. Two of Marilyn's siblings, who

had left the Catholic Church years before and joined non-denomina-
tional Evangelical sects, were especially critical of her investigation of the
Church. One of Marilyn's brothers sent a lengthy letter in which he wrote
that Marilyn was "on a sleigh ride to hell."

The negative reactions of her siblings hurt Marilyn, because she
couldn't understand why they would be so critical of a Christian religion she found to be so wonderful and spiritually uplifting. One of her
sibling's spouses had some brief experiences with the Church that led
her to misunderstand at least one doctrine, causing her to have strong
grievances against The Church of Jesus Christ of Latter-day Saints. The
vigor at which these siblings opposed her investigation was quite shock-
ing and disturbing to Marilyn. The fact that these individuals would
think so little of Marilyn's faith in Jesus Christ and distrust her ability
to discern truth from false doctrine was also a source of great frustration, pain, and disappointment.

Our Investigation Takes a Break

Despondent over her sibling's reactions, and feeling stressed out over
a number of related and unrelated things, Marilyn expressed a desire to
stop the investigation so we could gather our thoughts and relieve some
of the pressure she was feeling. There wasn't any pressure from the missionaries or members of the Church, but rather family and self-created
pressures from outside of the Church. Marilyn knew that I wanted to
be baptized, but I was not pressuring her into making any decisions that
she was not comfortable with. My feelings of wanting to move forward,
Marilyn's family pressures, our having a new baby in the house, and challenges at the prospect of leaving the Catholic faith was more than she
could bear at the moment.

With our newfound knowledge of the gospel, we decide to take all
that we learned in the Mormon faith and apply that to our lives as Catholics. We knew we had learned many wonderful things about how to raise
a family and how to live our lives that we could apply without joining The
Church of Jesus Christ of Latter-day Saints. We informed the missionaries that we were taking a break and that we did not want to meet with
them until further notice. The missionaries were disappointed but agreed
to stop contacting us unless they heard from us in the future.

The decision to cut our ties with the missionaries brought mixed feelings. On one hand we enjoyed meeting with the missionaries and other

Church members to learn and converse about spiritual things. On the other hand, we needed the time away to think about things on our own. We were on the edge and needed some time away to think.

The excited feeling of bringing new principles and activities to our Catholic lives didn't last long, as we quickly found little support, and sometimes intolerance, for such things as family home evening, refraining from alcohol, or doctrines that were somewhat out-of-step with traditional Catholic teachings. We were now in a strange position—we wanted to go to the next level in our spiritual understanding and living the gospel of Jesus Christ; however, we were associating with people who were fine with where they were at and weren't looking for anything more. We were changing and our Catholic friends weren't, and that was difficult.

One evening we met with a friend of ours who was deacon in the Catholic Church we attended. He and his wife freely drank wine during the evening, while their children ran around the house and made a considerable amount of noise and commotion. Later that evening Marilyn and I both found ourselves comparing their home to the home of our neighbors, where we always felt such an environment of peace and family unity. The Torgesen's children would play around the house and do what children do, but we never saw them in a chaotic state as we did in the home of our dear deacon friend. We asked ourselves what type of home we wanted and came to the quick conclusion that the Torgesen's home was what we desired for our family. Our dear friend the deacon was a wonderful person, but we simply wanted more.

During this same evening, our deacon friend tried passionately to dissuade us from embracing the doctrines and principles we had learned from our investigation of The Church of Jesus Christ of Latter-day Saints. He explained to us that there was no such thing as Satan, but rather an evil presence that was in opposition to that which was good. He said there was no such thing as angels, and that the Red Sea was not really parted by Moses in a literal sense, but rather it was an act of nature that allowed the Hebrews to cross. Upon hearing the deacon's logical explanations, I was immediately reminded of the words Heavenly Father spoke to Joseph Smith in the sacred grove: "They draw near to me with their lips, but their hearts are far from me, they teach for doctrines the commandments of men, having a form of godliness, but they deny the power thereof" (Joseph Smith—History 1:19).

One Sunday during Mass our pastor was speaking and referred to

John the Baptist as being the last of the prophets. Marilyn and I looked at each other and said contemptuously to each other, "That's not true."

During this same period, we decided to have our son Jason baptized into the Catholic faith. During the baptismal classes we found ourselves questioning the doctrine of baptism as presented in the Catholic Church. We had been taught during our investigation of the LDS faith that baptism followed repentance and that little children were pure and did not require baptism until eight years old. Despite our mixed feelings, we had Jason baptized.

During this period we were caught between two theological and spiritual worlds—the Catholic Church, and The Church of Jesus Christ of Latter-day Saints. We found ourselves torn between both. We loved and didn't want to let go of all we knew in the Catholic Church, but we were finding the spiritual lift and church home we were looking for in the Latter-day Saint faith. This went on week after week, and we began to realize that we had embraced a number of gospel truths and principles from the Mormon faith that were in contradiction to our lives as active and practicing Catholics.

As we contemplated all that had happened with our investigation there were three things that stood out to us:

1. Matthew 7:20 reads: "Wherefore by their fruits ye shall know them." We had met so many people from the LDS Church who all lived exceptional lives, had wonderful children, and were great examples of Christianity. What we witnessed was anything but evil and could only be characterized as solidly Christian and bearing an abundance of good fruit.

2. Each time we read the Book of Mormon we felt the presence of the Holy Ghost. We felt certain it was the work of God and therefore one could not dismiss the power of this book as being "Another Testament of Jesus Christ."

3. Joseph Smith, whom we were not certain was a prophet at the time, proclaimed that Jesus is the living son of God, came to the earth as man in the flesh, and is the Savior of the world. According to 1 John 4:2, "Hereby know ye the Spirit of God: Every spirit that confesseth that Jesus Christ is come in the flesh is of God." We had to be feeling the Spirit of God, and if so it was leading us into a different direction than the Catholic Church.

Those three things were the bulkhead of our belief that there was something more to The Church of Jesus Christ of Latter-day Saints that could not be denied. Despite having minor issues with a few doctrines, these issues were not so vexing as to make us forget the three aforementioned points. However, such issues remained as nagging thorns that kept us from fully embracing the restored gospel.

If there was ever something worth pondering in our lives as individuals and as a family, this was it. Was it true? Was The Church of Jesus Christ of Latter-day Saints a true church of God, and did Heavenly Father want us to join and be baptized? We knew that the answer to that question had eternal consequences to our lives, and the lives of our children and their children, and therefore we took it very seriously.

Our Wake-up Call to Take a Second Look

In May 1989, I received a call from an LDS Church member from the ward we had been attending from time to time—a *ward* is much like a parish from a size and geographical standpoint. The ward we had been attending was the Magnolia Ward in Magnolia, Texas. The member asked if I was available to accompany him on guitar for a wedding he had been asked to sing for at the Magnolia Ward building. I told him I was available, and we met on the day of the wedding and performed the songs.

During the reception I spoke with several of the ward members who wondered how we were doing. Everyone was extremely polite and didn't ask any questions relating to when we might join the Church, but rather their questions grew out of a genuine curiosity as to how Marilyn, Jason, and I were doing. I felt loved, valued, and I once again was reminded that these were solid Christian people, who were dedicated to their faith.

A few days after the wedding I found a message on our answering machine. The message was from a Joe Bailey, who identified himself as a member of the "Magnolia Ward bishopric." He said he wanted to come by to talk to us. We both wondered what a "bishopric" was. It turned out that Brother Bailey was the second counselor to the Magnolia Ward bishop. A bishop and his two counselors are referred to as a bishopric.

After briefly discussing various points of doctrine, Brother Bailey said he had "callings" to extend to us. We were not familiar with what a calling was, and so he explained that a calling was a duty to perform in the Church, which would be considered a "calling from God." The calling being extended to us was for Marilyn to lead the music for the Magnolia ward Relief Society, and for me to lead the music for the Magnolia ward priesthood. We were both a little stunned by the offer, as neither Marilyn nor I could read music. Furthermore, we were use to leading contemporary folk masses in the Catholic Church, and we felt the music of The Church of Jesus Christ of Latter-day Saints sounded more like dirges and music from a monastery (which is certainly not the case today!).

We told Brother Bailey we would think about the callings and he thanked us and left. Afterwards we found ourselves sitting on the couch a little in shock, feeling like the Lord was trying to tell us something. We had the feeling the callings extended to us were not to benefit the brothers and sisters of the Magnolia ward, but were instead extended to benefit us. We felt the Lord directed his servants to provide us an opportunity to serve the ward—not as a service call, but as a wake-up call. Our hearts were touched, and our feelings softened, and we wondered if we had really investigated the Church up to that time in the right way.

We were strongly reminded of the scripture from the eighteenth chapter of Matthew, verse three, which reads: "Verily I say unto you, Except ye be converted, and become as little children, ye shall not enter into the kingdom of heaven."

We asked ourselves the following questions:

- Had we really investigated the Church as little children who desired to know the truth in humility? Or, had we primarily relied on our adult intellect and allowed pride to keep us from more fully trusting our faith?

- Had we seriously considered what the Lord was trying to say to us through the Holy Ghost during our studies and meetings with the missionaries?

- Had we been too focused on not being "fooled" into changing religions and afraid of letting go of our traditions as Catholics?

- Had we really given the investigation a chance, relying on the Lord for guidance?

We could not honestly answer yes to any of the aforementioned questions. Because of that, we knew it was time to start our investigation all over again, but this time we needed to do less talking and more listening—listening not just with our ears, but with our hearts. We needed to trust in the Lord, allow faith to guide us, and pay attention to the promptings of the Holy Ghost.

To understand more about the music and the calling, we started attending the Magnolia Ward the following Sunday. The music did indeed feel a little stale and old to us, but the spirit we felt among the congregation was strong. Nearly every member in the church was singing, and singing in harmony! We weren't use to that in the Catholic Church, where so many would just watch us sing as a quartet, as if we were performing for them. We were touched and knew that something was happening here that couldn't really be denied any longer. We needed to go deeper, and do so with a different attitude.

We called Brother Bailey to let him know we wouldn't accept the callings (the only callings we have ever turned down since), and to ask him to send the missionaries back to our home.

Investigating by the Power of the Holy Ghost

Like most converts to The Church of Jesus Christ of Latter-day Saints, there's usually a special missionary who really makes a difference in the conversion process and sets the tone and pace of the baptismal process.

For us that missionary was Elder Abbott.

Elder Abbott was a tall, red-headed missionary with a smile that could light up a city and a simple disposition that was inviting and warm. Not that all missionaries didn't have much the same gifts as Elder Abbot, but for some reason his personality was exactly what we needed at this juncture of our investigation. I recall that he carried in his wallet a picture of a car he once owned. The car was a beautiful older model vehicle that he had fixed up, only to sell in order to obtain money to serve his mission if I can remember the story correctly. Elder Abbott understood sacrifice, and he understood the restored gospel.

There were no earth-shattering experiences as we worked with the missionaries during this next phase in our investigation and subsequent conversion. I can remember feeling more relaxed, and Marilyn feeling much calmer. We discussed the doctrines that we were most troubled with and resolved all of our concerns, with the exception of one. We agreed to deal with this last doctrine at a later time, as we felt it wasn't a core doctrine, nor critical to our salvation. We knew that God was our Heavenly Father and Jesus Christ our Savior—anything else was an appendage in terms of doctrine and theology (as Joseph Smith the prophet once said).

We started to think about baptism, but there was reluctance in both of us to commit, especially Marilyn. Because we didn't fully understand the importance of the authority of the Priesthood, we could not understand the need to be baptized again.

One day Marilyn, being concerned on the subject of baptism, sat down to continue her reading of the Book of Mormon. She opened up to the place where she had left off, which was Mosiah, chapter 18. In doing so Marilyn came first to verse eight, which reads: "And it came to pass that he said unto them: Behold, here are the waters of Mormon (for thus were they called) and now, as ye are desirous to come into the fold of God, and to be called his people, and are willing to bear one another's burdens, that they may be light."

Marilyn thought to herself, *Yes, I do want to help others and be a part of God's kingdom where everyone bears each other's burdens.*

She read verse nine: "Yea, and are willing to mourn with those that mourn; yea, and comfort those that stand in need of comfort, and to stand as witnesses of God at all times and in all things, and in all places that ye may be in, even until death, that ye may be redeemed of God, and be numbered with those of the first Resurrection, that ye may have eternal life—"

Marilyn thought to herself, *Of course, this is exactly what I want to do as a Christian . . . this is what it's all about!*

She read verse ten: "Now I say unto you, if this be the desire of your hearts, what have you against being baptized in the name of the Lord, as a witness before him that ye have entered into a covenant with him, that ye will serve him and keep his commandments, that he may pour out his Spirit more abundantly upon you?"

After reading this passage, Marilyn sat there stunned. She read it again, and again, and again. The answer she was praying for was given to her in no ambiguous terms. Marilyn desired to know what the Lord wanted her to do, and in plain and simple words, yet in a bold and powerful tone, the Lord gave her the answer. If she desired to build the kingdom of God, and follow the path of service that she had sought after since her conversion when she entered the convent, then why is she resisting being baptized? Her waiting was keeping her from enjoying an outpouring of the Spirit upon her and upon our family.

Unable to contain herself, Marilyn called me immediately at work to share what she had found. Although this powerful scriptural experience resolved her concern about being baptized again, it still wasn't enough to make her commit to baptism right away. Marilyn still didn't have a testimony of Joseph Smith being a prophet, nor of The Church of Jesus Christ of Latter-day Saints as the church the Lord wanted our family to join.

Looking back, even Marilyn is surprised at her stubbornness. For me, I wasn't going to be baptized without Marilyn, and therefore, I remained patient and supportive of Marilyn and her journey.

The Ward Fast

About a week later, toward the end of May, Brother Bailey came by to visit us again. This time Brother Bailey wasn't extending us a calling, but rather an invitation to join the Magnolia ward in a ward fast on our behalf. A bit confused I asked what a fast was, and why the ward would be fasting for our family.

Brother Bailey explained that a fast was abstaining from food and drink for a twenty-four hour period, or the equivalent of two meals. I immediately responded, "That can't be done," feeling such an act would make someone sick or die.

Brother Bailey assured me that their ward fasted a minimum of once a month as a means of helping the poor, and that adults and kids alike abstain from food and drink during that time and do just fine. Marilyn shared that she had taken part in fasting before, although not to the same degree, and understood the spirit of fasting as being a means of sacrifice in prayer.

Brother Bailey said that the ward would fast on our behalf so that we would receive a date for our baptism, and promised if we took part in the fast as well that the Lord would provide us a date for our baptism into the Church. The bishopric had set aside the following Thursday as the day of fasting. We reluctantly agreed to participate, feeling that we really had nothing to lose and might once and for all put to rest our nagging hesitation at making the commitment.

That Thursday I took the day off of work, having ceased eating and drinking after dinner the night before. Besides being extremely hungry by noon that day, it seemed to progress like any other day. Marilyn, being more familiar with fasting and the art of meditation, encouraged me to find time to sit and be still in order to discern what the Lord might be telling us. On and off during the day, we sat together as man and wife, and separately as individuals with the scriptures, praying that our Heavenly

Father would provide an answer to a baptism date.

By the end of the day, Marilyn and I counseled together to share our experiences of fasting. Despite the hunger and thirst, which wasn't nearly as bad as I thought it would be, I felt a peace and calm about what we did and an excitement about the prospects. I shared with Marilyn that I thought we should move forward with baptism, but did not have a date in mind. Marilyn shared that she was okay with the idea of being baptized, and offered late August as a time frame, which was about three months away. After talking about it some more, we felt good about the decision and were excited about sharing our news with Brother Bailey and the rest of our friends on Sunday.

That Sunday we went to the Magnolia ward enthusiastic about our news, but still feeling a bit nervous. Were we really ready to make this commitment?

Were we ready to give up our beloved Catholic Church?

Were we ready to tell our family and all of our Catholic friends, many of whom we had known for many years, that we were becoming Mormon?

Was Marilyn ready to let go of her dream of becoming a spiritual director she had for so many years and put her degree in Catholic theology on the shelf?

Though the answers to these questions may have been yes on that faithful Sunday, it was a very shaky and unsettling yes.

Upon seeing us Brother Bailey came up to us and asked us if we had received our answer. We enthusiastically told him we had.

With a big smile he said, "When's the baptism date?"

With an equally as big a smile, I said, "August 28."

The smile on Brother Bailey's face turned to a look of surprise and concern. Then he said, "That's not the right date." We were taken aback.

Hastily, Brother Bailey said he had to get ready for sacrament meeting and would talk to us later. We found a place in the pews and sat down together with Jason, surprised and bewildered by Brother Bailey's response.

"What does he mean that's the wrong date?"

"We were the ones who fasted for our date, not him," we thought.

"How does he know what's good for us?"

Of course, we had no idea that Brother Bailey's key concern was that once an investigator sets a baptism date that Satan immediately goes to work, trying to topple that investigator in any way possible. With the current date being the first part of June, and our proposed baptism date being the end of August, that would give Satan nearly three months to work on us. Brother Bailey didn't like the thought of that, and therefore, responded to our date with great concern.

The Temple and Committing to Baptism

After partaking of the sacrament we settled into our seats, still feeling depressed over our exchange with Brother Bailey. The speaker for that Sunday was introduced as Joseph Larkin, the stake patriarch. We really didn't know what a patriarch was, but it was clear that the man who stepped up to the podium was a man of God and someone who was familiar with conversing with the Lord.

Patriarch Larkin was as gentle of a soul as one could find, but as mighty of a man of God that you will ever meet. The look in his eyes and the tone of his voice let us know he was intimately familiar with the Savior Jesus Christ and possessed a testimony that was firm as the mountains.

From the podium Patriarch Larkin began speaking about the temple. I am not sure exactly what his words were, but he spoke of uniting ancestors, eternal marriages, and the opportunity for families to be together forever by virtue of the sealing powers of the holy priesthood in the sanctity of the temple. His words were powerful, bold, and unmistakably true.

I turned to Marilyn and saw tears streaming down her face. I took her hand and asked what was wrong. In a trembling, yet placid voice, Marilyn said, "What he is saying is true . . . we need to go to the temple . . . we need to be there as soon as possible."

My heart filled with joy when I saw a look in Marilyn's eyes that I had not seen before. It was a look of spiritual conviction and determination, mingled with love and humility that seemed to say, "It is time."

We savored the moment and agreed to keep the thought to ourselves for the time being. I'm not sure what happened during the rest of church that Sunday, but we kept that special moment to ourselves until we arrived back home that afternoon.

Shortly before sitting down to an early dinner, we heard a frantic knock on our door. I answered the door and saw an excited Elder Abbott, along with his companion Elder Merrill. I invited them in as Marilyn joined us in the foyer. Elder Merrill explained that Elder Abbott had had a dream the night before and wanted to share that dream with us.

Nearly out of breath and about to jump out of his skin, Elder Abbott proceeded to tell us about his dream, where Marilyn, Jason, and I were at the temple being sealed together as a family. After telling us more details about the dream he handed us a book about the temple and said that we should read the book to learn more. We thanked him for the book and wished the elders a good day.

Upon closing the door I looked at Marilyn and said, "Did you tell someone at the ward about our experience in sacrament meeting?" She responded that she did not. She asked me the same thing, and I answered likewise. Neither one of us said a thing to anyone about our experience in sacrament meeting, our feelings regarding the patriarch's talk on the temple, nor how it touched us deeply earlier that morning.

Marilyn, being a big believer in the Lord talking to us in dreams, was astonished. How could Elder Abbott have known about our experience in sacrament meeting, and how could he have known that sharing such a dream with us would carry such a powerful message from the Lord?

Unable to conjure up one more reason why we need to wait longer to be baptized, Marilyn and I embraced each other and decided to move forward with baptism. This was it! We were ready to take all that we had experienced and learned in our lives as Catholics, and join that with the abundance we had learned and experienced in our investigation of The Church of Jesus Christ of Latter-day Saints, and move our family to the next level in our spiritual lives. It was both scary and exciting at the same time! We knew it was what the Lord wanted.

We called Gerry and Allene to let them know. We then called Fred Davis, the ward mission leader, who then called the missionaries. The date was set for June 24, 1989, which was less than two weeks away. We were told to start thinking about individuals to speak at the baptism, those who would perform the ordinances of baptism and confirmation, and what music we would like to have. Although it was a bit overwhelming, we were filled with the Holy Ghost and felt the Lord guiding us every step of the way.

We received a number of phone calls that night from various ward members, each touching our heart; however, it was one of the phone calls that we made that was most memorable. I called our friend Alan Blankenship, the individual who helped us finish our bathroom, who gave us copies of the Book of Mormon, and who testified so boldly to us of the truthfulness of the restored gospel. The conversation went something like this:

"Hello, is Alan there?"

"Yes, this is Alan."

"Alan, this is Eric Shuster."

"Wow, what a surprise. How are you doing?"

"Well, thank you. What are you doing on Saturday, June 24?"

"I don't think I have anything planned, why?"

"We would like you to come down to Houston to baptize us."

There was a long silence, and then Alan said, "Into what church?"

"Into the LDS church, Alan."

There was a long silence again. Then Alan said, "Is this a joke?"

I responded, "No Alan, we are getting baptized, and we want you to perform the baptism."

Alan began to cry and was overwhelmed by the moment. We shared the experiences we had had during the many months since we had last seen him. I invited him and his family to all come down and stay at our house for the occasion.

That was truly a once-in-a-lifetime experience to spring something like that on a wonderful person like Alan. We couldn't wait for June 24 to come.

Being Baptized

When the time of the baptism came we were to be interviewed by the missionary zone leaders as was customary. I was interviewed first and answered a series of questions, including my belief in Jesus Christ, my commitment to the gospel, and belief that The Church of Jesus Christ of Latter-day Saints was led by a true prophet of God. Then came the question regarding my testimony of the Prophet Joseph Smith. I answered in the affirmative that I believed he was a prophet of God. In my mind however, I knew that Marilyn was unlikely to answer the same. Although she was ready to be baptized in to the Church, she was not ready to proclaim that Joseph Smith was the prophet of the Restoration.

After my interview, it was time for Marilyn's interview. I sat nervously in the chapel as the time dragged on. My fear was that the Elder was going to ask Marilyn the question about Joseph Smith, that she would answer in the negative, and the whole baptism would be cancelled. I pondered why such a question would be asked in a baptismal interview. After a few moments I realized it wasn't in the Church's best interest to baptize people who didn't embrace the full story of the Restoration, only to have such individuals fall away later.

After what seemed like a lifetime, Marilyn and the zone leader came into the chapel with smiles on their faces. Realizing that things must have gone okay, I asked Marilyn about the question on Joseph Smith. She said that the question came up and that she answered, "Joseph Smith was a great man," and that the zone leader graciously accepted the answer.

The Lord once again intervened, just as He had done so on so many occasions for us during our investigation. I wondered for a minute about the sequence of events that led up to that very moment. So much had happened. We had made so many changes in our lives and had come so far. I knew life was never going to be the same again. It was a satisfying space in time for me in a personal way.

The baptismal and confirmation ceremonies were a joyous and memorable occasion for us. Because neither Marilyn nor I could remember our baptisms as infants in the Catholic Church, how amazing it was to experience the exhilaration and deeply moving experience of baptism as adults. Then to experience confirmation with a full knowledge of the Holy Ghost and what we were receiving was joy on top of joy.

There were a number of people in attendance from the ward supporting us, including several priesthood holders who taught us with the missionaries. Alan who baptized us never stopped crying, our neighbors the Torgesens never stopped glowing, and the missionaries never stopped smiling. It was a very happy day indeed. Marilyn and I even sang a duet, Amy Grant's *El Saddai*.

We shall never forget that day. That was the day that we became totally clean and charted a new course for our lives in the gospel of Jesus Christ. That was the day that through our commitment, despite being so strongly devoted to the Catholic Church, that we let go of all of our anxieties and embraced the direction that we knew God wanted us to take, regardless of our fears. It was a choice day that was to be followed by years of spiritual growth, understanding, and sanctification that can hardly be described in words. Our lives took on new purpose, our joy became full, and our vision for the future became crystal clear. How grateful we were to have found the restored gospel of Jesus Christ.

The year following our baptism was another incredible experience altogether, full of ups, downs, challenges, and exhilarating events. Although important to complete the overall story, we will leave that for another book.

2

Doctrinal Preparation

B EFORE diving into the comparisons of Catholic and Latter-day Saint doctrine, I thought it would be helpful to prepare you first so that you will get the most out of the content. It will be helpful for you to have some background in the Restoration and how that formulates the basis of the need for The Church of Jesus Christ of Latter-day Saints. I will explain to you a process in understanding and reconciling doctrinal differences, which includes an explanation of our methodology of how I have gone about presenting the subject matter in this book.

The Restored Gospel

One of the key tenets of The Church of Jesus Christ of Latter-day Saints is that there has been a complete and total restoration of the gospel of Jesus Christ and a renewing of His Church on earth. One may ask *why* the gospel of Jesus Christ needed to be restored in the first place, especially when it has been in the hands of the capable and enduring Catholic Church for centuries.

Consider the over two thousand years that the Catholic Church has been in existence as the universal Church of Jesus Christ. During this celebrated period there have been numerous events—spiritual, political, and ecclesiastical—that have taken place. Historical records would strongly suggest that many of these events have been challenging, disconcerting, enlightening, revelatory, and even confusing. Because history can be written and rewritten, the interpretation of these many events can lead one to conclude a number of different things—including the solid and indestructible nature of the Catholic religion, or the falling away of the

38

Catholic Church and the need for a restoration.

I have not set out to provide the reader an exhaustive review of the apostasy. There are many books written by accomplished scholars on the topic of the apostasy of the Catholic Church and how such a falling away was prophesied in the Bible, validated by history, and demonstrated in the modern church. Therefore I will not attempt to add to these worthy texts and allow you as the reader to pursue such study on your own. I will, however, provide various thoughts to help frame the topic of the apostasy in order to bring context to the Restoration.

Catholic Teachings on the Apostasy and Restoration

The notion of an apostasy and restoration is completely rejected by the Catholic Church. The Catholic Church teaches that it can trace its origins to the original Christian community founded by Jesus, with its traditions first established by the Twelve Apostles and maintained through unbroken Apostolic Succession (Catechism 815). The Catechism of the Catholic Church teaches "the Lord Jesus endowed his community with a structure that will remain until the Kingdom is fully achieved" (Catechism 765). Such a teaching would suggest that the original church set up by Jesus Christ, which is historically thought of as the Catholic Church, would remain in tact until the Second Coming of Jesus Christ.

The Catechism continues: "This is the sole Church of Christ, which in the Creed we profess to be one, holy, catholic, and apostolic" (Catechism 811). As the sole Church of Jesus Christ, there is an inference of there not having ever been an apostasy, or a need for a restoration. Catholic doctrine boldly and plainly states that "outside of the Church, there is no salvation" (Catechism 846).

The Catholic Church rightfully turns to the testimonies of the early church fathers such as Clement, Hermas, Ignatius, Papias, Polycarp, Justin Martyr, and many others as a refutation of the apostasy and support for Catholic doctrine. These valiant individuals lived and exercised spiritual authority shortly after the Ascension of Christ and are thought to be in a strong position to provide first hand testimony.

Finally, most Catholic scholars that seek to nullify the notion of an apostasy point to the claim made by Jesus Christ as recorded in Matthew 16:18 that reads: "And I say also unto thee, That thou art Peter, and upon this rock I will build my church; and the gates of hell shall not prevail against it." The interpretation of this scripture is that an apostasy would be in contradiction to this claim made by Jesus.

The Catholic Church has built a strong case against any form of an apostasy having taken place and that the Church that remains today is as authoritative and true as the one left by Jesus Christ upon his Ascension over 2,000 years ago.

Putting the Apostasy into Context

Early on in our investigation of The Church of Jesus Christ of Latter-day Saints, we had to seriously consider whether or not we believed there was an apostasy of the Catholic Church. The very notion was somewhat preposterous to us at first, but we decided to keep an open mind and consider the facts. Here is what we found out and have come to understand ever since.

From a scriptural standpoint it's not difficult to locate a number of biblical references to a future apostasy (Amos 8:11; 1 Timothy 4:1–2; Hebrews 13:20; Isaiah 24:2–5; Jeremiah 2:13; 2 Thessalonians 2:3–4; and many others). These references, as compelling as they are, must be put into proper historical and spiritual perspective, especially since the New Testament was not canonized until approximately fifteen hundred years after the Ascension of Christ at the Council of Trent. No doubt, the Bible provides a foundation for an apostasy of some kind after the Ascension of Christ, depending on how one might interpret such scriptures.

From a historical standpoint, it is equally straightforward to identify the historical events that would suggest political and spiritual difficulties in Catholic Church, including the Crusades of the late 1000s, the great Schism of 1054, the Medieval Inquisition of 1184, the Spanish Inquisition of 1478, the Roman Inquisition of 1542, and the silencing of Galileo in the 1600s. Considering these and other instances of Church improprieties that have taken place, history provides a foundation for an apostasy depending on how one might interpret these events.

There are figures in history that have left an abundance of writings to suggest the apostasy of the Catholic Church including Eusebius (~275–May 30, 339), who was Bishop of Caesarea in Palestine, Martin Luther (November 10, 1483–February 18, 1546), and John Wesley (June 17, 1703–March 2, 1791) to name a few. According to these notable figures in history, there was indeed an apostasy of the Catholic Church as demonstrated through various historical events.

Modern events have cast a dark shadow of scandal and uncertainty on the Catholic Church and its leadership, mainly surrounding the abuse of individuals at the hands of priests with the hierarchy reportedly doing little to prevent, stop, or prosecute the offending clergy. These unfortunate events may be viewed as lagging indicators of the apostasy and the results of what can happen in the absence of priesthood authority.

While the Catholic Church has a strong and logical argument for there never having been an apostasy, there are equally as compelling arguments that the converse is true. Since there is no way to come to a definite conclusion, it is left up to the reader to decide. In the case of Marilyn and I, we spent a great deal of time pondering the issues; however, it was not until we comprehensively studied the doctrines (as we will share with you in this book) that Marilyn and I came to a firm testimony of the following:

> We believe that the Catholic Church evolved over the centuries and allowed political influences, committees, and individuals with ulterior motives to change the precious truths of the gospel and put into place ordinances and doctrines that are contrary to that which Christ intended. This led to the many unfortunate historical events that took place; the testimonies of many valiant individuals who opposed the heretical evolution (at the risk of their own lives), the bringing to pass the prophecies of the apostasy contained in the Bible, and the weakened state that the Catholic Church is in today.

While we were able to come to this conclusion based upon examination, study, and prayer, there was still one thing left that we needed to reconcile—the scripture from Matthew 16:18 regarding the Church and the gates of hell. Upon further study of this scripture we came up with the following:

We concluded that it is clear that the gates of hell did not prevail against Christianity itself, but that it was highly probable (even factual) that the vain ambitions of man, inspired by Satan, caused critical church doctrines to be distorted and changed, splintering Christianity into many different pieces. What was left were portions of truth scattered among different Christian sects, the absence of the authority of the priesthood (by way of lineage and worthiness), and no single church that had the fulness of the truth of the gospel of Jesus Christ.

A key issue that we came to understand is the misinterpretation of what "the rock" means in the scripture from Matthew. The Lord says that "upon this rock I will build my church." What is the rock the Lord is referring to? The name Peter in Greek is petros (a small rock), and the word for rock is petra (meaning a bedrock of sorts). The Greek text from Matthew 16:18 is to be read as the following: "Thou art Peter [petros, or small rock], and upon this rock [petra, or bedrock] I will build my church."[1]

One may conclude from this brief examination that the rock that the Lord was referring to was *revelation*, that the Church is built upon Christ, the "rock" of revelation. It was upon the principle of continuous revelation from God the Father and the Lord Jesus Christ that the church of Jesus Christ would be built, and that the gates of hell would never prevail against the revelation of the Lord, nor Christianity itself. Later we will explore the subject of revelation and the stark differences that exist in doctrine between the Catholic Church and The Church of Jesus Christ of Latter-day Saint on the subject.

Considering for a moment the likelihood of an apostasy, let us contemplate the chain of events that led up to the Restoration and the formation of The Church of Jesus Christ on the earth again in all of its fulness.

Christian Churches Abound in Early America

Fast forward to the early 1700s and the formation of the Americas, where freedoms led to a wide-open religious field. There existed the eventual creation and growth of numerous congregations of Christian churches. These various sects of Christianity often shared a great deal of common doctrine, while many evolved in their own doctrines that were different from other congregations. Combine this with the fact that many clergy and ecclesiastical leaders made their living through the donations of their congregations, the result was a fiercely competitive landscape between different Christian churches. These churches literally battled for members by tearing down one another through preaching and other forms of disputations.

This practice of competition among Christian sects continued for centuries across the globe and was accelerated with the establishment of the United States of America, where freedom of religion was guaranteed by the constitution. The opportunity to freely worship according to one's own faith was a strong allure for millions as they migrated to America.

Following the First Great Awakening among American colonial Protestants in the 1730s and 1740s came the Second Great Awakening between 1820 and 1835. The First Great Awakening made religion deeply personal to the average individual, while the Second Great Awakening coined the term "born again" and ushered in a period of feeling God without having to worry about doctrine. During this period there was a sharp increase in membership among the Baptists, Methodists, and Presbyterians in America, who often evangelized through tent revivals and religious tours.

It was during this period of religious fervor, among the freedom and liberty of the United States of America, when the Lord would restore his church on the earth again as promised in the scriptures.

The Prophecy of the Restoration

Just as the apostasy was foretold in the Bible, so too was the Restoration of the gospel of Jesus Christ foretold in the Bible. Consider the teachings of Peter the apostle as he spoke to those in the temple: "Repent ye therefore, and be converted, that your sins may be blotted out, when the times of refreshing shall come from the presence of the Lord; And he shall send Jesus Christ, which before was preached unto you: Whom the heaven must receive *until the times of restitution of all things*, which God hath spoken by the mouth of all his holy prophets since the world began" (Acts 3:19–21). The prophecy of the Restoration was foretold even before the apostles were taken from the earth, which restoration would come before the Second Coming of Jesus Christ.

Paul reinforces the restoration theme as he spoke to the Ephesians as recorded in Ephesians 1:10: "That in the dispensation of the fulness of times he might gather together in one all things in Christ, both which are in heaven, and which are on earth; even in him." Paul exclaims that in the dispensation of the fulness of times (which is the present dispensation), although there may be many different sects and doctrinal beliefs, they will all be gathered (or restored) into one great whole.

The book of Revelation describes the Restoration of the gospel in chapter 14, verse 6, which reads: "And I saw another angel fly in the midst of heaven, having the everlasting gospel to preach unto them that dwell on the earth, and to every nation, and kindred, and tongue, and people." If the fulness of the gospel of Jesus Christ was already on the earth there would be no need for an angel to bring the everlasting gospel to the earth.

Considering the incomprehensible love our Father in Heaven has for us as his children, we would surely conclude that such a Father would not let his children live in darkness and would restore all truth before the Second Coming of his son Jesus Christ.

The question would be how? How would the Lord restore His church, given the massive splintering of Christianity, given the "every wind of doctrine" (Ephesians 4:14) that existed; given that religious leaders across the globe were already predisposed to their own thoughts and inclinations? Such a restoration would surely cause uproar and lead to even more contention among Christian churches.

The answer may be found in a parable of Jesus, as recorded in Mark 2:21–22 which reads: "No man also seweth a piece of new cloth on an old garment: else the new piece that filled it up taketh away from the old, and the rent is made worse. And no man putteth new wine into old bottles: else the new wine doth burst the bottles, and the wine is spilled, and the bottles will be marred: but new wine must be put into new bottles."

The Restoration would not come from restoring an existing Christian sect. According to the parable, to restore an existing sect would cause that sect to fail and the Restoration itself to fail. The Restoration could only take place in the formation of an entirely new Christian church, or a "new bottle" as the Lord says. Furthermore, the individual who would facilitate such a restoration could not come from an existing sect, nor could they have a predisposition to any doctrines or affiliations or the same would hold true. The Restoration would have to be facilitated by an entirely "new bottle."

The Lord would have to raise up an individual who would be that new bottle and begin the Restoration in a land that would allow the formation of his restored holy Church amongst a free and liberated people. That individual was Joseph Smith, and the land in which this would take place would be America.

Joseph Smith and the Beginning of the Restoration:

Joseph Smith was born in December of 1805 in Sharon, Vermont, and with his family would later move to western New York just outside of Palmyra. Joseph was one of nine children born to Joseph Smith Senior and his wife, Lucy. Joseph was raised on a farm, and like many others during that period of time, worked hard with the family to sustain life. Joseph was said to be a curious individual who had a deep spiritual inclination from an early age and a spirit to ask questions when he felt it was necessary.

After an eventful childhood, which included a serious medical condition with one of his legs, Joseph found himself in the middle of the religious revival of 1820 as a fourteen year old boy. In Joseph's own words he describes the period of time:

> There was in the place where we lived an unusual excitement on the subject of religion. It commenced with the Methodists, but soon became general among all sects in that region of the country. Indeed, the whole district of the country seemed affected by it, and great multitudes united themselves to the different religious parties, which created no small stir and division amongst the people, some crying, "Lo, here!" and others, "Lo, there!" Some were contending for the Methodist faith, some for the Presbyterian, and some for the Baptist. (Joseph Smith—History 1:5)

While much of Joseph's family aligned themselves to the Presbyterian faith, Joseph was unsure which church taught the true gospel of Jesus Christ. Joseph found himself vexed by the contention between the various churches. He offered the following observation: "The Presbyterians were most decided against the Baptists and the Methodists, and used all the powers of both reason and sophistry to prove their errors, or, at least to make the people think they were in error. On the other hand, the Baptists and Methodists in their turn were equally zealous in endeavoring to establish their own tenets and disprove all others" (Joseph Smith—History 1:9).

Joseph observed the contention among the sects and knew that something was amiss. Perhaps Joseph knew in his heart that same spirit which Paul attempted to communicate the Ephesians: "There is one body, and one Spirit, even as ye are called in one hope of your calling; One Lord, one faith, one baptism, One God and Father of all, who is above all, and through all, and in you all" (Ephesians 4:4–6). If there was one faith and one baptism, how could there be so many churches? Which one was the true faith and the true baptism? Having a deep desire to find and join the true church of Jesus Christ, Joseph recorded an experience of reading the Bible that proved to be a turning point for the young man:

> While I was laboring under the extreme difficulties caused by the contests of these parties of religionists, I was one day reading the Epistle of James, first chapter and fifth verse, which reads: "If any of

you lack wisdom, let him ask of God, that giveth to all men liberally, and upbraideth not; and it shall be given him." Never did any passage of scripture come with more power to the heart of man that this did at this time to mine. It seemed to enter with great force into every feeling of my heart. (Joseph Smith—History 1:11)

This experience fueled Joseph's desire to know the truth and seek the guidance of the Lord in finding the answer to his question of which church to join. In the spring of 1820 Joseph decided to put his faith, and the promise of the Lord, to the test when he went into a grove of trees near his home to offer the most earnest prayer of his heart. Joseph records the experience of that day:

After I had retired to the place where I had previously designed to go, having looked around me, and finding myself alone, I kneeled down and began to offer up the desires of my heart to God. I had scarcely done so, when immediately I was seized upon by some power which entirely overcame me, and had such an astonishing influence over me as to bind my tongue so that I could not speak. Thick darkness gathered around me, and it seemed to me for a time as if I were doomed to sudden destruction. (Joseph Smith—History 1:15)

Embarking on the event that would usher in the Restoration of the gospel of Jesus Christ to the earth, Satan tried desperately to intervene and prevent the young boy Joseph from receiving revelation from God the Father. Joseph reached deep into his well of faith and pleaded with his Father in Heaven, in the name of Jesus Christ, for deliverance from the evil intercession. Joseph then remarks on the miracle that happened moments later:

Just at this moment of great alarm, I saw a pillar of light exactly over my head, above the brightness of the sun, which descended gradually until if fell upon me. It no sooner appeared than I found myself delivered from the enemy which held me bound. When the light rested upon me I saw two Personages, whose brightness and glory defy all description, standing above me in the air. One of them spake unto me, calling me by name and said, pointing to the other—*This is My beloved Son. Hear Him.* (Joseph Smith—History 1:16–17)

In what is commonly referred to in the Church as the "First Vision," this divine visitation from Heavenly Father and Jesus Christ began a series of events that would lead to the complete restoration of the gospel of Jesus Christ to the earth. Joseph's prayer was answered and he was instructed to not join any of the churches, as none of the churches taught the fulness of the gospel. The Lord was quoted as saying "they draw near to me with their lips, but their hearts are far from me, they teach for doctrines the commandments of men, having a form of godliness, but they deny the power thereof" (Joseph Smith History 1:19)

The new bottle was chosen in Joseph Smith, who would be tasked with restoring the Lord's church on the earth again. A fourteen-year-old boy, with no predisposition to any doctrines, who was willing to humble himself before the Lord to obtain guidance and direction. One is reminded of Samuel the boy prophet in the Old Testament, who at a young age received his own calling from the Lord.

The Restoration of All Things

Following the First Vision, Joseph Smith was given instructions and preparation through the angel Moroni, a messenger sent from the Lord. This was not unusual, as one must consider that the angel Gabriel was sent to the Virgin Mary as a messenger from the Lord about the coming of Christ. The angel Moroni instructed Joseph sparsely over a period of approximately seven years. During this period of preparation Joseph Smith was often admonished by the Lord for his decisions and refined in his thoughts and actions.

The admonishment Joseph received from the Lord, and the adversity of those around him, prepared the soon-to-be prophet to lead the world into the dispensation of the fulness of times, a time of preparation for the Second Coming of Jesus Christ that would include the restoration of all things and the reestablishment of the Lord's church on earth. Several chapters of this book include key components of the Restoration including the coming forth of the Book of Mormon, the restoration of the Aaronic and Melchizedek Priesthoods, the organization of the Church, and many other "plain and precious truths" that were lost as a result of the Apostasy.

This section can't begin to do justice in explaining the principle of the Apostasy, the miracle of the First Vision, and the magnitude of the Restoration. There are entire texts dedicated to exploring these subjects that will provide the reader with rich scriptural and historical support, along with spiritual and scholarly explanations that will fill in the gaps left by this brief chapter. The purpose of this book's explanation of these subjects is to provide the reader a framework of the Apostasy and Restoration so as have reference points in comparing Catholic and Latter-day Saint doctrines in the coming chapters.

Understanding and Reconciling Doctrinal Differences

During our investigation of The Church of Jesus Christ of Latter-day Saints, Marilyn and I did a great deal of studying, pondering, and praying. Some of our evaluations of doctrine were on the spur of the moment, while others were done more methodically and with great care. Our mind-set during our investigation of the Church was to study Latter-day Saint doctrine in comparison to that which we already knew to be, or at least thought to be, correct in the Catholic Church. We were not going to change our faith and lives based upon the urging of those who were teaching us—we had to find out for ourselves.

We therefore took the responsibility to study the doctrines for ourselves and decide what we thought was true. In the end, as it should be, it all came down to faith and what we believed to be true and where we thought the Lord was leading our family in terms of a faith community. At the same time, we knew the Lord expected us to utilize the facilities he had blessed us with in order to work out things in our own minds and hearts—both together as a couple and separately as individuals.

The purpose of this section is to help the reader understand how Marilyn and I went about reconciling the differences in doctrines between both churches during our investigation, while augmenting those experiences with supplementary study and analysis to provide additional clarity and insight to the reader.

The most dangerous thing about evaluating Christian religious doctrine is that, short of pure evil and without disciplined study and interpretation, one can find biblical support to rationalize just about anything. For centuries, man has found ways of extracting scriptures from the Bible, applying expansive interpretation with human philosophy, and walking away with questionable insights that turn into "man-made doctrine." Interpreting scriptures out of context is a rampant exercise that has led to the justification of murder, injustice, persecution, and all manner of sin. This is a far cry from what scripture was meant for. Paul wrote in his letter to Timothy "all scripture is given by inspiration of God, and is profitable for doctrine, for reproof, for correction, for instruction in righteousness" (2 Timothy 3:16).

What is required to avoid such pitfalls in religious doctrinal study is three fold: 1) having the Spirit of the Lord; 2) being intellectually prepared; and 3) using credible sources of information.

The Spirit of the Lord

The most important element in formulating truth from a doctrinal perspective is to have the Spirit of the Lord to guide the seeking individual. Paul spoke of the Spirit of God educating man when he told the Corinthians: "For what man knoweth the things of a man, save the spirit of man which is in him? even so the things of God knoweth no man, but the Spirit of God" (1 Corinthians 2:11).

Dallin H. Oaks of the Quorum of the Twelve Apostles of The Church of Jesus Christ of Latter-day Saints said the following with respect to having the Spirit of the Lord: "God teaches His sons and daughters by the power of his Spirit, which *enlightens their minds* and *speaks peace* to them concerning the questions they have asked. We also learn from these revelations that being taught by the Spirit is not a passive thing. Often the Lord's communication does not come until we have studied matters out in our own minds. Then we receive a confirmation."[2]

Only the Spirit of the Lord could have led Joseph Smith, a mere fourteen years of age and of little education when he began his ministerial journey, to translate the Book of Mormon and restore the Lord's church on earth.

I once served under a bishop who had little education but was able to grasp deep doctrinal concepts and effectively minister to those in his congregation. The Apostle Paul wrote, "But God hath chosen the foolish things of the world to confound the wise; and God hath chosen the weak things of the world to confound the things which are mighty" (1 Corinthians 1:27). It is often the small and unassuming things of our world that bring about great spiritual works through the Spirit of the Lord.

The Spirit of the Lord supersedes anything else intellectually or academically. From as far back as there have been scriptures available, the world has seen a vast array of scriptural interpretations. The same scripture from the Bible can be, and has been, interpreted in many different ways, leaving the reader confused and bewildered. The Spirit of the Lord can break through all of that and speak directly to the individual, providing answers to those who earnestly seek spiritual truth.

Intellectual Preparation

Although the Spirit of the Lord is most critical to understanding and reconciling doctrinal differences, one cannot dismiss entirely the value of intellectual preparation. The place of such knowledge in the seeking of spiritual truth is to properly place scriptural references into context, enable the comprehension of historical perspectives, and to recognize when additional research is necessary.

One need not be a theologian or scriptural scholar to be prepared intellectually. Such academic preparation can be a blessing or a curse, depending on the degree to which such knowledge is depended upon. We must remember that spirituality is about faith; therefore, the component of intellectuality takes a back seat to faith. If that were not the case, then the vast majority of Christians in the world today would be unable to participate in religion.

Intellectual preparation without having the Spirit of the Lord can be a hindrance in finding and understanding spiritual truth. Marilyn and I found this out during our investigation when we tried to rely on our intellectual ability and overlooked the component of faith. This is precisely the reason that the Lord said to his disciples: "Except ye be converted, and become as little children, ye shall not enter into the kingdom of heaven" (Matthew 18:3).

Marilyn holds a degree in Catholic Theology from Saint Thomas University in Houston, a well-know and prestigious Catholic University, and has been an avid student and teacher of Latter-day Saint doctrine since joining the Church in 1989. Marilyn is well-prepared to interpret scriptures and understand historical and spiritual context from both a Catholic and Latter-day Saint point of view.

As for myself, I hold a bachelor's and master's degree in Engineering and Business respectively, am the Chief Executive Officer of a market research firm, and have been a student and teacher of the scriptures since joining the LDS Church in 1989. I have had the unique experience of being robustly challenged by many individuals outside of the Church on points of doctrine, leading to my rigorous study of the Bible to answer such challenges.

Although there are individuals who were more likely prepared intellectually than Marilyn and I to conduct comparisons and analysis of doctrine, we believe our academic and spiritual preparation is substantial and provides a strong intellectual foundation on which to conduct these exercises and interpretations.

Credible and Authoritative Sources

Sir Isaac Newton said, "If I have seen a little farther than others it is because I have stood on the shoulders of giants."[3] Many individuals have come before Marilyn and I who have conducted enormous amounts of research, study, and meditation on the very doctrines we will explore in this book. We greatly benefit from their hard work and inspiration. Being an engineer and market research professional, I considered it a key responsibility to identify and utilize the most credible and authoritative sources of information for both churches, while employing a disciplined and structured methodology to carry out the doctrinal comparisons performed in this book. To accomplish this I utilized a variety of sources as required and appropriate, while focusing on a primary source for each religion:

Catholic Doctrine

The primary repository utilized was the Catechism of the Catholic Church, Second Edition (revised in accordance with the official Latin text promulgated by Pope John Paul II), copyright 1989. Other sources of reference included a variety of official Church documents, as well as books and articles from well respected Catholic authors and clergy.

Latter-day Saint Doctrine

The primary repository utilized was *Gospel Principles*, copyright 1997, published by The Church of Jesus Christ of Latter-day Saints. Secondary sources included *Mormon Doctrine*, copyright 1966 by Bruce R. McConkie, the official website of The Church of Jesus Christ of Latter-day Saints, and articles and talks written by past and present General Authorities of the Church.

The Bible as a Primary Source

In order to aid the reader and avoid confusion, I draw heavily from the Bible. For Catholic doctrine I used the *New Revised Standard Version*. However, the reader must keep in mind a qualifying statement given the Catechism: "Scripture quotations contained herein are adapted from the *Revised Standard Version of the Bible*, copyright © 1946, 1952, 1971, and the *New Revised Standard Version of the Bible*, copyright © 1989." Therefore, there will be times when I quote scriptures directly from the Catechism that may have been "adapted" by the authors of the Catechism, and therefore they will not match word for word with the *New Revised Standard Version of the Bible*.

For Latter-day Saint doctrine I used the King James Version of the Bible. Where non-Bible scriptures (Book of Mormon, Doctrine and Covenants, and Pearl of Great Price) could further illuminate Latter-day Saint doctrines and beliefs, they were used with care and explicit sourcing.

Following this threefold methodology with discipline has helped develop an objective review and comparison of the doctrines of the Catholic Church and The Church of Jesus Christ of Latter-day Saints. Although there will be a natural bias towards promoting the doctrines of the Latter-day Saint faith, I have done all that is possible to ensure that such subjectivity does not overpower objective spiritual analysis.

Belief Versus Doctrine

It bears mentioning that there are times when we as Christians may sometimes believe in something that may not be a part of our Church's doctrine or teachings. For instance, I've spoken to Christians who believe in reincarnation, Catholics who believe in birth control, and Latter-day Saints who believe in a little coffee every now and then. In each case, the belief system of the individual on a particular principle is in contrast to the teachings of their faith community.

Marilyn and I came across several teachings during our investigation of the Latter-day Saint faith that were not a part of Catholic doctrine. When this occurred we often already believed in the doctrine, or quickly embraced the teaching through study and prayer. An example of this would be the doctrine of being together forever in the eternities. Our belief was clearly in contrast to the teachings of the Catholic Church at the time. Once we heard this doctrine during our investigation, we immediately embraced it.

This contradiction of one's beliefs to the doctrine of the church they are affiliated with can happen for three reasons:

1. The Holy Ghost can bear witness to an individual from an early age of the truth of certain principles and doctrines. This typically happens when someone is seeking the truth from the Lord and is ready to receive such revelation, regardless of their religious affiliation. This was the case for Marilyn and I with respect to eternal families.

2. An individual can come across a true principle which fits with their way of thinking and therefore they quickly embrace it. Such was the case for Marilyn when we were told about the premortal

life from the missionaries. This was not a Catholic doctrine, but when she heard about it the doctrine seemed familiar and easy to accept.

3. An individual comes across a false principle and is deceived into believing its authenticity, usually by another deceived individual with reinforcement by Satan. Such is the case with reincarnation, which has absolutely no scriptural foundation and is completely out of step with Christian doctrine.

We will be dealing with doctrines of both churches in the coming chapters. Some of the doctrines discussed may ring familiar and align with the beliefs of the reader immediately. Some of the doctrines discussed may be foreign to the reader and inspire additional study and meditation.

Whatever the case, we believe that you as the reader will not only gain new insights into the doctrines of the Catholic Church, but will also gain new insights into the doctrines of The Church of Jesus Christ of Latter-day Saints.

Keep in mind that even though an individual may not believe a certain doctrine, if the doctrine is a true doctrine of the gospel of Jesus Christ, then that individual must find a way to align their belief to that doctrine. There were some Latter-day Saint doctrines which Marilyn and/or I struggled with; however, after "becoming as a child," with prayer, reading the scriptures, and further pondering, we were able to understand and embrace each one of the doctrines being taught to us. Never did we allow ourselves to be "convinced" of a doctrine. In each case, we relied on the Lord to guide our study and allowed the Holy Spirit to help us discern what was true.

Understanding Simple Doctrine before Advanced Doctrine

The apostle Paul admonished the early Christians to learn simple doctrines first, followed by more advanced doctrines. In his first letter to the Corinthians he wrote: "I have fed you with milk, and not with meat: for hitherto ye were not able to bear it, neither yet now are ye able" (1 Corinthians 3:2). Paul wrote a similar passage in his letter to the Hebrews as recorded in Hebrews 5:12. In a book such as this that explores a variety of doctrines, many of them advanced in spiritual nature, it is prudent to point out that care must be taken and preparations made to understand the simple first and then to progress on to the more advanced. For this reason I have organized this book in such a way that each chapter is somewhat preparatory to the next in logical succession. You can use the book as a reference to skip from one chapter to another, but in doing so, you may find yourself trying to digest *meat* when you have skipped the *milk* of earlier chapters (see 1 Corinthians 3:2).

Jesus Christ counseled the Pharisee Nicodemus on this same issue as recorded in John 3:12 when he said: "If I have told you earthly things, and ye believe not, how shall ye believe, if I tell you of heavenly things?" When one desires to understand the deep spiritual doctrines of Christianity they must be prepared to exercise faith and understanding in the more basic doctrines of the gospel of Jesus Christ first. If you come across something in this book you don't understand, we recommend prayer, earnest study, and the exercising of as much faith as you can muster. By doing so you will have the opportunity to receive personal revelation through the Holy Ghost that will answer your prayer and provide the understanding you are looking for.

Prepare to be Challenged

This book is meant to be both a story of conversion, as well as a reference of the comparison of doctrines between the Catholic Church and The Church of Jesus Christ of Latter-day Saints. Although it is not intended to do so, there may be instances where through the explanation of doctrines or the sharing of experiences you may find yourself spiritually challenged as we were—and that can sometimes be uncomfortable. If this happens, may we suggest that you turn to God in prayer and seek the guidance of the Holy Ghost for direction and understanding. We did so and were never let down, although some answers came more slowly than others.

With this in mind, having the Spirit of the Lord, being intellectually prepared, and utilizing credible sources, we will now set out to share with you our own insights and perspectives into a large number of church doctrines, practices, and principles, and how they compare between the Catholic Church and The Church of Jesus Christ of Latter-day Saints.

The Format of Each Section and Chapter

The format of each section and chapter will be to present to you the Catholic doctrine; followed by the Latter-day Saint doctrine; and then conclude with our thoughts and commentary on how we came to accept through prayer and study the Latter-day Saint doctrine as a restored truth in the fulness of the gospel.

Because of copyright issues, it was necessary for me to summarize the doctrines and content of both churches in our own words, using direct quotations only where absolutely necessary. In all cases vigorous attempts were made to keep the Catholic and Latter-day Saint content as pure as possible without any subjectivity.

It should be noted that Catholic doctrine in its native form is very proper, legalistic, and often technical in nature. On the other hand, Latter-day Saint doctrine in its native form is simple and often casual in nature. In summarizing the doctrines of both churches, it will often appear as if the Catholic doctrine is formal and the Latter-day Saint doctrine is informal. It was not my intent to purposefully do so; it is simply the native doctrines are often radically different in structure and wording between both churches.

It was not possible to cover all of the doctrines, practices, and principles that made an impression on us; therefore, we selected forty doctrines to focus upon. Perhaps in another book, we can discuss and compare such things as social issues, church practices, and the plan of salvation—all of which deserve the reader's attention.

Come join us as we take you through part of what we've learned during our journey in conversion from Catholics to Latter-day Saints—as individuals, as a married couple, and as a family—and how we took the deep and formidable roots of our Catholic past, and transformed those into an abundant harvest of spiritual fruit as Latter-day Saints.

NOTES

1. James A. Carver, "I Have a Question," *Ensign*, Jan. 1986, 54–56.
2. Dallin H. Oaks, "Teaching and Learning by the Spirit," *Ensign,* Mar. 1997, 7.
3. This quote is generally attributed to a letter that Newton wrote to Robert Hooke in the eighteenth century. Wikiquote, "Isaac Newton," http://en.wikiquote.org/wiki/Isaac–newton#Quotes_about_Newton.

3

Premortal Life

HAVE you ever wondered where you came from? I don't mean your mother's womb, your hometown, or your country of origin; rather, I mean your original state of being. Did you exist in a spiritual state of being with God before this life, or did your life simply begin at conception or birth?

Could there have been, for you and me, a spiritual birth before there was a physical one? Have you ever met someone for the first time and thought you had somehow known them before? Have you ever heard something for the first time and found it eerily familiar? Do these experiences not hint at your having lived before? If so, where did you live, and where did you have your beginning? Was it on this earth or in some place altogether different?

This chapter will explore these questions and suggest some answers that will enlighten you. We will examine the concept and theology of premortal life, which for our purposes we will define as a spiritual existence before our life on earth. Much has been said and much written about the afterlife; we will in this chapter venture in a new direction and say a few words about the before-life.

CATHOLIC DOCTRINE

My study of Catholic doctrine found no direct discussion of a premortal life although Origen (AD 185–AD 254), a theologian and early father of the Christian Church, taught the pre-existence of the soul. The Catechism of the Catholic Church alludes to the soul of each man and woman as "immediately created" by God (Catechism, glossary, 366, and 382). Although the term "immediately" is not specifically defined, its use implies that God creates the human soul at the moment of conception—and not before. The possibility of a premortal life seems not to be considered.

The Catholic doctrine which holds that life, both physical and spiritual, begins at conception can be supported from the writings of Isaiah (Isaiah 44:2, 24), where the prophet speaks of the Lord "forming one from the womb." Isaiah's words could be taken to mean that the soul (or spirit) is created at the time of conception, or shortly thereafter. This doctrinal position is said to have been supported by some of the early Church fathers; hence, the word *immediately* in the Catechism. In this context at least, the doors of Catholicism may be closed to the belief in a premortal life.

LATTER-DAY SAINT DOCTRINE

The doctrine of premortal life is a key element of The Church of Jesus Christ of Latter-day Saints and helps tie together a number of principles that are taught in several advanced doctrines. It is the doctrine of the premortal life that distinctly answers the many questions that were posed at the opening of this chapter.

The doctrine of the premortal life begins with the basic belief that every person ever born to the earth is a spirit child of Heavenly Parents, reared in the premortal life, and endowed with a unique set of talents and capabilities toward a specific purpose in life on earth. Our purpose on earth is but a continuation of our eternal progression, which began in the premortal life but required us to come to the earth since we could progress no further in a premortal state.

Life on earth is viewed as a testing ground prior to the eternities. Each of us as God's children is sent by design to experience mortality, progress in knowledge and understanding, and gain a testimony of our Lord and Savior Jesus Christ. As a testing ground, our memory of the premortal life is "veiled," so we may choose good or evil for ourselves without any predisposition or knowledge of our premortal state. Because our Heavenly Father knew of the challenges we would face on earth, he has given us the capability to recognize eternal truth when we hear it again on earth, while providing us a Savior in Jesus Christ to help us gain forgiveness from our sins and overcome physical and spiritual death. In our premortal state we were presented the plan of salvation in its entirety by our Heavenly Father as part of the Grand Council in heaven.

See *Gospel Principles* 11–15.

THOUGHTS AND COMMENTARY

For us, finding the doctrine of premortal life was like finding lost car keys in a place where we then remembered we had left them. We simply looked again and found this doctrine in plain sight.

Although we had not heard the doctrine of the premortal life taught in the Catholic Church, the doctrine seemed somehow familiar, and we were immediately comfortable with it. It was a conclusion for which we had seen much evidence—but never the conclusion. We went back to the scriptures, studied them prayerfully, and examined the experiences of our own lives: "Furthermore we have had fathers of our flesh which corrected us, and we gave them reverence: shall we not much rather be in subjection unto the Father of spirits, and live?" (Hebrews 12:9).

In this scripture Paul personalizes the role of Heavenly Father as not just the Creator, but as the Father of our spirits. Since he is our Father, it is completely consistent that we would have been with him before coming to the earth. This personalization is further supported in Acts 17:29, where men and women are referred to as "the offspring of God"; in Psalms 82:6 where we are referred to as "children of the most high"; and in Deuteronomy 14:1 where we are referred to as "children of the Lord your God."

From Jeremiah 1:5 we read (God speaking to Jeremiah): "Before I formed thee in the belly I knew thee; and before thou camest forth out of the womb I sanctified thee, and I ordained thee a prophet unto the nations." God as the Father of our spirits knows us—long before we came to this earth. We were with God before being "formed in the belly." As his spirit children, we dwelt with him. He *knows* us. Jeremiah was sanctified and called as a prophet before his journey in mortality, before his physical conception. In like manner we are called to our own unique missions, out of a past that is unremembered.

From Revelation 12 we read about a war in heaven (verse 7). Satan (the dragon in verse 3) drew away a third of the stars (spirit children of our Heavenly Father) from heaven, and they were cast to the earth for their rebellion. You will read later (see chapter 7) that this event took place in the premortal life and that the third of the stars that were cast to the earth were the followers of Satan who, because of their rebellion, would not gain a body of flesh and bone. The remaining two-thirds include you and me, we who chose Jesus Christ and were granted the opportunity to come to the earth, receive a body, and live in mortality.

Outside of scriptural references, there was our common experience. Have you ever met someone you felt you knew, even knew well, though this was your first meeting. We have fanciful ways of explaining this, but always in the background is the doctrine of the premortal life—a sort of spiritual unified theory of unexplained acquaintances.

The importance of the premortal life will become clearer as you read the following chapters. For now, we offer it to you as the short answer to the first of the three fundamental questions that should occupy the lives of every human who lives today, has ever lived, or will yet live: Where did I come from? Why am I here? And where am I going?

To neglect any of these questions is to live an unexamined life. If you will examine your life, Marilyn and I are confident you will find, as we did, that the game is larger than you thought, and that it did not begin where you live now—not even close. Could the doctrine of the premortal life have been lost throughout the centuries, or perhaps never formulated properly as Origen seemingly attempted to do in the early church, given its far-reaching implications to many other doctrines of Christianity?

4

The Creation and the Fall

THE Creation of the world and the expulsion of Adam and Eve from the Garden of Eden are well-known biblical stories. Although the story is well known and oft repeated, the underlying theology is not. This is particularly true of the part that Christ plays in this story and in the larger plan of God the Father.

This chapter will explore the creation of the earth and of man, with particular emphasis on the role of Jesus Christ in these events. We will examine the Fall of Adam and Eve and its frequently overlooked implications. We will discuss how the concept of original sin, as commonly understood, is inadequate to explain the profound impact of what actually transpired. We will invite you to consider how the Fall of Adam and Eve became an essential step in the eternal progression of all of us, the starting point of our journey back to our heavenly home.

Creation

As a Catholic, I remember being taught the story of the Creation with a focus on the events of the six days of creation and on characteristics of the Garden of Eden. Although I never doubted the story's authenticity as a theological milestone, I was never led to believe, nor did I seriously consider, its critical relevance outside of sin and the deception of Satan. It was more or less a story.

After being introduced to Latter-day Saint doctrine on the Creation and the Fall, I realized this was not a mere story, not simply inspirational biblical narrative, but instead core doctrine giving vital illumination to all that came before and all that would follow. With this realization came a new understanding of the origins of man, of his purpose—and of my purpose as a child of God.

CATHOLIC DOCTRINE

The Catechism of the Catholic Church outlines the doctrine of creation as being carried out by the word of God being facilitated by the Holy Trinity. This coordination between the Holy Trinity and the word of God is described with reference to God as "the One who *alone* made heaven and earth" (Catechism, 287, emphasis added) for the purpose of showing forth the glory of God (see also Isaiah 43:1 and Psalms 115:15, 124:8, and 134:3). The creation of the universe, although splendid and magnificent, is not complete but continually evolving towards a state of future perfection as designed and destined by God.

The creation of man was accomplished in the image of God (Genesis 1:27), with our first parents, Adam and Eve, being composed "in an original state of holiness and justice" (Catechism 375), amalgamating the spiritual and material worlds as male and female within the friendship of God. As individuals, humans are of great worth, having dignity, "self-knowledge," and the ability to interact and commune one with another. The earth and all creation are given to and purposed for man; conversely, the purpose of man is to "serve and love God and to offer all creation back to him" (Catechism 358).

As God's creations, man is given freedom to choose for himself, with the ultimate hope that he will choose intelligently and with love that will perfect the work of the creation and lift up others towards their ultimate destinies in mortality and beyond.

LATTER-DAY SAINT DOCTRINE

Latter-day Saint doctrine purports that Jesus Christ created the earth and all that is upon it (plants, animals, seas, and so forth), while having created many other worlds in the process (sun, moon, stars, and other material things that constitute the universe). Jesus performed the Creation, which was done spiritually before being executed physically, through the power of priesthood and by delegation from God the Father.

After the creation of the physical environments and non-human creatures came the greatest of all creations—mankind. Mankind, both man and woman, were created in the image of God with spirits clothed in bodies of flesh and blood. Adam and Eve were the first man and woman to be put upon the earth, physically patterned after our heavenly parents, whom we left in the premortal life. The creation of the earth and of mankind demonstrates the power, wisdom, and love of Jesus Christ and Heavenly Father.

See *Gospel Principles,* 27–29.

THOUGHTS AND COMMENTARY

The Latter-day Saint doctrine on the Creation arises from the doctrine of the premortal life. This linkage of the Creation to the premortal life is essential. We lived as spirit children with our heavenly parents and were told about the plan of our Heavenly Father. This plan called for us, his children, to follow him and become more like him. Is this not much the way of a wise child on earth, following and seeking to become more like a righteous biological parent?

My wife and I could envision our premortal joy in the counsels of heaven as we heard about this plan (Job 38:7). But to fulfill this plan, there needed to be a place for us to be tried, to gain experience, and thus to become more like our Heavenly Father. This would take place in a state called mortality in the physical surroundings of earth. This additional knowledge of creation and its purpose and mechanisms gave us an expanded understanding of our own purpose here on earth. This expanded understanding was not only comforting, it was essential. It was also plain and simple in ways we had never before experienced.

The Catholic doctrine of God and the word of God creating the earth, and the creation being the work of the Holy Trinity is somewhat confusing, especially in light of biblical scripture. The Latter-day Saint doctrine of the earth being created by Jesus Christ under the direction of Heavenly Father is consistent with John 1:1–3: "All things were made by him [Christ]"; Colossians 1:16–17: "for by him [Christ] were all things created"; and Hebrews 1:1–3: "by whom [Christ] also he [the Father] made the worlds." (The place of the priesthood, the form through which the Father delegates his work, will be further explored in chapter 9.)

The Creation conformed precisely to God's master plan, which included all things being created spiritually before being created physically.

Latter-day Saint doctrine holds that the universe was *formed* and *organized,* not created *ex nihilo,* "out of nothing," as Catholic doctrine holds. This is not an insignificant difference.

Catholic and Latter-day Saint doctrines again diverge on what it means to have been created in the image and likeness of God. Whereas Catholic doctrine describes the "image of God" as being spiritual and characteristic in nature (Catechism 357), Latter-day Saint doctrine takes the meaning in simpler terms. We believe our bodies are created in the physical as well as the spiritual image and likeness of God. This doctrine is consistent with the definition of image and is supported by a number of biblical passages including Genesis 9:6, Exodus 24:10, and Acts 7:55–56.

Finally, a stark contrast between the Catholic and Latter-day Saint doctrines of creation lies in the concept of "heavenly parents." When we first heard this, we were startled, as we had never considered the possibility of there being a Heavenly Mother. There are no scriptural references referring to a Heavenly Mother (though a Latter-day Saint hymn makes reference), but knowing the eternal importance of families we could not dismiss the idea. We considered the scripture from Ephesians 3:14–15: "For this cause I bow my knees unto the Father of our Lord Jesus Christ, of whom the whole family in heaven and earth is named."

In Catholicism there is a yearning for a divine mother, hence the emphasis on Mary, the mother of Jesus, who is often referred to as the "Blessed Mother." This yearning is instinctive, a natural extension toward feminine spiritual comfort and nurturing. Heavenly Father intended to provide for each of us a mother and father in mortality, and if things are to be on earth as they are in heaven, then the notion of there being a Heavenly Mother is not difficult to embrace.

The Fall of Adam and Eve—Original Sin

The Fall of Adam and Eve is commonly referred to as the original sin in Catholic doctrine. Our earliest memories of the narrative describe Adam and Eve being tempted by the devil to eat an apple they shouldn't have, leading to the destruction of the Garden of Eden. Like the story of the creation, it was another story. As a Catholic I accepted it without looking beyond the simple facts presented in the Bible. In light of Latter-day Saint doctrine, Marilyn and I both came to realize that the Fall was not just a story: It was a complex event of tremendous significance for all mankind, reaching far beyond the concept of original sin.

CATHOLIC DOCTRINE

Catholic doctrine suggests that the fall of Adam and Eve, commenced through their own temptation in the Garden of Eden at the hand of the devil, led to decay in their trust in God, the abuse of free will, and outright disobedience. Because of their breaking the commandment against partaking of the fruit of the tree of knowledge of good and evil, Adam and Eve were immediately stripped of the holiness they obtained through the Creation and developed a distorted image of God of whom they then became much afraid. The Fall of Adam eventually led to spiritual disharmony across a broad life spectrum, including interpersonal tensions, loss of spiritual control, lust, and obsession with domination. This decay included the world and all that was in it.

The Catholic Church links man's proclivity toward evil and destruction to the Creation and Fall of Adam, spawning the doctrine of original sin, in which all humans are born afflicted with a sin transmitted from Adam as a result of his and Eve's fall. Original sin, as well as the justice of Christ through his infinite Atonement, comes through the "unity of the human race" in which the transmission of the sin is thought to be a mystery and beyond the comprehension of man (Catechism 404). Original sin can only be removed through baptism, including infants who have not committed personal sin themselves. Even after baptism the Fall of Adam creates a dynamic whereby the devil has assumed "certain dominion" over man, despite his agency.

See Catechism 397, 399, 400, and 403–408.

LATTER-DAY SAINT DOCTRINE

Latter-day Saint doctrine on the Fall begins with the understanding that Adam and Eve were valiant spirits in the premortal life and given the assignment to be the first man and woman to live on the earth. It was their mission to bring mortality into the world according to our Heavenly Father's plan. When they assumed their places in the Garden of Eden, Adam and Eve had physical bodies but were not yet mortal, and therefore, unable to have children and exempt from death. Because they were in the presence of God, Adam and Eve had a spiritual life but were unable to understand the difference between good and evil.

Adam and Eve were given two key commandments by God: (1) to "multiply and replenish the earth," and (2) to not eat of the tree of knowledge of good and evil. Just as he does today, Satan influenced Adam and Eve to transgress the commandments of God, seeking to destroy the plan of our Heavenly Father. When Adam learned that Satan persuaded Eve to eat of the tree of knowledge of good and evil, he chose to do likewise in order to remain with Eve, leading to what we refer to as the Fall. As a result of the Fall, Adam and Eve became subject to the consequences of their disobedience: they were cast out of the Garden of Eden, became mortal beings, and were consigned to live in a world much different from the garden. In this world, Adam and Eve and all their descendants would be subject to suffering and physical death. The trial and training of mortality had begun. Perhaps more important, the fall brought about a spiritual death that created a separation from God. Adam and Eve and their posterity lost the opportunity to have face-to-face communication with God. That separation from God was further aggravated by Satan's introduction of evil into the world. The fall brought about both physical and spiritual death that would eventually be reconciled through the Atonement of Jesus Christ.

Despite the introduction of physical and spiritual death and its consequences, the Fall is seen as the commencement of Heavenly Father's plan of salvation. This commencement is a great blessing to all of mankind. This blessing included the obtaining of physical bodies of flesh and bone, the prospect to choose between good and evil, and the opportunity to take full advantage of the Atonement and Resurrection of Jesus Christ. Considering the state of Adam and Eve before the Fall in the Garden of Eden, none of these blessings would have been available without the Fall. The transgression of Adam and Eve belongs solely to Adam and Eve and is not inherited by any of the descendants of Adam. The second article of faith states: "We believe that men will be punished for their own sins, and not for Adam's transgression." The Fall of Adam brought forth mortality, but man does not carry Adam's transgression.

THOUGHTS AND COMMENTARY

As we pondered the doctrine of the fall from the Latter-day Saint doctrinal perspective, we realized that there was far more to the doctrine than sin coming into the world as a result of Adam's decision. There are five key points of interest we developed over time that caused us to reconsider our previous beliefs as Catholics:

1. We know that Adam and Eve before eating of the tree of knowledge of good and evil were not even aware that they were naked. Since they were told by God to "be fruitful, and multiply, and replenish the earth" (Genesis 1:28), one might wonder if

the human race could have ever been propagated had they not become aware that they were naked and had the opportunity to procreate.

2. We feel strongly that God wants each of his children to know and understand the difference between good and evil. That being the case, one must wonder why the tree that they were commanded to not eat of was named the tree of knowledge of good and evil as opposed to something less meaningful.

3. One must question whether God intended for Adam and Eve to remain in a sinless state for all eternity. If God intended this, why was Satan's influence allowed in the garden at all? Satan's eternal objective is to have all of God's children break the commandments of the Lord and become Satan's subjects; therefore, God knew that Satan's presence would lead to sin. Through God's omnipotent power in creating the earth, he could have easily kept Satan from entering the garden, thus reducing or even eliminating the threat of sin to his beloved creations.

4. We know that Jesus Christ was the chosen Savior before the foundation of the world (1 Peter 1:20), and therefore, God knew that we would need a Savior before Adam and Eve were ever sent into the garden.

5. We know that God is a just God and would never hold a person accountable for the transgressions of another person. So how could it be possible that the transgressions of Adam could be attached to his descendants?

When considering these five key points, the Latter-day Saint doctrine of the Fall has much greater spiritual impact and application than the doctrine of original sin. Whereas Catholicism views the Fall as inherently negative, The Church of Jesus Christ of Latter-day Saints views the Fall in a much broader spiritual perspective. Although the transgression of Adam and Eve had dire consequences for us physically and spiritually, as documented in the Bible, the event had far greater reach in launching the Lord's plan of salvation for all mankind.

God, in his infinite wisdom, set into motion a plan that would establish the principle of agency (the freedom to choose—sometimes referred to as free will); introduce the struggle between good and evil as a proving ground for faith; institute a state of mortality among humankind; and lay the foundation for the Atonement and Resurrection of his son Jesus Christ. This plan is in full operation today among the children of God.

We know that the serpent told Eve that if she ate of the tree of knowledge of good and evil that she would not die, but that "God doth know that in the day ye eat thereof, then your eyes shall be opened, and ye shall be as gods, knowing good from evil" (Genesis 3:5). Satan was actually correct (although perhaps not truthful) in telling Eve that she would not die an instant physical death, but that her eyes would be opened, and that she would become like the gods. In Genesis 3:22, God says: "Behold the man is become as one of us, to know good and evil." Curiously, in tempting Eve as he did, Satan, the great dissembler, was delivering a strong element of truth, and in doing so Satan did exactly what God knew he would do and helped launch the plan of salvation. Satan's punishment for doing so was to be cursed all the days of his life and be conquered by Christ (Genesis 3:14–15).

Knowing these fantastic truths about the Fall of Adam and Eve, we are able to understand a number of important gospel principles that have an impact on our own lives today. The simplistic story of Adam and Eve that we grew up with is actually a major spiritual milestone in which the plan of our Heavenly Father for all humankind was kicked off and put into play—the same plan that we are a part of today.

5

Communication to and from God

COMMUNICATION to and from God is essential during our journey through this life and into the next. As in any form of communication, there is a sender and a receiver. We as God's children find ourselves in both roles: we send our petitions to our Heavenly Father through prayer, and we receive our answers through personal revelation, the scriptures, and prayer. This chapter explores these three elements of communication with our Heavenly Father to understand how both churches utilize and instruct its members on these invaluable mediums of divine communication.

Revelation

The word revelation is defined as making something manifest, especially something of great significance that was not previously known. Revelation can come to an individual on a personal matter, to a father for his family, to an ecclesiastical leader for an entire congregation, or to a designated person of God for the entire world.

CATHOLIC DOCTRINE

Catholic doctrine on revelation is clearly summarized as the following: "God has revealed himself fully by sending his own Son, in whom he has established his covenant for ever. The Son is his Father's definitive Word; so 'there will be no further Revelation after him' " (Catechism 73).

Catholic doctrine thus asserts that God, in sending Jesus Christ to the earth, along with the inspiration of the Holy Spirit, has revealed all that he intends to reveal to the human race. Man can come to know God through Jesus Christ by study and meditation upon the works and words of God the Father as found in nature and the scriptures.

Prior to the coming of Christ, God manifested himself to Adam and Eve in the Garden of Eden. He communicated directly with them and made covenants with them. He later manifested himself and made covenants with Noah, Moses, and Abraham in what certainly can be called revelations. But since the coming of Christ such communication has not been necessary. This does not mean there have not been "private" revelations that have been recognized by the Catholic Church as serving to help Catholics live the revelations of Jesus Christ more completely, but these do not add to or take away from anything Christ revealed more than two thousand years ago.

See Catechism 50, 67 to 72, and glossary.

LATTER-DAY SAINT DOCTRINE

Latter-day Saints believe that the Prophet Joseph Smith, by command from God the Father and his only begotten son, Jesus Christ, restored the Church of Jesus Christ upon the earth in 1830. The direction given to Joseph Smith was not to establish a new church, a reformed church, or a breakaway church. It was his direction to restore the church that Christ had established on the earth some two thousand years earlier, a church which had been lost to apostasy as explained in chapter 2.

The Church of Jesus Christ of Latter-day Saints was established by modern revelation—not revelation improving upon or completing or surpassing or correcting that of Christ, but revelation restoring to men the revelation of which Christ was the fulfillment some two thousand years earlier.

The ninth article of faith of The Church of Jesus Christ of Latter-day Saints clearly states the Church's position on revelation: "We believe all that God has revealed, all that He does now reveal, and we believe that He will yet reveal many great and important things pertaining to the Kingdom of God."

In the spirit of Hebrews 1:1–2, the Church of Jesus Christ is to be directed by God, with revelation being the "rock" upon which the Church is to be built (Matthew 16:16–18). Such was the case when

Jesus instructed and directed leaders in establishing his Church, while receiving direction from God the Father. Though Christ left his earthly existence, he remains with us always unto the end of the world according to the promise given before his Ascension (Matthew 28:20). He is with us through the Holy Ghost (Luke 12:23 and John 14:26).

Christ spoke directly to Saul in a vision (Acts 9:3–6) and to Peter in like manner (Acts 10). These were revelations after the Ascension of Christ. Christ gave many revelations to John in what came to be the Book of Revelation in the New Testament. These were given after the Ascension of Christ. Prophets and others can have the gift of prophecy (1 Corinthians 14:39), in each case given in its proper order and in agreement with the scriptures.

Bruce R. McConkie, a Latter-day Saint apostle, defined revelation in two parts: personal revelation and revelation for the Church. Personal revelation is given to individuals for their own personal guidance; revelation for the Church is given to Church-appointed leaders for the entire Church body.

See *Gospel Principles,* 101–104; and *Mormon Doctrine,* 643–47.

THOUGHTS AND COMMENTARY

When the principle of revelation was first introduced to us during our investigation of the Church, Marilyn and I couldn't fathom why a loving Heavenly Father would not provide this ability to his children individually and certainly to the Church collectively. Frankly, we were not aware that the Catholic Church does not believe in any further revelation—that was, and still is, quite a surprise to us.

To limit revelation to that which was provided by Jesus Christ before his Ascension into heaven would be akin to saying that God no longer speaks to his children or has no further instruction to provide. I am reminded of a saying I once heard concerning a quiet God and how preposterous such a notion is: "Is God the great I am, or the great I was?"

We found comfort in the Latter-day Saint doctrine about a living God who would interact with his children on a personal level while providing broader guidance through appointed Church leaders. The doctrine of continuous revelation gave new meaning to prayer and to the importance of divine counsel. It made God and his Son Jesus Christ more alive to us.

Upon studying the writings of the Apostle Paul, we were even more convinced of the truthfulness of the Latter-day Saint doctrine regarding revelation. In 1 Corinthians 2:9–10 Paul writes: "But as it is written, Eye hath not seen, nor ear heard, neither have entered into the heart of man, the things which God hath prepared for them that love him. But God hath revealed them unto us by his Spirit: for the Spirit searcheth all things, yea, the deep things of God."

Paul provides similar insights in chapter 14 of his first letter to the Corinthians and in chapter 3 of his letter to the Ephesians. Paul wrote these letters long after the Ascension of Christ. He did not consider himself or others to be without the gift of continuing revelation, and neither did we.

Our family enjoys our own personal revelation today, along with the confidence of knowing our Church leaders are continuously receiving revelation from our Heavenly Father. Such doctrine and practices are completely in line with the Bible and what we personally believe to be true as children of a loving Father in Heaven. Given the wonderful experiences we have had with revelation since our baptism, both individually and Church-wide, we could never imagine being without this revelation. It has not led us away from the core doctrines of our Christian faith, it has led us deeper into them.

Scriptures

God speaks to us through sacred scriptures—something Marilyn experienced long before we joined the Church. He speaks continually through the flow of his sacred Word, providing guidance and answers to questions that come up in our daily lives.

Necessary to God's communication with us is our interpretation of his sacred scriptures. But, sadly, it is these interpretations that have led religious people to contend with one another, often violently, over many centuries. Differences of interpretation were sometimes quite challenging to Marilyn and me during our investigation of the Church. On many occasions we utilized Marilyn's Catholic University education and familiarity with the scriptures to guide us.

Catholic Doctrine

The Catholic Church accepts as scripture the Bible, including the Old Testament (forty-six books) and the New Testament (twenty-seven books), with an emphasis on the Christ-centered four gospels. There are seven books in the Old Testament that are unique to the Bible used by the Catholic Church: 1 and 2 Maccabees, Ecclesiasticus (also known as Sirach), the Wisdom of Solomon, Baruch, Tobit, and Judith.

The Old and New Testament are in full unity with God's plan and revelation, are built upon one another as the inspired true Word of God, and should be thought of as one book of Christ. Although the Bible and its saving truth was written by the hand of man, God is still seen as the scriptural author, as the writing was inspired by God and teaches without error.

The Catholic Church teaches that interpretation of scripture must take into account what God intended to be revealed through the author, with an understanding that the Holy Spirit may also provide additional insights to the reader. Church members are urged to read the scriptures regularly.

See Catechism 134–141.

LATTER-DAY SAINT DOCTRINE

The eighth article of faith of The Church of Jesus Christ of Latter-day Saints states: "We believe the Bible to be the word of God as far as it is translated correctly; we also believe the Book of Mormon to be the word of God."

This article helps lay the Latter-day Saint doctrinal foundation for scriptural interpretation. The standard scriptural works of The Church of Jesus Christ of Latter-day Saints include the Bible, the Book of Mormon, the Doctrine and Covenants, and the Pearl of Great Price. The Church also accepts inspired words of its living prophets to be scripture.

From earliest times, the Lord has commanded his prophets to keep records of events that are both historical and spiritual. Often these records have become scripture. Whenever the servants of the Lord "speak or write under the influence of the Holy Ghost, their words become scripture."[1]

The Bible covers the period from the creation through shortly after the Ascension of Jesus Christ. The thirty-nine books of the Old Testament foretell of the coming of the Savior, while the twenty-seven books of the New Testament provide a record of the life of the Savior, with an emphasis on his public ministry. Geographically, the Bible records the lives of people living in the Middle East. The Bible was authored by several inspired individuals and has been translated from its original Greek and Hebrew text by numerous scholars and organizations into many different versions and languages.

The Book of Mormon complements the Bible in providing a record of people living in the Americas between approximately 2200 BC and AD 400. As the subtitle of the Book of Mormon says, it is "Another Testament of Jesus Christ," providing, in particular, a record of the visit of Jesus Christ to the inhabitants of the Americas shortly after his Resurrection. The Book of Mormon was authored by several inspired individuals, abridged onto gold plates, and translated into English from its original reformed Egyptian text by the prophet Joseph Smith. It was later translated from English into many different languages.

The Doctrine and Covenants (D&C) is a collection of revelations given to modern-day prophets. It was compiled from 1823 to 1978. The purpose of the Doctrine and Covenants is to prepare the inhabitants of the earth for the Second Coming of Jesus Christ by providing direction and guidance. Among other things, the Doctrine and Covenants gives written details for the organization and operation of the Church and the offices of the priesthood and their ecclesiastical and spiritual functions.

The Pearl of Great Price contains three different compilations: the Book of Moses, the Book of Abraham, and a collection of inspired writings by Joseph Smith. The Book of Moses is a work revealed to Joseph Smith pertaining to visions and writings of Moses that focus on the creation of the earth. The Book of Abraham is a translation from a papyrus scroll originating from the Egyptian catacombs, translated by Joseph Smith, and containing insights and information on creation, the priesthood, the gospel, and the nature of God. The writings of Joseph Smith include a portion of Joseph Smith's inspired translation of the Bible, a brief history of the Church, and the Articles of Faith.

Because Latter-day Saints believe that whenever the servants of the Lord speak or write under the influence of the Holy Ghost, their words become scripture, the words of the living prophets are also considered scripture. Such words can come through Church publications, conferences, and other forms of inspired instruction. One must still give consideration to those scriptures that are canonized, which today are the Bible, the Book of Mormon, the Doctrine and Covenants, and the Pearl of Great Price.

Church members are exhorted to study the scriptures every day, as individuals and as families. In doing so Church members are told they can avoid evil and grow closer to God—especially when members read the scriptures in conjunction with pondering, praying, and asking God for further understanding through the Holy Ghost.

See *Gospel Principles*, 52–56.

THOUGHTS AND COMMENTARY

As Catholics, Marilyn and I together were quite active in regularly reading the Bible. Marilyn also read frequently on her own—a regiment she formulated in the convent and continues to this day. Saint Jerome said the Church "forcefully and specifically exhorts all the Christian faithful . . . to learn 'the surpassing knowledge of Jesus Christ,' by frequently reading of the divine Scriptures. 'Ignorance of the Scriptures is ignorance of Christ.' "[2]

Despite such an exhortation by an early church father, we cannot ever recall being encouraged by Catholic Church leaders to read the Bible, nor were we aware of any sustained effort to promote earnest study of the Bible. Most of our Catholic friends seemed to have little interest in studying the scriptures outside of occasional reading. This may be a lingering result from past history where the reading of the Bible was strictly done by clergy, with little involvement of the laity.

In our investigation of The Church of Jesus Christ of Latter-day Saints, one of the first things we had to come to terms with was the idea of the "Bible being the word of God as far as it is translated correctly," as stated in the eighth article of faith. As frequent Bible readers, we never considered that translations could affect the meaning of the Bible. I discovered there were multiple translations of the Bible but didn't think there might be serious imperfections in translation. I was surprised to learn that there were at least seventeen *English* translations of the Bible in active use, with dozens of other translations in circulation. These include the English Standard Version, Good News Bible, Holman Christian Standard Bible, J. B. Phillips New Testament, King James Version, the Living Bible, the Message, New American Bible, New American Standard Bible, New International Version, (New) Jerusalem Bible, New King James Bible, New Living Translation, (New) Revised Standard Version, Today's English Version, the Amplified Version, and Today's New International Version.

As a Christmas present Marilyn gave me a parallel Bible many years ago with four side-by-side simultaneous translations. I found the translations in many instances to be very different from one another. Not only the translations, but the plain meanings they conveyed were in many cases different. It became quite clear why Latter-day Saint doctrine puts a small disclaimer on the correctness of the translation of the Bible. Although we felt an affinity toward the New Jerusalem translation of the Bible, over time we came to appreciate the proper nature of the King James Version, despite its awkward language from time to time. It took some getting use to!

The second thing we needed to come to terms with was the question of whether there was additional scripture—mainly, of course, the Book of Mormon, the Doctrine and Covenants, and the Pearl of Great Price. Having the Apocrypha as Catholics was a small primer to having these additional books of scripture for our use and benefit. However, some, who were somewhat unfriendly toward the LDS faith, were quick to point out to us the scripture from Revelation 22:18 which states: "For I testify unto every man that heareth the words of the prophecy of this book, If any man shall add unto these things, God shall add unto him the plagues that are written in this book."

Their interpretation of this scripture was that any additional scripture outside of the Bible was blasphemous. We found similar scriptures in Deuteronomy 4:2 and 12:32 that spoke of not "adding to" the word of God. These Old Testament scriptures called into question the validity of the New Testament itself, since they were written hundreds of years earlier. Therefore, we concluded that the scripture from Revelation 22:18 must be referring to adding to the revelation and prophecy of John, not to adding scripture outside of the Bible itself. Thus, the possibility of additional scripture was opened to us, but we remained cautious.

In our quest to understand, we started with a simple question: Could the word of God be confined to a single book? John 21:25 casts a serious doubt on this notion: "And there are also many other things which Jesus did, the which, if they should be written every one, I suppose that even the world itself could not contain the books that should be written."

We next considered how a single book could testify of itself as being true. Matthew 18:16 suggests that one book cannot testify of itself—it takes at least two: "But if he will not hear thee, then take with thee one or two more, that in the mouth of two or three witnesses every word may be established."

With these two questions soundly answered, we cautiously read the Book of Mormon along with the Doctrine and Covenants.

Almost immediately, given her extensive background in the scriptures,

Marilyn found that many of the principles and teachings she knew well in the Bible were more simply illuminated and expounded upon more fully in the Book of Mormon and the Doctrine and Covenants. Marilyn felt strongly the presence of the Holy Ghost as she studied and prayed upon these two works of scripture. The same was true for me, although, at first, at a slower pace than Marilyn. It was clear that the Book of Mormon witnessed of the Bible being true (1 Nephi 13:23–24), and that the Bible witnessed of the Book of Mormon being true (Ezekiel 37:16–20)—both being testaments of Jesus Christ. We experienced an enhanced peace, comfort, and understanding of the gospel of Jesus Christ that we had not enjoyed up to that time. Our testimony of the Book of Mormon as a true scriptural witness of Jesus Christ allowed us to extend our spiritual confidence to the prophet Joseph Smith, the Doctrine and Covenants, and the principles of the restored gospel.

Further study helped us formulate the place of modern revelation in the form of scripture. It is clear that God is continually calling man to live a higher law and that it became necessary to restore laws that were lost; hence, it is necessary for the Lord to provide additional scripture, to speak to us again, adding here a little, there a little, and enriching our understanding. For example, Exodus 21:24 from the Old Testament provides justification of taking revenge on one's enemies; however, Matthew 5:44 from the New Testament calls for the loving one's enemies—thus a higher law. Jesus set the example of this practice when he moved the Jews to a higher law in divorce from allowance (Deuteronomy 24:1–3) to forbiddance (Matthew 5:31–32).

As we continued our study we found several instances where the three additional standard works being used by The Church of Jesus Christ of Latter-day Saints helped illuminate and bring clarity to topics covered in the Bible, but not reconciled or explained in a way we could understand or comprehend. In our Catholic experience, such irreconcilable differences had been explained away as "mysteries." In many cases, these topics were of great importance, and we couldn't accept that a loving Father in Heaven would want to keep his children in the dark about such sacred matters.

Consider the following examples of how Latter-day scriptures provide spiritual support and understanding of matters addressed, but not reconciled, in the Bible:

Cain and Satan

Genesis 4:8 in the Bible mentions that Cain slays his brother Abel after becoming angry when the Lord did not respect his offering. The Bible doesn't provide a reason for the killing or what motivated Cain to do such a thing. Moses 5 in the Pearl of Great Price provides important details on how Satan influenced Cain to commit the murderous act, providing vital spiritual insights for us to liken to ourselves in the struggle with evil.

Communal Sustenance

Acts 2:44–45 and 2 Corinthians 8:14 in the Bible discuss the virtues of communal living where there is economic equality in sharing all things in common; however, the Bible doesn't provide any details on how this can be accomplished or administered. In Doctrine and Covenants 42:30–36, the "law of consecration" is laid out in detail to the point of being operational.

Clean Living

1 Corinthians 6:19 and Proverbs 20 in the Bible warns that God's children are to respect their physical bodies and refrain from certain substances; however, the Bible is light on specifics. Section 89 of the Doctrine and Covenants, often referred to as the Word of Wisdom, provides exceptional detail concerning these matters and describes associated blessings.

Baptism

Baptism is first mentioned in the Bible in Mark 1:4, and later in John 3:5 as being essential to entering the kingdom of God. Paul in 1 Corinthians 10:1–2 states metaphorically that the Israelites were "baptized . . . in the cloud and in the sea." However, the Bible doesn't provide facts of when baptism started and how the requirement of baptism from John 3:5 applies to those who lived on the earth before John the Baptist. Such cryptic references to baptism leave huge gaps in spiritual understanding. One can read from 1 Nephi 20:1 in the Book of Mormon that baptism existed at or around the time of Isaiah (740 BC). With further help from the Book of Moses in the Pearl of Great Price, one can gain a full understanding of the origin of baptism on the earth—traced literally back to the time of Adam.

Unforgivable Sin

1 John 1:7 states that the Atonement of Jesus Christ can cleanse us all from sin. Conversely, Matthew 12:31–32 states that blasphemy against the Holy Ghost shall not be forgiven in this world or the next. These two scriptures from the Bible not only contradict one another, but the Bible doesn't provide any definition of blasphemy against the Holy Ghost. This paradox is reconciled through modern-day revelation and scripture found in Doctrine and Covenants 132:27, where blasphemy against the Holy Ghost is defined in detail.

On an intellectual and spiritual level, Marilyn and I both gained powerful testimonies of Latter-day scriptures as God's word and forming with the Bible the fulness of the gospel of Jesus Christ. Many years later to the present, after exhaustive study and spiritual experience with these standard works of scripture, we can testify confidently that their value in our own lives and the lives of our children is incalculable. Our Christian faith has been reinforced by these additions to the canon. We move and act with deeper understanding and commitment than would have been possible without them. By the light of these sacred texts, our faith has been strengthened, we have fully embraced the truth, we live the Lord's commandments, and we love Him fully in service.

Prayer

Before investigating The Church of Jesus Christ of Latter-day Saints, prayer to me consisted of three things: the "Our Father," the "Hail Mary," and whatever other petitions I might have to offer my Heavenly Father in prayer. Marilyn on the other hand had far more experience in prayer, given her background as a nun and the spiritual life that she had developed.

After being married, Marilyn and I prayed together each day, using the scriptures, music, meditation, and other means of enhancing our prayers. Our prayer practices as Catholics fully prepared us for a more comprehensive prayer life as Latter-day Saints. The Latter-day Saint doctrine on prayer prompted us to make important refinements to our prayers that gave them deeper meaning. As we taught our children to pray, we ourselves prayed with greater simplicity and directness.

CATHOLIC DOCTRINE

God earnestly calls every one of his children to pray daily (even constantly) and through the liturgy, with Jesus exhorting his disciples to do so with great motivation, faith, and a pure heart in his name.

The method and mechanics of prayer are many. Prayers should start with the Sign of the Cross, "In the name of the Father and of the Son and of the Holy Spirit. Amen," while invoking Holy Spirit (1 Corinthians 12:3). Prayer is primarily addressed to the Father, but can also be addressed to Jesus Christ. Prayer can be done "in communion with the Virgin Mary," and through intercession (on behalf of another) with the saints.

The most fundamental Christian prayer is the Our Father (or Lord's Prayer), entrusted to all of the world by Jesus Christ. The Our Father is the "quintessential prayer of the Church."

The basic form of prayer includes blessing, petition, intercession, thanksgiving, and praise. There are "three major expressions of the life of prayer: vocal prayer [the body joining the heart and soul], meditation [thought and imagination], and contemplative prayer [attentiveness]" (Catechism 2721).

Other sources of prayer can be the scriptures, the liturgy, and the three virtues (faith, hope, and charity). Prayer is most appropriately conducted in four specific places: personal or family locations, monasteries, places of pilgrimage (holy places), and the church.

The Church calls its members to focus on faith, conversion, and "vigilance of heart" in order to avoid difficulties in prayer—mainly "distraction and dryness." A lack of faith and certain forms of depression leading to discouragement can be a threat to effective prayer. This can be especially harmful to the process of prayer when there is a feeling that prayers are not heard. Then one must call out to the Holy Spirit for help in offering prayer.

See Catechism 2166, 2590, 2591, 2621, 2644, 2647, 2662, 2680, 2681, 2682, 2692, 2696, 2720–2724, 2754–2757, 2773, 2776.

LATTER-DAY SAINT DOCTRINE

Latter-day Saints consider prayer one of the greatest blessings we will have during our journey in mortality. Prayer is "sincere, heartfelt talk with our Heavenly Father."[3] Prayer has been taught and practiced since the beginning of time, affects all of our thoughts and actions, and will bring us closer to God than anything else we can do as humans.

The Church instructs that we are to pray whenever we feel the need to do so, and always "with a sincere heart, with real intent." The times we don't feel like praying are likely the times we need it the most. All prayers should be directed to God the Father, *only*, and can be done in silence or out loud as we feel directed. We are directed to have personal prayers each morning and night (as a minimum), while having a prayer in our hearts at all times. We are also directed to have prayers as a family each morning and night. In addition, we are admonished to have prayers before eating as an individual or as families. All Church meetings and events begin and end with prayers, typically offered by individuals from the congregation.

The form of Latter-day Saint prayer usually includes addressing Heavenly Father, expressing feelings from the heart as if to "confide in him," asking forgiveness, giving thanks, praying for others, and expressing love for Heavenly Father and for Jesus Christ. The highest and most reverent language possible should always be used. In all instances of prayer Latter-day Saints are asked to avoid "vain repetition" and ask for and submit themselves to God's will, understanding that God knows what is best for us. Latter-day Saints close every prayer in the name of Jesus Christ.

Somewhat unique to Latter-day Saints is the prayer position that some take of having their arms folded. Although not any means a requirement or suggested action, many use this position as a means of avoiding fidgety hands, especially with children, and allowing one to embrace the prayer from deep within the heart.

The genuine prayers of the faithful are always answered, but not always in the way or timing we desire. We are to accept the influence of the Holy Ghost, which often manifests itself with warm comfortable feelings of confirmation, to understand the answer to our prayers. We are counseled to do all we can to bring about that which we desire and not ask God to do all of the work. God is not our butler; he is our Heavenly Father, and he has given us power to make things happen. Finally, we must be ever aware that answers to prayers frequently come through other people.

See *Gospel Principles*, 41–44.

THOUGHTS AND COMMENTARY

Before investigating the Church, prayer was already a vital part of our lives—especially Marilyn's. She was use to praying for guidance, for direction, for healing, and for the other events of life, both large and small. The act of pouring out her soul to the Lord was an integral part of her life that she placed great value in. When we were first introduced to the method in which Latter-day Saints prayed, it was a bit foreign to us. Latter-day Saint prayer was more formal in language than we were used to and generally more rigid in posture and execution. This applied to both public and personal prayers.

Although different from what we were used to, over time Marilyn and I found the Latter-day Saint doctrine and practice on prayer to be meaningful and reverent. Up to that time we never thought about how we prayed and the principles and doctrine behind prayer. We found Latter-day Saint prayer practices down-to-earth, functional, highly expressive, and conversational. We found we could readily put the doctrine on prayer into everyday practice as individuals and as a family. The guidance provided on how and when to pray, what to pray for, and how prayers are answered provided detailed insight into the process and value of prayer in our lives.

Six key things stood out to us as we pondered the differences in the doctrines: 1) conducting personal prayers morning and night (at a minimum); 2) praying to our Heavenly father exclusively; 3) using the most reverent language possible; 4) always ending prayers in the name of Jesus Christ; 5) avoiding meaningless words and repetitions; and 6) the emphasis on praying as a family.

Although the principle of intercessory prayer is biblically sound and comforting, we didn't have any issues with the practice of praying exclusively to our Heavenly Father—the source of all life. He is our Father, our God, and the deity to whom all prayers should be directed. We thought to ourselves, "Why pray to Mary or a saint, when you can go right to the Father himself with prayers?" When Jesus taught his disciples to pray, he addressed his Heavenly Father and set the perfect example for all of us on prayer. He did not invite anyone to pray to him. He always deferred to the Father—always!

Over time we found that praying to our Heavenly Father exclusively avoided confusion with our children. I can remember in my younger days thinking, "How do I pray? Who do I pray to: Mary, Jesus, God, the Holy Ghost, a particular saint?" I even found myself praying to particular statues in the Catholic Church as a child, seeing many other members do the same as they knelt before certain images. Although the prayers may not have been directed at the statues physically, it was difficult to understand the difference as a child.

Our children are confident that their Father in Heaven is the right one to direct prayers to all of the time no matter where they might be. There is no confusion or ambiguity.

As a Catholic, I gave little thought to the language of prayer because the formulas were set—otherwise, I was free to chat with whomever I chose. I grew up voicing my prayers silently or out loud in a casual language, since this was most comfortable to me. I found the Latter-day Saint practice of using "higher" language in prayer to be foreign, even odd. I was accustomed to saying "you" and "your" when addressing Heavenly Father. Using "thee" and "thou" seemed quaintly old-fashioned at first. Soon I became aware of a shift in myself. Language is powerful. I was showing greater reverence and respect. My love and awe for my Heavenly Father grew, as did my feeling of closeness and of having a deep personal relationship. I came to understand, along with my family, that language can enhance prayers and the spirit behind prayers.

As Catholics Marilyn and I were familiar with congregational prayer and communal proclamations during the course of the liturgy, or Mass, much of which is repetitive. The Mass from start to finish has a number of passages that are said repetitively by the presiding priest and the congregation. It is easy to recite these passages without much thought or any spiritual involvement. Perhaps too easy.

I remember reciting the Nicene Creed and the Mystery of Faith over and over. I remember hearing the Eucharistic prayers being recited by the priests, and of the constant repetition—perhaps to the point of being meaningless at times when our minds might wander. The rosary itself is a series of repetitive prayers that can easily fall into the same dynamic of reciting words without comprehending the importance of their meaning.

While pondering these Catholic rituals during our investigation of the Church, we were reminded of the counsel from Jesus as recorded in Matthew 6:7: "But when ye pray, use not vain repetitions."

Recalling our prayers as Catholics we would always cross ourselves, but we may or may not end our prayers by invoking the name of Jesus Christ ("in the name of Jesus Christ"). In John 14:6 Jesus proclaimed: "I am the away, the truth, and the life: no man cometh unto the Father, but by me." Therefore it was simple to accept that all prayers should be ended in the name of Jesus Christ, as only through him can our prayers to our Father in Heaven gain access.

Finally, the Latter-day Saint focus on praying as a family seemed obvious to us. Although there is no mention of family prayers in the Catechism, this doesn't mean that Catholic families don't pray as families—they do! However, having emphasis on family prayers built into the doctrine and regular practice of The Church of Jesus Christ of Latter-day Saints is exceedingly helpful in developing this discipline.

We are certain that our Heavenly Father wants us to pray as a family every day. The Latter-day Saint focus on family prayer reinforced our belief that God continues to speak to his children through the process of revelation and prayer. It also reinforced our belief that God speaks to the leaders of his church and that those leaders listen and apply the Lord's counsel.

While I can recall many sacred moments of reciting the rosary and the beauty of the Hail Mary prayer, I came to understand that these prayer experiences during my days as a Catholic prepared me for life as an even more prayerful Latter-day Saint. Like so many other things, I wasn't giving up anything in becoming a Latter-day Saint and was in fact gaining so much more in reaping the harvest.

NOTES

1. *Gospel Principles,* 52.
2. DV 25; cf. Phil 3:8 and St. Jerome, *Commentariorum in Isaiam libri xviii,* prol.: PL 24, 17b.
3. *Gospel Principles,* 41.

6

The Father, Son, and Holy Spirit

ALTHOUGH Jesus Christ is the core figure in our lives as Christians, a full understanding of the Father, the Son, and the Holy Spirit (or the Holy Ghost) is essential to reaching our full potential in the gospel.

This chapter will explore Catholic and Latter-day Saint doctrines on the nature of the Father, Son, and Holy Spirit. Finally, we will consider Catholic doctrine on the Trinity in comparison to Latter-day Saint doctrine on the Godhead.

God the Father

God is the central figure in the spiritual lives of all humans who believe there is a God. God is referred to by many different names across a variety of religious sects, but among Christians he is most often referred to as "God the Father." For many, God is an incomprehensible being without form or substance, immaterial—a pure spiritual essence who created heaven and earth and all that are in it and who was then, is now, and forever will be the sole governor of all that is. He is the prime mover, the alpha and the omega—and he is alone.

For others, God is a more personal and approachable being—though still all-powerful. This being gave us life, allowed us to enter this mortal realm, and will welcome us home to his heavenly realm, which is our eternal home, when our mortal existence reaches its inevitable end.

Although we may not reach a perfect understanding of God the Father, we must seek to know him. The doctrinal foundation of God the Father can either help or hinder the process of knowing God, and is therefore worthy of our careful study.

CATHOLIC DOCTRINE

Catholic doctrine presents a God who is living, the creator of all things, a being who is the first and the last (Isaiah 44:6). God is merciful and gracious, the essence of love and "truth itself, whose words cannot deceive" (Catechism 215). God's love is described as being that of a father's toward his son, even stronger than a mother's love for her own children. In his omnipotence, God is from "everlasting to everlasting" (Catechism 207).

While the characteristics of God can be described in earthly terms, the physical nature of God is less comprehensible to mankind—a mystery: "In no way is God in man's image. He is neither man nor woman. God is pure spirit in which there is not place for the difference between the sexes" (Catechism 370).

Thus, in Catholic doctrine, the word *father* and the masculine pronouns used to refer to this word, are entirely metaphorical, and this metaphorical reference is exceedingly—one might say, infinitely—broad.

God cannot be thought of as being a father in the physical sense, since he is without form or gender. So, although there are "characteristics" ascribed to God, God remains a "mystery beyond words" (Catechism 230). Saint Augustine said, "If you understood him, it would not be God."[1] Saint Augustine's mixture of the pronouns "him" and "it" is noteworthy.

See Catechism 200–207, 210, 211, 215, 219, 230, 338, and 370.

LATTER-DAY SAINT DOCTRINE

Latter-day Saint doctrine describes God as the one supreme being and creator of all things, the father of Jesus Christ, and the ruler of heaven and earth.

God is ascribed the characteristics of love, mercy, charity, truth, power, faith, knowledge, and judgment, having all power, all knowledge, and from whom all good things come.[2] This mixture of tangible and intangible characteristics does not negate that God is our Heavenly Father; it affirms this truth. God is the Heavenly Father of all men and women who have ever lived on the earth; all of us are the spiritual sons and daughters of the living God.

With all mankind being created in the image of God (Genesis 1:26–27), it follows that God has some form of the physical characteristics of man: a body of flesh and bones. However, unlike our bodies, his is glorified, perfected, and beyond our ability to comprehend.

See *Gospel Principles*, 8–10.

THOUGHTS AND COMMENTARY

The Catholic doctrine on God the Father describes an omniscient and all-powerful being from whom/where everything that is righteous and good comes. Furthermore, God is a mystery and beyond the understanding of man, laying a foundation of reverence for his majesty and dominion. Catholic doctrine focuses on reverence for God while protecting his sanctity and dominion.

Although the Latter-day Saint doctrine mirrors Catholic doctrine in reverence and awe for God, we felt the Latter-day Saint doctrine also gave God a more intimate nature and more closely resembled a doctrine that reveals a loving Father in Heaven. We must remember that God in the New Testament is referred to by Jesus and Paul as "Abba" (Mark 14:36; Romans 8:15; Galatians 4:6), which literally translated means "father," but a personal form of father, approaching a meaning more like "daddy." The idea of God being our father was revealed to Marilyn as she was reading the Bible and praying during her time in the convent. The concept was pure revelation to her soul and she knew from that point forward that God was her Heavenly Father. Interestingly, when she shared this with her fellow sisters, they appeared disinterested in her newfound revelation.

Marilyn and I grew up, as do many Catholics, being told that in many ways God is a mystery and beyond our comprehension. Such a doctrine can put distance between us and God, making it more difficult to know and love God more fully.

Catholic doctrine describes God as without gender ("neither man nor woman"), creating confusion both spiritually and intellectually. In numerous biblical passages God is referred to as "He" and "Father." I found it impossible take scripture seriously while holding in my mind the image of God without gender. He is our Heavenly Father, a being male in essence, a loving Father to us all.

Paul writes that God is the Father of Spirits (Hebrews 12:9). We found Latter-day Saint doctrine much closer than Catholic doctrine to what we read in scripture and to the intimate relationship we have with God.

Turning the word *father* into pure metaphor; denying the fatherhood of God; and dispensing with humans being created in God's physical image as a fanciful notion or a mysterious abstraction were simply too much for us. We were seeking intimacy with God, not with an abstraction. In the seeking, we found our Heavenly Father, a "he," a male.

The real shock for Marilyn and I was the Latter-day Saint doctrine that God has a body of flesh and bones. For awhile we had to put this doctrine on the back-burner as it was so different from the Catholic doctrine of God being spirit only. We realized that acceptance of the doctrine was not critical at the moment and decided to move on. Over time, as startling as that doctrine was to us, we had to consider several passages from the Bible that supported such a doctrine, passages that now made perfect sense once we knew the truth.

We Are in God's Image

There are several scriptures in the Bible that mention our being created in the "image and likeness" of God. Genesis 9:6 refers to "man's blood" and the image of God in the same verse, strongly suggesting a physical likeness between God and man's blood. While some may interpret such scriptures metaphorically, we had to consider the possibility of the literal meaning. Up until that time we had focused on the "spirit" nature of God as mentioned in John 4:24: "God is a Spirit: and they that worship him must worship him in spirit and in truth." Since humans are spirits with flesh and bones in the image and likeness of God, one must consider that God is *spirit* with flesh and bones as well. This consideration begs a profound question: In what form, then, are the "flesh and bones" of God. One need not dispense with the plain language of scripture to imagine a God of infinite power who is also in the form he gave to man. What we don't know are the processes that generate bodily glorification. This is where the mystery lies, not in the fatherhood of God.

Those Who Have Seen God

The Bible mentions those who have seen God in one way or another. Stephen (Acts 7:55–56) looked up to Heaven and saw Jesus standing on the right hand of God. Although God has appeared to man in many forms, one must consider that some references clearly imply God having a tangible body as opposed to a being without form. How does Jesus stand to the right or to the left of nothingness? If we let metaphor take over, we will be left with no God at all.

God Having Shape

Jesus refers to God having "shape" (John 5:37), while Paul refers to Christ in comparison with God when he tells the Hebrews "being the brightness of his glory, and the express image of his person" (Hebrews 1:3). With God being referred to as having shape and "person," one must seriously consider the physical nature of God.

The doctrine of God having a body was indeed new to us; however, after exhaustive study of the Bible, we found this doctrine to be sound and further reinforced the intimacy of God as our Father—especially for our children. Jesus himself said, "He that hath seen me hath seen the Father" (John 14:9). Joseph Smith was blessed to have this doctrine revealed to him firsthand when he saw the Father and the Son in the sacred grove as part of the First Vision.

The ultimate benefit to our spiritual lives from the Latter-day Saint doctrine on God the Father is that we have come closer to our Father in Heaven through a more intimate understanding of his character, while maintaining a reverence that is appropriate when praising and praying to the Almighty. We have again gained everything and lost nothing, relying on plain and simple truths as far as they will take us and being content to leave the rest to our Heavenly Father.

Jesus Christ, Our Savior

As do many Christians (Catholics included), we grew up never questioning the existence of Jesus Christ, although our understanding of who he is and what he did evolved over time. The Catholic churches we attended and the homes of our families had various versions of the crucifix depicting Christ hung on the cross. Such images for us projected a suffering Christ with an emphasis on the passion, further reinforced through the Eucharist and various Catholic holidays.

Although we knew Jesus Christ as Catholics, our examination of the doctrines of Jesus Christ between the Catholic Church and The Church of Jesus Christ of Latter-day Saints revealed subtle differences that later became significant and enhanced our spiritual understanding of the Savior and his role in our lives, nourishing the roots we developed as Catholics that would later bloom brilliantly as Latter-day Saints.

CATHOLIC DOCTRINE

Catholic doctrine is beautifully articulate in defining the name of Jesus and his glorified titles as the foundation of who the Savior is:

- The name *Jesus* means "God Saves" as "there is no other name under heaven given among men by which we must be saved" (Acts 4:12) (Catechism 452).

- The title *Christ* means "Anointed One" or the Messiah (Catechism 453).

- The title *Son of God* denotes the special relationship and place that Jesus Christ has as being the only begotten son of the Eternal Father. "He is God himself" (Catechism 454).

- The title *Lord* connotes the "divine sovereignty" of Jesus (Catechism 455).

Jesus Christ as the only son of God, born of the Virgin Mary, took on the physical characteristics and nature of a human without losing his divine stature—thus becoming both God and human as the Son of God. Although having the physical characteristics of man, including a "human intellect and will," Jesus is perfectly in tune with God and the Holy Spirit (Catechism 482). In doing so Jesus becomes the perfect and only intermediary between God and mankind.

Jesus Christ in his ministry illuminated the true meaning of the Mosaic law and fulfilled it through his ultimate sacrifice for the redemption of mankind (Matthew 5:17–19; John 8:46; Matthew 5:33; and Hebrews 9:15). Jesus taught his disciples in all he did from the smallest of words and actions to his Atonement on the cross and glorious Resurrection. Jesus revealed himself to be the "Savior God himself" (John 5:16–18) through his many acts, although many did not recognize his Messiahship and wrote him off as a blaspheming man (Catechism 594).

Jesus willingly submitted to the will of the Father and was crucified, fulfilling his mission on earth to "make many righteous; and he shall bear their iniquities" (Isaiah 53:11; Romans 5:19), ultimately manifesting God's eternal love for us by reconciling ourselves to himself. Jesus suffered death where his soul and his body were separated from one another without corruption (Acts 13:37).

Before his Resurrection, Jesus "in his human soul united to his divine person" visited the dead that died before him to "open heaven's gates for the just" (Catechism 637).

Jesus was resurrected on the third day as "the first-born from the dead" (Colossians 1:18), laying the foundation for our own Resurrection at the appointed time through him. Through his Atonement and Resurrection, Jesus Christ assumed his divine position as Lord and Christ. Before his Ascension, Jesus imparted the Holy Spirit to his apostles and all of the Church. Upon his Ascension, Jesus enters into "God's heavenly domain" where no one can see him (Colossians 3:3), and from where he constantly mediates for us, pours out the Holy Spirit, and from where he will come again (Catechism 665 and 667).

From his divine existence, Jesus Christ leads his church as the first to enter heaven before us, setting the example and hope of our one day doing the same and being with him forever. Despite his sovereign reign as Lord, not everyone has subjected themselves to Jesus Christ. Such subjection will not happen in its fulness until after a final battle with evil before the judgment day.

Christ will come in glory to facilitate the final judgment where the living and the dead will be given their just grace and rewards according to their works. It is here where the final triumph of good over evil will take place.

See Catechism 452–455, 479–482, 592–594, 620–637, 658–682, 746, 1019.

LATTER-DAY SAINT DOCTRINE

The mission of Jesus Christ and his role in our salvation was established in the spirit world long before he came to the earth. The plan of salvation called for us to leave our heavenly existence and come to the earth where we would need a savior to teach us how to return to our Heavenly Father and redeem us from our sins. The chosen savior was Jesus Christ, who willingly accepted his mission despite the grief and sorrow that he would suffer (Isaiah 53:3–7).

Jesus Christ was born of the Virgin Mary, whereby the Holy Ghost came upon her and the power of the Highest overshadowed her (Luke 1:35). Through this act "God the Father became the literal father of Jesus Christ,"[3] being the only person to ever be born of an immortal father and a mortal mother—thus the "Only Begotten Son." While his divinity would be inherited from his Father, his mortal characteristics would be inherited from his human mother.

Although little is known about his youth, we know Jesus "grew and waxed strong in spirit, filled with wisdom" (Luke 2:40), and at twelve years old, he had knowledge of his divine mission (Luke 2:46–49). At about thirty years old, Jesus was baptized "to fulfill all righteousness" (Matthew 3:15). This was followed by a fast and temptation by Satan for forty days in the desert to prepare Jesus for a public ministry that would change the course of man's salvation forever.

During the public ministry of Christ, he set the example of service, performed a variety of stirring miracles, demonstrated human love with divine nature, established his church, and taught the gospel to all who would hear. Although declaring himself to be "the way, the truth, and the life" (John 14:6), Jesus gave glory to God and proclaimed, "I came down from heaven, not to do mine own will, but the will of him that sent me" (John 6:38), the will of his father being "that every one which seeth the Son, and believeth on him, may have everlasting life: and I will raise him up at the last day" (John 6:40).

At the end of his public ministry, Christ fulfilled his ultimate mission on earth by performing the great Atonement. Jesus first went into the garden of Gethsemane. There he took upon himself the sins of every human who has ever (and will ever) walk the earth. It was here that Jesus endured what no mortal could ever endure, saying "my soul is exceeding sorrowful unto death" (Mark 14:34). The pain was so great that "being in an agony . . . his sweat was as it were great drops of blood falling down to the ground (Luke 22:44). While Jesus asked Heavenly Father to relieve him of this pain, he freely submitted to it, continuing according to the will of Heavenly Father (Mark 14:36).

From Gethsemane Jesus allowed himself to be taken by the Pharisees and the Romans, physically and verbally abused, and then crucified at Calvary. The sacrifice made by Jesus upon the cross was accepted by God the Father to reconcile all mankind to him—hence the "Atonement" (at-one-ment) between God the Father and each one of us. Such was the greatest and "most important event that has ever occurred in the history of mankind."[4]

Jesus was buried in a tomb and during the three days before his Resurrection, his spirit entered the spirit world to organize and commence the teaching of his gospel to those who had died before him and for those who would die in the future (1 Peter 3:18–20).

After three days Jesus was resurrected. His spirit and his body were reunited in perfection and glory, demonstrating his power over physical death. Through the fulfillment of his mission, Jesus made it possible for each one of us to be resurrected, giving every person who accepts the

Atonement the gift of being saved from spiritual death.

Following his Resurrection, Jesus appeared to many individuals, including his apostles in Jerusalem and the people of the Americas, to expound upon his teachings and strengthen those in need. Following this brief period on earth, Jesus ascended into heaven and now sits at the right hand of God the Father. Jesus Christ will come again in fulfillment of the scriptural prophecies, will reign in righteousness during the millennium, and will oversee the final judgment.

See *Gospel Principles*, 17–18, and 61–74.

THOUGHTS AND COMMENTARY

Although we did not find significant differences between Latter-day Saint and Catholic doctrines on Jesus Christ outside of the Trinity, there were small differences on the Latter-day Saint side that added significance and understanding to the life of Christ, while providing insight into our own lives as well. The Latter-day Saint doctrine helps explain in more detail the mission and significance of the Savior as part of God's master plan, which is referred to by Latter-day Saints as the "plan of salvation." Jesus is not only our Savior, but our brother—an important distinction that is rarely mentioned among Catholics, although 100 percent supported by the Bible.

Very important, and that which will receive more attention in the section on the Crucifixion (Atonement), is the emphasis placed by Latter-day Saint doctrine on Christ's experience in the Garden of Gethsemane, as well as that which happened on the cross. The Catholic Church, like much of the Christian world, puts a great emphasis on the Crucifixion and less emphasis on the agony in the garden. The great Atonement of Jesus Christ includes the events of the garden and the Crucifixion—you cannot have one without the other; however, to put excessive emphasis on the Crucifixion without equal or greater emphasis on what happened in the Garden of Gethsemane is to misunderstand the process of the Atonement of Christ.

The understanding of Christ coming to the Americas (as outlined in great detail in the Book of Mormon) helped explain the scripture from John 10:16: "And other sheep I have, which are not of this fold: them also I must bring, and they shall hear my voice; and there shall be one fold, and one shepherd."

Christ coming to the Americas opens up a dialogue that begins to connect the dots for a number of historical and cultural traditions passed down by past civilizations. His ministry in the Americas, like that of the Old World, produced valuable insight into important doctrines that would never have come forth without the Book of Mormon.

The doctrine of The Church of Jesus Christ of Latter-day Saints on Jesus Christ helped Marilyn and I better understand how we fit into our Heavenly Father's plan, how our time here in mortality is significant, and how Jesus Christ is a central part of that plan in the redemption of all mankind. Such understanding, much like the doctrine of Heavenly Father, personalizes the relationship with our Savior and elevates our spiritual awareness and sensitivity.

The Holy Spirit

As a Catholic, the Holy Spirit (or the Holy Ghost as this personage is more commonly referred to among Latter-day Saints) was one of the three entities to which I crossed myself after each prayer since my childhood. I can't remember learning much about the Holy Spirit as a child, and therefore, I didn't really know what it was growing up.

When I was confirmed at thirteen years of age, the visiting cardinal, his Eminence Dominic Cardinal Ignatius Ekandem, mentioned becoming an adult in the Catholic Church and receiving the Holy Spirit for further guidance in my life. Although being confirmed by a Cardinal was one of the great experiences of my Catholic upbringing, my lack of understanding about the doctrine of the Holy Spirit minimized my appreciation for the ordinance of Confirmation.

It was not until I studied Latter-day Saint doctrine on the Holy Ghost that I came to fully understand the role and significance of the Holy Spirit. This chapter will explore the doctrine of both churches on the Holy Spirit, and invite the reader to learn more about this very important aspect of Christianity.

CATHOLIC DOCTRINE

In the glossary of the Catechism of the Catholic Church, the Holy Spirit is defined in this way: "[The Holy Spirit is] the third divine Person of the Blessed Trinity, the personal love of Father and Son for each other. Also called the Paraclete (Advocate) and Spirit of Truth, the Holy Spirit is at work with the Father and the Son from the beginning to the completion of the divine plan for our salvation."

The Holy Spirit is equal to the Father and the Son in the Trinity, is the spirit of both the Father and the Son, and according to the creed of the church from the Council of Constantinople, the Holy Spirit is to be worshipped and glorified.

The Holy Spirit fulfills multiple missions in the Church. The Holy Spirit "reveals that, with them, the Spirit is one and the same God" (Catechism 263). Within the liturgy, the Holy Spirit is to "prepare the assembly to encounter Christ; to recall and manifest Christ to the faith of the assembly; to make the saving work of Christ present and active by his transforming power; and to make the gift of communion bear fruit in the Church" (Catechism 1112). The Holy Spirit instructs and guides the Church in prayer, is linked to the forgiveness of sins, sanctifies the Church, and provides inspiration in praise, thanksgiving, and blessings. The Holy Spirit prepares the faithful of the Church to receive Christ in all things and guides them to all truth.

It was the Holy Spirit that anointed Jesus to be consecrated as Christ, and it was Jesus, referring to the Holy Spirit as another comforter, who poured out the Holy Spirit onto his apostles and the Church. Through the Holy Spirit, the being of the Father and the Son and the mystery of the Trinity is revealed in its fulness.

The Holy Spirit is present in the liturgy and in many spiritual aspects of Church rite. The Holy Spirit is received through the sacrament of confirmation by anointing of the forehead with oil and the laying on of the minister's hand. As the Holy Spirit is received, there are seven gifts the Holy Spirit can confer upon those who believe in Christ. These include "wisdom, understanding, counsel, fortitude, knowledge, piety, and fear of the Lord" (Catechism 1845).

The Holy Spirit abides within each believer to teach, expound, and inspire them to live the gospel in its fulness. Within the soul, the Holy Spirit heals that which is scarred from sin, and renews the person "through a spiritual transformation" (Catechism 1695). Through this transformation comes an increase in faith, by which the Holy Spirit provides help, encouragement, and sanctification to the soul.

See Catechism 179, 243–246, 264, 685, 744–747, 984, 1111–1112, 1133, 1316, 1320, 1695, 1845, 1982, 1983, 2026, 2661, and 2644.

LATTER-DAY SAINT DOCTRINE

From the time of Adam and Eve, the presence and importance of the Holy Ghost (or Holy Spirit as it is commonly referred to by the Catholic

Church) has been felt. After Adam and Eve were cast out of the Garden of Eden, the Holy Ghost was given to comfort, help, and guide them and their descendants—all the children of God.

The Church of Jesus Christ of Latter-day Saints defines the nature and mission of the Holy Ghost as the following: "The Holy Ghost is a member of the Godhead (1 John 5:7). He is a spirit that has the form and likeness of a man. He can be in only one place at a time, but his influence can be everywhere at the same time. . . . The Holy Ghost is our Heavenly Father's messenger and is a special gift to us. . . . The mission of the Holy Ghost is to bear witness of the Father and the Son and of the truth of all things."[5]

The Holy Ghost testifies that Jesus is the Christ, and through the power of the Spirit (a common Latter-day Saint reference to the Holy Ghost), we are given guidance and knowledge to live the gospel.

God allows his children to feel and experience the Holy Ghost and gives them the opportunity to posses the "gift of the Holy Ghost" through faith, baptism, and confirmation. The gift of the Holy Ghost provides *continual* guidance and inspiration if one lives the precepts of the gospel in righteousness. Temporary guidance can be obtained through the Holy Ghost without baptism and confirmation; however, such guidance and influence is not made constant until faith and commitment are exercised in their fulness through the receiving of these sacred ordinances.

The gift of the Holy Ghost is given through the laying on of hands by Melchizedek Priesthood. This is called the ordinance of confirmation which takes place following baptism, frequently the day of, or shortly thereafter. Although the gift of the Holy Ghost is given, the person receiving the gift must exercise faith, live worthily, have a desire to receive help and guidance, and learn to feel and heed the promptings of the Holy Ghost to experience the effects of this gift.

The gift of the Holy Ghost can bring peace to our souls and confidence of understanding the deep things of God (1 Corinthians 2:9–12). In addition we can be blessed with the gifts of the spirit for the benefit of ourselves and others in returning back to our heavenly home. These gifts include, "The Gift of Tongues; The Gift of Interpretation of Tongues; The Gift of Translation; The Gift of Wisdom; The Gift of Knowledge; The Gift of Teaching Wisdom and Knowledge; The Gift of Knowing That Jesus Christ Is the Son of God; The Gift of Believing the Testimony of

Others; The Gift of Prophecy; The Gift of Healing; The Gift of Working Miracles; and The Gift of Faith."[6]

Each of us has one or more of these gifts of the Spirit and must learn to recognize, develop, and use these gifts while on the earth. Satan has his own imitations of these gifts and hopes to use them to deceive the children of God. We are called to be wise in our administration of the gifts of the Spirit.

See *Gospel Principles*, 36–38, and 137–147.

THOUGHTS AND COMMENTARY

Our Catholic heritage prepared us to understand more fully the mission and role of the Holy Ghost. Whether it be our crossing ourselves after prayers in mentioning the Holy Ghost, or our confirmation, we knew there was a Holy Ghost; we simply needed to know more about the Holy Ghost.

Of course, the first major change for Marilyn and me was the idea of referring to the Holy Spirit as the Holy Ghost. This was not difficult, given the scriptural foundation for doing so. Although odd at first, it eventually felt like going back in time, recapturing something lost, and feeling it restored. Marilyn and I made an earnest effort to make the transition and over time it became a natural thing for us to do.

The differences between Holy Spirit and Holy Ghost are not theological, but rather a matter of linguistics. The term Holy Ghost appears in the King James Version of the Bible and comes from the traditional English word *gast,* which is taken from German noun *geist.* We can still find the word *gast* in the English words *aghast* and *flabbergasted.* In later translations of the Bible, the word *ghost* was changed to *spirit* to be more in line with the meaning of the day—thus the term Holy Spirit. Oddly enough the word *spirit* has now taken on multiple meanings prompting some scholars and theologians to suggest going back to the term Holy Ghost.

Beyond the term itself, the most positive difference was the degree of emphasis placed on the Holy Ghost by The Church of Jesus Christ of Latter-day Saints. From the time of our investigation of the Church to this very day, this emphasis has remained constant. All members of the Church are encouraged to listen to the promptings of the Holy Ghost continually, and urged to follow the Holy Ghost in all we do. This emphasis has led to a greater awareness of the Holy Ghost, augmented by a significantly enhanced understanding of the role of the Holy Ghost in our lives.

By accepting the Holy Ghost as a member of the Godhead (in perfect oneness with the Father and the Son), but a separate being with the mission of revealing all truth, we better understand the role of the Holy Ghost in our lives. We felt the Catholic doctrine on the Holy Spirit as part of the Trinity was more difficult to comprehend. In Catholicism, the Holy Spirit is another "mystery," and mysteries are hard to access, let alone apply. We had been inhibited from understanding the real value of the Holy Ghost in our lives.

The doctrine of the constant companionship of the Holy Ghost was the final component that made an impact on us. We knew from our experiences as Catholics that we could feel the presence of the Holy Ghost in our lives and the guidance it provided in leading us closer to Christ; however, after receiving the confirmation ordinance in The Church of Jesus Christ of Latter-day Saints, we could feel the constant companionship of the Holy Ghost as a guiding force, helping us understand spiritual matters, directing our decision making, and revealing to us the inspiration of the Lord. It's like clearing the fog from your faith and gaining clear spiritual sight.

This brings life to the scripture "know ye not that your body is the temple of the Holy Ghost which is in you" (1 Corinthians 6:19). The difference was dramatic to Marilyn and me and also confirmed the truth of the Latter-day Saint doctrine on the Holy Ghost—a restoration of the gospel truth of the Holy Ghost. Where we once had the gospel in our lives, we now had the fulness of the gospel of Jesus Christ

The Trinity

The Catholic doctrine of the Trinity is in many respects an advanced doctrine and one of the most difficult pieces of Christian theology to understand and comprehend. Like so many elements of Catholic doctrine, it is explained essentially as a "mystery," and requires the faith and patience of the individual to accept. In the Trinity, the Father, Son, and Holy Ghost combine in a mysterious way to form a single God entity. After learning the Latter-day Saint doctrine on the Godhead, we came to view the oneness of the Father, Son, and Holy Ghost differently, providing intimate insight into the unity of the three. We learned it wasn't so mysterious at all.

CATHOLIC DOCTRINE
The Catechism of the Catholic Church describes the Trinity as the

following: "The mystery of the one God in three Persons: Father, Son, and Holy Spirit. The revealed truth of the Holy Trinity is at the very root of the Church's living faith as expressed in the Creed. The mystery of the Trinity in itself is inaccessible to the human mind and is the object of faith only because it was revealed by Jesus Christ, the divine son of the eternal Father" (Catechism Glossary).

Catholic doctrine on the Trinity is critical to maintaining the theology of "one God," while at the same time revealing the power and presence of the Father, Son, and Holy Spirit: "inseparable in what they are . . . in what they do. But within the single divine operation each shows forth what is proper to him in the Trinity" (Catechism 267). The Trinity is a doctrine that is shrouded in theological explanation and historical lore. God can reveal himself as three separate beings (Father, Son, and Holy Spirit) while still being God in "one essence, substance, or nature."[7]

See Catechism, 200, 261, 262, 266, 267, 292, and glossary.

LATTER-DAY SAINT DOCTRINE

The Latter-day Saint doctrine of the Godhead can be summarized in a single quote from the Prophet Gordon B. Hinckley, which is in perfect harmony with similar content from the *Gospel Principles* manual:

> They [the Godhead] are distinct beings, but they are one in purpose and effort. They are united as one in bringing to pass the grand, divine plan for the salvation and exaltation of the children of God. In His great, moving prayer in the garden before His betrayal, Christ pleaded with His Father concerning the Apostles, whom He loved, saying: "Neither pray I for these alone, but for them also which shall believe on me through their word; "That they all may be one; as thou, Father, art in me, and I in thee, that they also may be one in us" (John 17:20–21). It is that perfect unity between the Father, the Son, and the Holy Ghost that binds these three into the oneness of the divine Godhead.[8]

God the Father, Jesus Christ, and the Holy Ghost are three distinct beings who are one in purpose, but not one in being. While their distinctiveness is manifest in their separate missions and presence, they are unified and inseparable in how they carry out God's plan of happiness for his children.

See *Gospel Principles*, 37.

THOUGHTS AND COMMENTARY

The Catholic doctrine of the Trinity has become the standard in nearly all Christian sects that have arisen since the Council of Nicaea in AD 325. In fact the Roman Emperor Constantine convoked this council to resolve disputes about this very matter, leading to the doctrine of the Trinity used by most of Christendom today.

The Catholic doctrine of the Trinity is not one that Marilyn and I as Catholics spent much time trying to understand, nor did we feel inspired to contemplate. Like selected other doctrines of the Catholic Church, the Trinity was said to be a mystery and not something that could be comprehended by any human. Although we accepted that faith was required because the oneness of the Father, the Son, and the Holy Ghost was beyond human comprehension, we didn't believe that confusion needed to be added by proclaiming that the Father, Son, and Holy Ghost are "one essence, substance or nature." How could a council called into being by a Roman emperor decide this so definitively—when the very reason for the council being called was disputation on this very topic?

The confusion about how three beings can be three beings but not be three beings but only one being, God, leads to some important questions. Perhaps primary among them is this: How can God the Father give up himself as his only begotten son to be sacrificed for our sins? Rather circular, we came to think, even nonsensical.

Why was Jesus Christ praying to himself in the Garden of Gethsemane, calling himself father? Why did Jesus have to depart in order for the Holy Spirit to come upon his Apostles if he was or had in him the Holy Spirit? Was the Father talking to himself when he proclaimed at the baptism of Jesus, "This is my beloved Son, in whom I am well pleased" (Matthew 3:17)? Does the distinction between the Father and the Son in the Bible mean nothing? Is it a no-distinction distinction, and if it is, why does God in his holy word make it clear, again and again?

Such questions are certainly as valid as the doctrine that gives legitimate rise to them. Truth-seeking Christians must consider them, and so we did.

Upon hearing the Latter-day Saint doctrine of the Godhead—the Father, Son, and Holy Ghost are three distinct beings profoundly unified in purpose—we immediately understood what was being taught and were able to see the doctrine expressed and implied repeatedly in the New

Testament. Explaining the Catholic doctrine of the Trinity using the Bible is possible; however, to adequately defend the doctrine requires yielding to pure metaphor and the acceptance of questionable abstractions. Further study of the doctrine of the Godhead revealed the following biblical truths that support the Latter-day Saint doctrine of the Godhead:

Distinct from God Before Christ Came to the Earth

From Genesis 1:26 ("Let us make man in our image") and Genesis 3:22 ("Behold, the man is become as one of us"), we can see that Heavenly Father and Jesus Christ, by whom the creation was carried out (Colossians 1:16), were separate beings, thus the use of the plural pronoun, *us*. In John 7:29, Jesus says, "For I am from him [Heavenly Father]," and Paul says in Romans 8:29 that Jesus is the "firstborn" (also seen in Colossians 1:15). Jesus, being the Son of God, was born of God and distinct from God before coming to the earth. It may not fit perfectly the commonly held views of the monotheistic model, but the scriptural passages are difficult to refute.

Distinct from God during the Time of Christ's Ministry

When Christ was baptized, Heavenly Father's voice was heard from heaven (Matthew 3:17). Jesus, as recorded in John 8:18, told his disciples that "the Father that sent me beareth witness of me." Jesus in praying to the Father in John 17:3 calls for man to "know thee the only true God, *and* Jesus Christ" (emphasis added). There are numerous scriptures from the Bible where Jesus either demonstrates or proclaims the distinction between himself and his Father during his mortal ministry. Perhaps most important to note is not only the distinction that Jesus makes, but the deference with which he makes it. Christ taught us to know two personages, himself and Heavenly Father, to whom he repeatedly defers—and invites us to do likewise.

Distinct Differences in Knowledge

Although a perfect oneness exists among the Godhead, there is also a separation of knowledge, which would not exist if there was one in essence of being. Jesus said, "But of that day and that hour knoweth no man, no, not the angels which are in heaven, neither the Son, but the Father" (Mark 13:32). In John 7:16 Jesus says, "My doctrine is not mine, but his that sent me." Jesus clearly demonstrates that God still reigns and has knowledge that he, the Son of God, does not have.

Distinct Differences in Power and Dominion

Christ declared that he did not have the power to grant the honor of anyone sitting on his left or right hand, but that his Father in Heaven alone had the dominion to grant such a request (Matthew 20:23). Jesus proclaimed, "The Son can do nothing of himself, but what he seeth the Father do" (John 5:19). Jesus said further, "The servant is not greater than his lord; neither he that is sent greater than he that sent him" (John 13:16). In John 14:28, Jesus says, "I go unto the Father: for my Father is greater than I." In Revelation 3:21 Christ says "I also overcame, and am set down with my Father in his throne." These are only a few examples where Jesus Christ proclaims that the power and dominion of Heavenly Father exceeds his own.

Distinctly Different Punishments for Blasphemy

Jesus points to a striking separation between himself and the Holy Ghost when he says, "And whosoever speaketh a word against the Son of man, it shall be forgiven him: but whosoever speaketh against the Holy Ghost, it shall not be forgiven him, neither in this world, neither in the world to come" (Matthew 12:32). If Jesus and the Holy Ghost were one essence, then the punishment for speaking against either would be the same. The distinction between Jesus and the Holy Ghost is also made clear in John 16:7, when Jesus tells his Apostles that when he departs the "comforter" (Holy Ghost) will come to them. Unless Jesus did not know whether he was coming or going, he was telling his disciples that another personage was coming to take his place, one profoundly unified with him in purpose.

Heavenly Father is the God of Jesus Christ, and Jesus Worshipped God

Perhaps the most powerful testimony of the Godhead comes from those Bible passages that declare Heavenly Father as being the God of Jesus Christ. In Ephesians 1:17, Paul refers to Heavenly Father as "the God of our Lord Jesus Christ, the Father of glory." When Jesus Christ was on the cross, he referred to Heavenly Father as his God in saying, "My God, my God, why hast thou forsaken me?" (Matthew 27:46). On many occasions Jesus prayed to Heavenly Father as his God and Father. Jesus worshipped God as written in Matthew 4:10 when Jesus tells Satan "Thou shalt worship the Lord thy God, and him only shalt thou serve." God is our God and our Heavenly Father, while also being the God and

Heavenly Father of the Lord Jesus Christ. Jesus Christ is the Son of God. When Jesus prayed, it was not God the Father of himself talking to himself. Jesus and Heavenly Father are one in purpose, not one in essence or substance of being.

Distinct from God After Christ's Resurrection and Ascension

We read in Acts 7:55 a vision from Stephen: "But he, being full of the Holy Ghost, looked up steadfastly into heaven, and saw the glory of God, and Jesus, standing on the right hand of God." This vision came after the death, Resurrection, and Ascension of Christ. Paul provides numerous passages where he makes very clear distinctions between God and Jesus Christ (1 Corinthians 8:6; 2 Thessalonians 2:16; 1 Timothy 2:5; 1 Corinthians 5:6, and others). Paul says, "And the head of Christ is God" (1 Corinthians 11:3). Although one in purpose in all that they do, the Father, Son, and Holy Ghost are three distinct and separate beings.

Because the doctrine of the Godhead is such a crucial part of the gospel and because this doctrine differs markedly from the Catholic Church and, indeed, most other Christian sects, much study and prayer is warranted. To that end Marilyn and I spent a good deal of time ensuring the Latter-day Saint doctrine was on solid ground. Beyond study, the Holy Ghost testified to us that the doctrine of the Godhead was true. Heavenly Father, Jesus Christ, and the Holy Ghost are distinct beings unified in purpose and effort, but distinct in form, substance, and nature—such is our testimonies of the Godhead.

The doctrine on the Godhead has generated considerable consternation among other Christians. This consternation has been expressed in the form of claims that the Church practices polytheism (worship of multiple gods) and has diminished the divinity of Jesus Christ. Many critics point to a number of scriptures where Jesus Christ declares that the Father and he are one (John 10:30, for example). This and other references to "oneness" are perfectly consistent with the Latter-day Saint doctrine of the Godhead, where perfect oneness of purpose and effort is achieved among the Father, Son, and Holy Ghost. Just as my wife and I become one in any decision we make together ("one flesh" according to Mark 10:18—speaking symbolically, of course), God is one with Jesus Christ and the Holy Ghost.

The perfect oneness of the Godhead is exquisitely defined in John 17 where Jesus, praying to Heavenly Father, says, "That they all may be one;

as thou, Father, art in me, and I in thee, that they also may be one in us" (John 17:20–21). Jesus Christ is the Son of God. He is divine, and we praise him as our Redeemer and Savior. We worship Jesus Christ as the Son of God, and we worship Heavenly Father as the father of Jesus. Jesus Christ is in perfect oneness with our Heavenly Father and sits on his right hand. The doctrine of the Godhead as taught by The Church of Jesus Christ of Latter-day Saints takes nothing away from Jesus Christ. Instead it clarifies his role as the Son of God and the role of God the Father as his father and the father of our spirits. No metaphors, abstractions, or mysteries there. No stretching our doctrines out of shape to conform to someone's idea of the perfect monotheistic model. Jesus did not do this in his time on earth, and neither do we in ours.

In reflecting how the doctrine of the Trinity came about, I have personally hypothesized that in the early days of the Church, great strife existed between the Christians and Jews over the nature of Jesus Christ. This was complicated by continual acts of heresy and individuals inside and outside of the church, who made things up as they went along. At the same time, there were disagreements in the Church of Alexandria over the nature of Jesus in relationship to the Father; in particular, whether Jesus was of the same or merely of similar substance as God the Father. For these reasons, the First Council of Nicaea was held in Nicaea in Bithynia under the direction of Constantine I in AD 325. From this council of approximately 300 bishops (out of 1,800 invited) came the creation of the Nicene Creed. The creed seemed to ignore the biblical evidence of the Godhead and instead formulated a compromise between the spiritual and the political, rendering the doctrine of the Godhead lost for centuries until the Restoration of the gospel through the Prophet Joseph Smith.

The doctrine of the Godhead has helped our family understand the roles of each member of the Godhead—Father, Son, and Holy Ghost. This understanding supports the structure of prayer whereby we pray to our Heavenly Father in the name of Jesus Christ, calling on the Holy Ghost for inspiration and guidance. Such an understanding of the Godhead brings greater meaning to prayer, to the importance of becoming close to our Savior Jesus Christ, and to the objective of returning to our Father in Heaven when our work in mortality is finished. The Latter-day Saint doctrine of the Godhead has clarified that which we learned as Catholics, and has made a profound impact on our spiritual lives—all of it for the good.

NOTES

1. St. Augustine, *Sermo* 52, 6, 16: PL 38:360 and *Sermo* 117, 3, 5: PL 38, 663.
2. *Gospel Principles*, 9.
3. *Gospel Principles*, 64.
4. *Gospel Principles*, 71.
5. *Gospel Principles*, 37.
6. *Gospel Principles*, 141–147.
7. Lateran Council IV: DS 800.
8. Gordon B. Hinckley, "The Father, Son, and Holy Ghost," *Ensign*, Mar. 1998, 2.

7

Angels and Satan

*A*NGEL is a word commonly reserved for describing benevolent spiritual entities—a meaning I will use here. But the painful fact is that Satan, the prince of darkness, the father of lies—is an angel, albeit a fallen one. We are told that he "drew the third part of the stars of heaven with him into his fallen state (Revelation 12:4). So, while it may make us uncomfortable, no discussion of angels is complete without a discussion of Satan and his followers.

However, I will by convention refer to the spirit entities who are aligned with God, who serve God and man in countless ways, and who contribute to our salvation, as simply angels.

Angels have been depicted in art for centuries. They are mentioned frequently in the Old and New Testaments and in many other writings, sacred and profane. Angels have delivered vital comfort and messages of great importance to men and women on earth. Yet their existence today is frequently denied, or their roles discounted.

Do angels still exist? Who are they? Can we communicate with them? What is their purpose? Does Satan really exist? Who are Satan's minions? This chapter will explore these and other questions about angels and Satan.

Angels

Outside of the many beautiful works of art belonging to the Catholic Church, Marilyn and I had not given much thought to angels before investigating The Church of Jesus Christ of Latter-day Saints. We, like many other Catholics, pictured angels as heavenly beings (usually with wings), who possessed divine powers they used to help the children of God. We casually discussed "guardian angels" from time to time because of Marilyn's experiences that would strongly suggest the presence of these divine beings. However, angels in general were far removed from us and not a part of our everyday lives. We came to understand through our study of Latter-day Saint doctrine that there was much more to angels than we thought.

CATHOLIC DOCTRINE

Catholic doctrine defines angels as "spiritual creatures who glorify God without ceasing and who serve his saving plans for other creatures" (Catechism 350). This definition is given in the present tense: Angels exist today and are hard at work. Saint Thomas Aquinas said, "The angels work together for the benefit of us all."[1]

Angels are venerated in the Catholic Church as both surrounding Jesus Christ and helping to fulfill his mission. "Guardian angels [are] assigned to protect and intercede for each person" (Catechism, glossary). While guardian angels are singled out as protectors, Catholic doctrine calls for each of the faithful in Christ to have an angel by his or her side to intercede, to protect, and to guide. The help of angels is seen as powerful and mysterious, yet beneficial to the entire Church, including the liturgy.

See Catechism 334–336; 350–353; and glossary.

LATTER-DAY SAINT DOCTRINE

Latter-day Saint doctrine provides extensive detail on angels, defining different types of angels and their origin. Angels are broadly defined as "messengers sent from God" (*Gospel Principles* Glossary). President Joseph F. Smith revealed: "When messengers are sent to minister to the inhabitants of this earth, they are not strangers, but from the ranks of our kindred, friends, and fellow-beings and fellow-servants."[2]

Joseph Smith taught that angels are connected to the earth. He said they are beings "who belong to it [the earth] or have belonged to it."[3]

Elder Bruce R. McConkie describes five specific types of angels in his book *Mormon Doctrine*:

> **Premortal Spirits**: These are the spirits of those who have not yet come to the earth.
> **Spirits of Just Men Made Perfect**: These are the spirits of those

who have lived righteously on earth, have died, and are awaiting their Resurrection. These individuals are referred to as "just men made perfect" (Hebrews 12:22–24). The visit of Gabriel to Zacharias and to Mary illustrates this kind of being.

Translated Beings: These are translated beings that function as angels, as was the case with the appearance of Moses and Elijah on the Mount of Transfiguration (Matthew 17:1–3). The Apostle John was translated and became a ministering angel (John 21:22–23)

Resurrected Personages: These are resurrected beings that serve as angels (Matthew 27:52-53). The appearances of Moroni and John the Baptist to Joseph Smith illustrate this type of angel.

Righteous Mortal Men: These are holy men living on earth that are occasionally referred to as angels as they act as ministers for God such as those that appeared to Lot to warn him of the destruction of Sodom and Gomorrah (Genesis 19).[4]

Suspiciously absent from this list of angelic types is the "guardian angel." President Joseph Fielding Smith taught that help may be rendered by ministering angels during times of need, but that the true guardian angel for the children of men on earth is "the power and direction available through the Light of Christ and the Holy Ghost."[5]

Moroni (a Book of Mormon prophet) proclaimed that "It is by faith that angels appear and minister unto men" (Moroni 7:37). Faith is the prerequisite for the appearance and ministry of angelic beings.

The purposes of angels are many. Consider the following list of angelic actions compiled by Larry E. Dahl, Associate Professor of Church History and Doctrine, Brigham Young University:

- Announce and testify of events pertaining to God's work and glory (Matthew 1:20–21, Matthew 28:1–6; Luke 1:11–20, Luke 2:8–14; Revelation 14);

- Preach the gospel and minister "unto the children of men, to make manifest concerning the coming of Christ" (Moroni 7:22; Moses 5:58);

- Declare "the word of Christ unto chosen vessels of the Lord, that they may bear testimony of him" (Moroni 7:31; Mosiah 3:1–27);

- Bring to earth "their rights, their keys, their honors, their majesty and glory, and the power of their priesthood" (D&C 128:21; D&C 27:12; D&C 110:11–16; Joseph Smith—History 1:68–70);

- Protect and guide the servants of God in times of trouble so that they may accomplish his purposes (Acts 5:18–20; Daniel 3:28; 1 Nephi 3:29; Helaman 5);

- Bring comfort, instruction, and warnings to faithful individuals in times of need (Genesis 16:7; Exodus 23:20–23; Matthew 2:13, 19–20; 1 Nephi 11:14–15, 30; Alma 8:14–18).[6]

Church leaders have affirmed the reality of angels in numerous blessings, sermons, and other accounts.

THOUGHTS AND COMMENTARY

Catholic and Latter-day Saint doctrine differ on the nature and mission of angels in ancient and modern times. Latter-day Saint doctrine provides valuable detail on the character of angels and their interactions with us on earth. With this doctrine, our eyes were opened to the many passages in the Bible that shed light on angels and our relationships with them. The Latter-day Saint doctrine opened up spiritual possibilities, not only from a scriptural standpoint, but from the reality of countless experiences of many who have been aided by divine intervention from spiritual beings. How many times have you heard of someone claiming to have been helped by an ancestor or a person they didn't know? The Latter-day Saint doctrine helps tie together various instances where individuals were given divine help from heaven-sent beings in various forms.

Marilyn had an experience in college while crossing the street. She felt pressure against her chest that kept her from crossing. At that very moment, a car ran the light and sped through the intersection where Marilyn would have been walking. She attributes this incident to the intervention of an angel.

Another thing that struck Marilyn and me was the fact that Latter-day Saint Church leaders acknowledge in a very public way the nearly constant activity of angels in the present day. The Catholic Church does not discount present-day activity of angels, but we had the distinct impression as Catholics that vigorous angelic activity was not readily acknowledged by Catholic Church leaders. It was downplayed as an infrequent occurrence and requiring official Church intervention to validate the event.

The vibrant Latter-day Saint doctrine on angels spoke to Marilyn and me as a strong proclamation that God lives and his power is at work in the lives of his children. Now, today! Our exposure to angels in Catholic art and folklore prepared us well for the comprehensive doctrine on angels in the Latter-day Saint faith. It was reassuring, even exciting, to understand this tangible doctrine in our own lives and to teach our children.

Satan and His Followers

Satan, or the devil, was a topic that Marilyn and I discussed together privately from time to time, and with less frequency and in a more guarded manner with fellow Catholics. When addressing this topic with other Catholics, we would get a wide variety of reactions. Some seemed to embrace the reality of Satan and his works of evil in the world. Others, even a Catholic deacon who was a dear friend of ours, viewed Satan as more of an "evil presence" in the world, an abstraction rather than a real, living, tangible being. A Barna Research Group study in 2001 confirmed this feeling when it revealed that only 17 percent of Catholics believe in the reality of Satan.

This section will examine the doctrine of Satan and those who follow him, discussing the differences and similarities of evil and those who dispense it.

CATHOLIC DOCTRINE

The Catechism defines Satan and those who are led by him as the following: "Satan or the devil and the other demons are fallen angels who have freely refused to serve God and his plan. Their choice against God is definitive. They try to associate man in their revolt against God" (Catechism 414).

Once a good angel created in the order of God, Satan willfully committed sin against God by rejecting his divine rule and became "a liar and the father of all lies" (John 8:44). Satan's followers, called demons, were also righteous before becoming evil by their own free will. For Satan and his followers, there is no opportunity for repentance in this world or the next, as their sin against God is unforgivable and outside of the mercy of God.

Satan is a creature of pure spirit, giving him power and influence over God's children as the "ruler of this world" (Catechism 2864). As the evil one, Satan (or the devil) sought to lead away Christ from his ministry on earth, just as he and his followers today seek to lure man into disobedience against God. In this he was successful with Adam and Eve—bringing upon them sin and death. Satan desires to block the plan of God through deception and sin, steeping the world in wickedness and corruption.

God allows Satan to have influence and power:

> Satan may act in the world out of hatred for God and his kingdom in Christ Jesus, and although his action may cause grave injuries—of a spiritual nature and, indirectly, even of a physical nature—to each man and to society, the action is permitted by divine providence which with strength and gentleness guides human and cosmic history. It is a great mystery that providence should permit diabolical activity, but "we know that in everything God works for good with those who love him." (Catechism 395)

Although a force of evil, Satan's power is not infinite: He lacks the ability to prevent the building of the kingdom of God. Christ came to destroy the works of the devil (1 John 3:8) and will triumph, dealing Satan a clear defeat at the appointed time. The triumph of man over evil is petitioned by all Christians in the Lord's Prayer, "but deliver us from evil," showing the confidence of the victory already won by Christ in the defeat of Satan.

See Catechism 391–395, 414, 2851, 2852, 2864, and glossary.

LATTER-DAY SAINT DOCTRINE

Latter-day Saint doctrine on Satan and his followers begins with the following definition of Satan from the Apostle Bruce R. McConkie: "Satan (or the Devil—literally meaning *slanderer*), is a spirit son of God who was born in the morning of the pre-existence (D&C 76:25–26). Endowed with agency, the free power of choice, he chose the evil part from the beginning, thus placing himself in eternal opposition to the divine will. He was 'a liar from the beginning.' "[7]

God created all things, including all beings as his spirit children. Satan, or Lucifer as he was once called, was a spirit son of our Heavenly Father in the premortal life and enjoyed great stature as a valiant spirit. Satan became angry when Jesus Christ was chosen to be our Savior, as Lucifer wanted the glory of this role for himself. Satan's anger led to a war in heaven (Revelation 12:7). The spirits who followed Satan fought against Jesus Christ and his followers—we were among those who chose Jesus Christ.

Because of Satan's rebellion, he and his followers—one-third of the spirits of heaven (Revelation 12:4)—were cast out. Their punishment was separation from God and loss of any opportunity to take on a mortal body. As the "sons of perdition," these evil spirits were and are eternally damned; there is for them no possibility of forgiveness.

Revelation 12:4 says that these evil spirits were cast down to the earth, the same earth we live in today. Without a mortal body, these spirits retain their knowledge of their premortal life and suffer constantly from the knowledge of their loss, which they know is hopelessly eternal. Thus, with Satan as their leader, they seek to destroy the plan of our Heavenly Father by persuading us continually to break the commandments of God and to do evil. Satan's plan is to deceive us, keep us from returning to our Heavenly Father, and make us miserable as he and his followers are. The Book of Mormon states that Satan seeks "the misery of all mankind . . . for he seeketh that all men might be miserable like unto himself" (2 Nephi 2:18, 27).

Satan accomplishes his goals through deception and cunning, leading away many into sin. He is the master deceiver. He is able to imitate the gifts of the spirit, including prophecy, tongues, healings, visions, and other miracles (*Gospel Principles*, 149 and Exodus 7:8–22). Satan's army of seduced mortals includes false prophets, false healers and miracle workers, fortune tellers, paranormal mediums, and others who engage in practices that lead us away from Christ and the plan of Heavenly Father. God will reveal to those who seek discernment the falsehood of these seduced mortals—people who are under the influence of Satan and are an abomination to the Lord (Isaiah 47:12–14; Deuteronomy 18:9–10).

Satan can use the most subtle means to deceive us. In doing so, he can cause us to give up our freedom of choice: he can tempt us into following him in ways that have terrible—and frequently inevitable—consequences. For instance, Satan leverages our passions and human emotions to lead us into breaking the law of chastity through pre-marital sex, adultery, and yielding to the enticement of same-sex attraction. Satan can accomplish this in degrees by leading people into wearing immodest clothing, encouraging immoral or improper thoughts, viewing or listening to inappropriate movies and music, and performing suggestive acts. He uses lewd distortions of dancing, music, and other delightful activities to bring us into sin. Satan preys especially upon those who are "lonely, confused, or depressed. He chooses this time of weakness to tempt us."[8]

Satan will have the power to tempt us until the Second Coming of Jesus Christ. During the thousand-year reign of Christ before the final judgment (known as the Millennium), Satan will be bound and have no power to tempt those living on the earth at that time (Revelation 20:2). At the end of Millennium, Satan will have power and influence once again (Revelation 20:3) as part of a last epic struggle before the final judgment. In that final battle, Satan and his followers will be soundly defeated and cast into outer darkness for all eternity.

Our Heavenly Father has given us clear guidance on how we can avoid the temptation and bondage of Satan. We will never be tempted beyond our capacity to resist (1 Corinthians 10:13), but only if we put forth the effort ourselves to pray regularly, rely on the Atonement of Christ, and petition God for help in resisting the temptations of Satan.

See *Gospel Principles*, 18, 19, 23, 24, 149, 249, 250, 284, and 286.

THOUGHTS AND COMMENTARY

In our study of Latter-day Saint doctrine, we were introduced to Satan as an angelic being who fell from God's presence. This idea created in us a valuable new awareness of evil. Although not altogether different from that of Catholic doctrine in that respect, it was the way the doctrine was taught, the details given, and the constant reinforcement that helped us gain a stronger testimony of the reality of Satan (59 percent of Latter-day Saints reported believing in the reality of Satan in the same Barna Research Group study cited earlier). This awareness helped us and our children better understand how to identify evil and avoid being caught in Satan's snares.

Latter-day Saint doctrine provides valuable details on the specific act of disobedience that caused Satan and his followers to fall, along with insights on how Satan and his followers regularly tempt us today. Through modern-day scripture we came to understand Satan's error— how he rebelled against our Heavenly Father's plan of salvation; how in this rebellion, he desired to become the Savior of the world in a way that would have robbed mankind of agency and brought us as slaves to universal salvation; and how for this he wished to claim glory for himself, with no acknowledgement of Heavenly Father. In short, Satan's great sin was pride, and thus he fell from being a son of the morning to being the master of evil.

These details about the nature and mission of Satan gave us new weapons against him. We understood he was a powerful spirit, and we understood the cause of his spectacular fall in the premortal life. The modern-day scriptures that provide this understanding illuminated several ambiguous scriptures found in the Bible. We knew better how to combat evil, because we knew more about its source.

Our roles in the plan of salvation became more clear with Latter-day Saint doctrine. We ceased to be spiritual spectators. We became soldiers for Christ here-and-now, having been informed of the side we had already taken, the choice we had already made in the premortal life. We gained confidence in knowing our choice allowed us to ultimately come to the earth and gain a body, while Satan and his followers were cast to the earth without bodies—thus explaining the scriptural accounts of demons taking control of earthly bodies. This knowledge helps us understand the fight that we are in. It helps us stay committed to the fight when times are tough, and memory of our choice begins to fade.

When I ponder that these spirits who follow Satan retain their knowledge of their premortal life, including their knowledge of precisely who I was then and am now, I understand the seriousness of the struggle. I know with a deeper understanding the power of temptation and the potential danger from weapons available to Satan to tempt us. This doctrine helped me finally understand why unclean spirits in the Bible knew that Jesus Christ was the son of God long before Jesus declared it himself: "And unclean spirits, when they saw him, fell down before him, and cried, saying, Thou art the Son of God. And he straitly charged them that they should not make him known" (Mark 3:11–12).

The unclean spirits knew Jesus as the Son of God because these spirits retained their knowledge of the premortal life. This was an incredible revelation to us! Imagine the great influence Satan can exercise over us because of his clear memory of us in the premortal life. We have no such clear memory of him or his minions. No wonder we see so much evil in the world today! Until our memory is restored, we must rely on faith in God and the Atonement of Jesus Christ. With these and the many spiritual tools available through Christ's Church, we can overcome the memory advantage of Satan. This hope, this confidence sustains us in the fight.

The doctrine of The Church of Jesus Christ of Latter-day Saints on Satan provides details and insights that helped Marilyn and I fully understand and to further the understanding of our children; this knowledge helps each of us in our own personal struggles with evil. Satan lives, and he and his wicked followers, both spirits and mortals, are hard at work. We must match this work with our own to protect ourselves against Satan and his minions.

NOTES

1. St. Thomas Aquinas, *STh* I, 114, 3, *ad* 3.
2. *Gospel Doctrine*, 435–36.
3. Dean Jarman, "Questions and Answers," *Liahona*, Apr. 1984, 22.
4. *Mormon Doctrine*, 35–37.
5. Joseph Fielding Smith, *Doctrines of Salvation*, comp. Bruce R. McConkie, 3 vols. (Salt Lake City: Bookcraft, 1954), 1:54.
6. "I Have a Question," *Ensign*, Mar. 1988, 21.
7. *Mormon Doctrine*, 192.
8. *Gospel Principles*, 250.

8

The Crucifixion and
Resurrection of Jesus Christ

MOST Christians consider the Crucifixion and Resurrection of Jesus Christ as the two most important events in the history of the world. These events are at the very center of Christian life: Had they not occurred, man would be lost in sin, with no chance for eternal life.

Despite the importance of these events, many Christians have only a superficial understanding of them. Profound peace and a powerful spiritual awakening are available to those willing to go beneath the surface in search of a deeper knowledge of these infinite acts of love by the Savior.

The Crucifixion or Atonement

CATHOLIC DOCTRINE

The Crucifixion, or *Expiation*, is defined as the following from the Catechism: "The act of redemption and atonement for sin which Christ won for us by the pouring out of his blood on the cross, by his obedient love 'even to the end' (Jn. 13:1) The expiation of sins continues in the mystical body of Christ and the communion of saints by joining our human acts of atonement to the redemptive action of Christ, both in this life and in Purgatory" (Catechism glossary).

Jesus Christ, in complete harmony with the scriptures, freely offered himself in death for the sins of all mankind (1 Corinthians 15:3). It was because of God's infinite love for us that he sent his son to be the repara-tion for our sins (1 John 4:10), and in doing so "God was in Christ recon-ciling the world to himself" (2 Corinthians 5:19).

Christ "symbolized this offering and made it really present" (Cat-echism 621), before and during the Last Supper when he said, "This is my body which is given for you" (Luke 22:19).

The offering of himself, made by Jesus at the Last Supper, is later accepted by Jesus from his Father in the Garden of Gethsemane, show-ing Christ's obedience unto death—fulfilling the "Cup of the New Cov-enant." Through the obedience of Christ to the Father in bearing the iniquities of all (Isaiah 53:11), Jesus accomplished the great Atonement (Isaiah 53:10). The death of Christ (the Paschal Sacrifice) redeems man from sin and reunites and reconciles man unto God (the sacrifice of the New Covenant).

The sacrifice of God in giving his only son, and the sacrifice of Christ in giving himself to his Father through the Holy Spirit, supersedes all other sacrifices for redemption of man. Jesus offers his obedience to replace the disobedience of man—wherein Adam we are all made sinners through his disobedience, through Christ we are made righteous through his obedience. Christ did what no other man, however righteous, could do for himself. The Atonement was done out of love, and it is by that same love that we are now compelled.

As the "one mediator between God and men," Christ unites himself to all men and calls each of his disciples to take up their cross and follow him as the only way in which man can achieve entrance into heaven (Cat-echism 618).

See Catechism 612–623, and glossary.

LATTER-DAY SAINT DOCTRINE

Latter-day Saints refer to the suffering of Jesus in the Garden of Geth-semane, combined with his crucifixion on Calvary, as the Atonement. Jesus offered himself up as a sacrifice for our sins. He paid for our sins and overcame death through his incomprehensible suffering—the suffering of God in human flesh. The Atonement "is the most important event that has ever occurred in the history of mankind."[1]

The Atonement was the primary reason that Jesus came to the earth. Without the Atonement of Christ, we could not have a hope of salvation and would be eternally burdened with physical death (separation of the body and spirit) and spiritual death (separation from God) brought about by the fall of Adam.

The Atonement is something we could not do for ourselves because of the weaknesses brought on by sin and mortality. As the Only Begotten Son of God and the only sinless person to ever live on the earth, only Jesus Christ could perform the great Atonement. Jesus told his disciples: "I lay down my life, that I might take it again. No man taketh it from me, but I lay it down of myself. I have power to lay it down, and I have power to take it again" (John 10:17–18). It is difficult to fathom the love that our Heavenly Father has for us in giving up his only begotten son (John 3:16), and the love of Jesus in willingly suffering on our behalf.

The Atonement brings forgiveness into our lives and gives strength to those who believe in its enabling powers. The Apostle David A. Bednar spoke of the enabling power of the Atonement: "The enabling and strengthening aspect of the Atonement helps us to see and to do and to become good in ways that we could never recognize or accomplish with our limited mortal capacity. I testify and witness that the enabling power of the Savior's Atonement is real. Without that strengthening power of the Atonement, I could not stand before you this morning."[2]

We are able to enjoy the eternal benefits that result from the Atonement through our faith in Jesus Christ. This faith leads to repentance, baptism, confirmation, and keeping the Lord's commandments. In doing so we can become true disciples of Jesus Christ, receive power to endure, be cleansed from our sins, and return to live with our Heavenly Father to enjoy eternal life.

See *Gospel Principles*, 71–74.

Thoughts and Commentary

At their foundations, the doctrines of both churches on the Atonement are the same: Christ, as the perfect sacrifice, died for the sins of the world so that all mankind may be saved. Marilyn and I were happy to see these similarities and felt well prepared in the Catholic faith to accept the Latter-day Saint doctrine that took us to a more detailed yet more easily understood and more spiritually fulfilling doctrine.

As mentioned in chapter 6, we found it fascinating that The Church of Jesus Christ of Latter-day Saints placed more emphasis on the Garden of Gethsemane than did the Catholic Church. It may seem a small point, but it made a significant difference to us. By seeing in their separate contexts the various events that together constitute the Infinite Atonement, we reached a broader and deeper understanding of the Atonement and the infinite love it expresses.

Christ's agony in the Garden of Gethsemane, the beatings and humiliations that followed, and finally the Crucifixion are horrors at the human level. There are no words adequate to describe these horrors at the level of God in the form of a man.

We can read biblical accounts of crucifixion dating back to the time of the Egyptians (Genesis 40:19) and the time of Esther. Historical records document that crucifixion was practiced among the Assyrians, Scythians, Indians, Germans, Greeks, and Romans. Alexander the Great was said to have had two thousand Tyrians crucified as a consequence of their resistance following the conquest of Tyre.

While thousands have experienced the brutality of physical crucifixion, only Jesus Christ has ever taken upon himself the sins of the world. The agony of this ultimate act of selfless love is described in Luke 22:42–44, where Christ's sweat is described "as great drops of blood." The fear of Christ before taking upon him the sins of the world and the resultant pain and suffering are clearly described in scripture.

The Atonement wasn't complete until the Crucifixion, when Christ carried the sins of the world to the cross into the final sacrifice. The Crucifixion was the capstone of a process Latter-day Saints refer to as the Atonement, not in and of itself the Atonement. When we saw this, we were awakened to a deeper spiritual understanding of the infinite sacrifice of Jesus Christ and Heavenly Father.

An entirely new principle was introduced to us through Latter-day Saint doctrine: the principle of the "enabling power of the Atonement." We were quite familiar with the "forgiving power of the Atonement," but spent little time in pondering the enabling power—mainly because such a doctrinal concept does not exist in Catholicism as far as we know it.

This added granularity to the principle of the Atonement proved invaluable in helping our family gain a deeper and richer testimony of the Atonement and what our Savior Jesus Christ did for us. Perhaps most important, it allowed us to apply this enabling power in our daily lives. Like so many times before, we felt like we stumbled onto a treasure trove of powerful principles that must have been present at one time in the history of Christianity—they were simply too important to have never been understood in the first place.

The Resurrection of Christ

The Resurrection of Jesus Christ is celebrated annually in all of Christendom. In English this celebration is called Easter. Any active Catholic can recall the wonderful Easter Sundays where daughters are dressed in bright Easter attire with hats and ribbons. With smiles and bright faces, even the excitement of baskets and Easter eggs, the liturgical celebrations leading up to and including Easter were always memorable and joyous.

This section will examine the Resurrection from Catholic and Latter-day Saint perspectives to reinforce the similarities and identify the subtle, yet significant differences in this all-important event.

CATHOLIC DOCTRINE

The Catechism defines the Resurrection of Christ in simple and straightforward language and testifies of the importance of the event: "The bodily rising of Jesus from the dead on the third day after his death on the cross and burial in the tomb. The resurrection of Christ is the crowning truth of our faith in Christ" (Catechism glossary).

The Resurrection of Christ, testified of by Jesus and the prophets, glorifies the Savior and projects his supreme power and majesty over all, opening the heavens to all who believe on his name. Before being reunited to his body on the third day after his physical death, Jesus "in his human soul united to his divine person" visited the dead and "opened heaven's gates for the just who had gone before him" (Catechism 637). There, Jesus proclaimed the good news of the gospel to the spirits in bondage, fulfilling the messianic mission.

Although the Resurrection of Christ is a mystery to the human intellect, the reality of the event is historically verified and documented. There were witnesses to the Resurrected Christ, including Mary Magdalene, who was the first to see the resurrected Jesus; other holy women; Peter; and the remainder of the Twelve Apostles. Paul states that more than five hundred persons saw the resurrected Christ.

Christ rose from the dead in a physical body. He invited people to touch him, and even ate meals. Jesus pointedly told his apostles that he was not a ghost, but a resurrected and perfected being, despite the imprints in his hands and side. As such Christ was not resurrected back into earthly life, but into a glorified state full of the power of the Holy Spirit. The Resurrection confirms the divinity of Christ as both the son of God and as God himself. The three divine persons of the Trinity act as one while maintaining their own unique characteristics.

The Resurrection of Christ lays the framework for our own resurrection as outlined in the Catechism: "Christ, 'the first-born from the dead' (Col 1:18), is the principle of our own Resurrection, even now by the justification of our souls (cf. Rom 6:4), and one day by the new life he will impart to our bodies (Rom 8:11)" (Catechism 658).

See Catechism 434, 632 to 639, 641–653, 658, 1026, and glossary.

LATTER-DAY SAINT DOCTRINE

Three days following his Crucifixion, Christ's spirit was eternally reunited to his body and was resurrected. Before his Resurrection, after his crucifixion, Christ descended into the spirit prison to preach the gospel. The Apostle Peter describes this act of love by the Savior: "For Christ also hath once suffered for sins, the just for the unjust, that he might bring us to God, being put to death in the flesh, but quickened by the Spirit: By which also he went and preached unto the spirits in prison" (1 Peter 3:18–19).

President Joseph F. Smith recorded a vision in which he saw Christ visit the righteous spirits in the spirit world. It was there that Christ organized missionary work for the dead, including the appointment and endowment of messengers to "carry the light of the gospel to them that were in the darkness, even to all the spirits of men" (D&C 138:20).

Through the Atonement and the Resurrection, Christ was able to overcome physical death and open up the pathway of Resurrection to us all (1 Corinthians 15:21–22). The Prophet Alma taught that everyone who has ever lived will be resurrected, "both old and young, both bond and free, both male and female, both the wicked and the righteous" (Alma 11:44). As resurrected beings we will be in a state of immortality, where we "can die no more" (Alma 11:45).

See *Gospel Principles* 74, and 291.

THOUGHTS AND COMMENTARY

Catholic doctrine on the Resurrection of Jesus Christ puts greater emphasis on the spiritual nature and historical verification of the Resurrection of Jesus Christ than does Latter-day Saint doctrine. In the early days of Christianity, the Catholic Church bore the burden of "proving to the world" that the Resurrection took place. This burden likely led to a greater emphasis on historical events and their validation.

One must also appreciate the Catholic emphasis on the broader nature and meaning of the Resurrection as it relates to Christ's divinity and physical presence—another burden borne by the early Church in asserting that Christ was the messiah of the Old Testament. All Christians are indebted to the Catholic Church for its unwavering commitment and testimony on the Resurrection of Jesus Christ.

Even so, I don't remember any sermons, discussions, or educational events as a Catholic where the intimate details of Christ's Resurrection were comprehensively addressed. I was surprised to read the details offered in the Catechism on the doctrine of the Resurrection. I suspect the details provided in the Catechism would surprise many Catholics. These details offer a deep spiritual glimpse into the miracle of the Resurrection and the events leading up to it.

A key difference between the doctrines of both churches lies in the added detail supplied by the Prophet Joseph F. Smith. He described how Christ, during the time between his death and resurrection, organized the preaching of the gospel in the spirit world. This effort not only took place when he was there, but it was organized to continue after he left.

Notes

1. *Gospel Principles,* 71.
2. David A. Bednar, "In the Strength of the Lord," *Ensign,* Nov. 2004, 76.

9

Priesthood

THE priesthood of God is the ministering arm for the Lord's work on earth. It is noteworthy that the Catholic Church and The Church of Jesus Christ of Latter-day Saints are the only Christian institutions that claim to hold the authoritative priesthood of Jesus Christ, both declaring an unbroken succession of apostolic authority.

While the two churches share some common beliefs regarding the priesthood, other beliefs, some significant, are not shared. We will explore these similarities and differences in four parts: 1) structure and authority; 2) healings and blessings; 3) marriage and celibacy; and 4) wages and earnings.

Structure and Authority

God is orderly: Reading the scriptures and patiently observing the natural world brings this comforting assurance into full view. God gives authority to certain men to act in his name. In this way he organizes and administers his Church and avoids the confusion that comes when many claim to have authority from God. Slowly, methodically, this process has proceeded over the millennia, and it has been painstakingly recorded in the Old and New Testaments and other sacred texts. The methodology of this structure and authority of the priesthood differs between the Catholic Church and The Church of Jesus Christ of Latter-day Saints.

CATHOLIC DOCTRINE

The Catechism defines the Priesthood of Christ as the following: "The unique high priest, according to the Order of Melchizedek. Christ fulfilled everything that the priesthood of the Old Covenant prefigured. (cf. Hebrews 5:10, 6:20). He offered himself once and for all (Hebrews 10:14), in a perfect sacrifice upon the cross. His priesthood is made present in a special way in the Church through the ministerial priesthood, conferred through the Sacrament of Holy Orders" (Catechism glossary).

The priesthood is the power to act for Christ in his person, given to his apostles and their successors. The priesthood was on earth before the coming of Christ. The priesthood of the Old Covenant was called the Aaronic Priesthood and was established to administer in the ordinances of the Old Testament and to prepare man for the priesthood and ministry of the New Covenant, the Melchizedek Priesthood. The Aaronic Priesthood lacked the power to bring about salvation and therefore was fulfilled in Christ Jesus in the Melchizedek priesthood as part of God's New Covenant with man.

Melchizedek is the "king of Salem [who] brought forth bread and wine: and he was the priest of the most high God" (Genesis 14:18). Psalm 110:4 says, "Thou art a priest for ever after the order of Melchizedek." This is echoed by Paul in his letter to the Hebrews when he refers to Christ as the "high priest after the order of Melchisedec" (Hebrews 5:10).

Priests in the Catholic Church are ordained through the sacrament of Holy Orders, which is bestowed (or conferred) by the laying on of hands by a bishop, followed by a prayer in which God is petitioned to provide the graces of the Holy Spirit to the ordained. Holy Orders can only be conferred upon baptized men who have been recognized by Catholic authority as suitable for the ministry.

The priesthood of the Catholic Church is granted and practiced in three degrees: bishops, priests (or presbyters), and deacons. Each of the three degrees has distinct responsibilities and authority within the ministry, with only bishops and priests holding the priesthood:

BISHOPS: "The bishop receives the fulness of the sacrament of Holy Orders, which integrates him into the episcopal college and makes him the visible head of the particular Church entrusted to him. As successors of the apostles and members of the college, the bishops share in the apostolic responsibility and mission of the whole Church under the authority of the Pope, successor of St. Peter" (Catechism 1594).

PRIESTS (or presbyters): "Priests are united with the bishops in sacerdotal dignity and at the same time depend on them in the exercise of their pastoral functions; they are called to be the bishops' prudent co-workers. They form around their bishop the presbyterium which bears responsibility with him for the particular Church. They receive from the bishop the charge of a parish community or a determinate ecclesial office" (Catechism 1595).

DEACONS: "Deacons are ministers ordained for tasks of service of the Church; they do not receive the ministerial priesthood, but ordination confers on them important functions in the ministry of the word, divine worship, pastoral governance, and the service of charity, tasks which they must carry out under the pastoral authority of their bishop" (Catechism 1596).

Although only a small percentage of Catholic men hold the priesthood, all baptized and faithful members of the Catholic Church are able to share in the priesthood through the "common priesthood of the faithful" (Catechism 1591). The first form of the priesthood—the ministerial priesthood—is granted only to men who have completed Holy Orders and been given the sacred duty to dedicate their lives to service within the Catholic Church. The second form, the common priesthood of the faithful, does not involve the taking of vows or the dedication of one's life to service within the Church. However, all who share in the "common priesthood of the faithful" are able to minister in a spiritual sense through the Holy Spirit to the Catholic community.

The academic requirements to become a Catholic priest generally include an undergraduate degree, including courses in philosophy and psychology, followed by an additional four years minimum of master's related courses on ministry, divine studies, and administration.

See Catechism 935, 1541, 1544, 1591–1598, 1600, and glossary.

LATTER-DAY SAINT DOCTRINE

The Church of Jesus Christ of Latter-day Saints defines the priesthood as "the power and authority of God."[1] It was by the power of the priesthood that the heavens and earth were created and the universe is maintained in its perfect order. Through the power of the priesthood, the Lord achieves his ultimate mission "to bring to pass the immortality and eternal life of man" (Moses 1:39).

A priesthood of God existed before, during, and after the ministry of Jesus Christ. When Christ was upon the earth, he ordained Apostles to lead his Church and "gave them the power and authority of the priesthood to act in his name" (Mark 3:13–15; John 15:16; *Gospel Principles,* 82).

Priesthood authority is required to perform the ordinances such as baptism, confirmation, the blessing and passing of the sacrament, administering to the sick, performing special blessings, and the administration of temple ordinances.

The priesthood is divided into the Aaronic Priesthood (the lesser priesthood) and the Melchizedek Priesthood (the greater priesthood). The Aaronic Priesthood is sometimes referred to as the "preparatory priesthood."

Aaronic Priesthood

The Aaronic Priesthood originated in the time of Moses and was conferred upon Aaron and his sons to administer in the ecclesiastical duties of God (Numbers 18:1). Today, Aaronic Priesthood holders administer the outward ordinances of repentance and baptism (D&C 107:13–14, D&C 107:20).

The offices within the Aaronic Priesthood today include deacon, teacher, priest, and bishop. Within a ward, the Aaronic Priesthood is organized into a deacons quorum, a teachers quorum, and a priests quorum.

DEACON: Deacons perform duties such as passing the sacrament, ushering during Sunday services or special occasions, helping to maintain and clean Church buildings and grounds, assisting priesthood leaders, and fulfilling special Church assignments such as the collection of fast offerings.

TEACHER: In addition to the duties of a deacon, teachers take an active role in helping Church members live the commandments, including home teaching. Teachers are also tasked with the preparation of the bread and water for the sacrament.

PRIEST: In addition to the duties of a deacon and teacher, priests may baptize members, bless the bread and water of the sacrament, and actively preach the gospel. A priest, in preparation for the Melchizedek Priesthood, may ordain deacons, teachers, and other priests. If there are no Melchizedek Priesthood holders available, a priest may officiate at Church meetings.

BISHOP: A bishop holds the Melchizedek Priesthood in the office of a high priest and presides over the Aaronic Priesthood within the ward he is assigned—specifically as the president of the priest's quorum. The bishop is the leader and presides over the entire ward and is responsible for the spiritual well-being of every individual who lives within the geographic boundaries of his ward—regardless of their religious affiliation. Bishops are given the gift of discernment in order to act in their stewardship as the Common Judge in Israel.

Melchizedek Priesthood

Melchizedek Priesthood holders are given the power and authority to lead the spiritual work of the Church, including the preaching of the gospel and the administration of the ordinances within temples. The President of The Church of Jesus Christ of Latter-day Saints is the presiding high priest over the world-wide Melchizedek Priesthood.

The offices within the Melchizedek Priesthood include elder, high priest, patriarch, seventy, and Apostle. Within a ward, the Melchizedek Priesthood is organized into an elders quorum and a high priest group. The high priest group is part of a stake-wide high priest quorum presided over by the stake president.

ELDER: Each Melchizedek Priesthood holder can be referred to as an elder, and all elders are called to "teach, expound, exhort, baptize, and watch over the Church."[2] Elders can lead or participate in the ordinance of confirmation in which the gift of the Holy Ghost is bestowed by laying on of hands. Elders can administer to the sick, bless children of record, and preside at Church meetings as appropriate in the absence of a high priest. They can also do all the duties of the Aaronic Priesthood.

HIGH PRIEST: A high priest is a Melchizedek Priesthood holder who is put in charge of the spiritual affairs of a particular entity or geographic area. Members of bishoprics, stake presidencies, mission presidencies, high councilors, and other selected leaders of the Church must be ordained high priests. A high priest retains all of the spiritual privileges of an elder.

PATRIARCH: A patriarch is called to give special blessings to the Church. "Patriarchal blessings" provide guidance and insight to those who receive them.

SEVENTY: Seventies are General Authorities of the Church who are called as "special witnesses" of Jesus Christ to the entire world and help administer in the affairs of the Church. At the time of this writing there are eight quorums of seventies that currently serve within The Church of Jesus Christ of Latter-day Saints.

APOSTLE: Like the Seventies, Apostles are also special witnesses of Jesus Christ to the world and administer in the affairs of the Church as prophets, seers, and revelators. There are Twelve Apostles and together they form the Quorum of the Twelve Apostles; however, members of the first presidency may also be set apart as members of the Quorum of the Twelve Apostles. Apostles are given all of the keys of the kingdom of God on earth, but only the President of the Church "actively exercises all of the keys. The others act under his direction."[3]

The priesthood is available to all worthy male members of the Church. It is granted "by the laying on of hands by those who are in authority, to preach the Gospel and administer in the ordinances thereof" (Articles of Faith 1:5).

There are no academic or professional requirements to hold the priesthood, nor are there any such requirements to hold any leadership position within The Church of Jesus Christ of Latter-day Saints. However, readiness for any leadership calling takes into account reliable evidence of such readiness, and this evidence can include educational and professional achievements.

See *Gospel Principles*, 81–91, and 238.

THOUGHTS AND COMMENTARY

It didn't take long for Marilyn and I to realize that the single most important component of the Lord's Church on earth is the authority of the priesthood. As we learned about the significant differences in the structure and organization of the priesthood in The Church of Jesus Christ of Latter-day Saints, we began to see how the priesthood in the Catholic Church had evolved over time, leading to the difficult state that exists in some parishes today. During our investigation we came to the conclusion that there was a need for a complete restoration of the Catholic priesthood, based upon our life experiences and history. Not because all priests in the Catholic Church are bad, but because we couldn't help but feel that the current difficulties among a good percentage of the Catholic priesthood may have come from a broken Apostolic succession and subsequent apostasy. It was important that we had seen the Catholic priesthood in action and compared that to our observations of the Latter-day Saint priesthood in action. Now many years later the comparison still stirs up the very deepest emotions within us. We finally found the priesthood described in the scriptures and hoped for as Catholics.

I once felt a strong desire to become a priest in the Catholic Church in my early twenties, spending one weekend in a seminary to sort out my personal feelings. Even stronger, however, was my desire to be married and raise a family in the Lord. As a Catholic the two vocations—priest and husband/father—are mutually exclusive. I had to choose one, and I chose marriage and children.

When I considered becoming a Latter-day Saint, I saw I could combine both destinies: I could hold the priesthood and be a husband and a father. I saw that this combination was indeed the Lord's intention and felt that at last that I had come home to the truth.

The division of the priesthoods into two parts, the Aaronic and the Melchizedek, is a wise and correct organization of these powers. Although it is clear that Jesus fulfilled the Law of Moses, he did not do away with everything under the Law of Moses—such as the Ten Commandments, for example. However, since perfection cannot be obtained through the Aaronic Priesthood alone (Hebrews 7:11–12), there is a need for the Melchizedek Priesthood in combination with the Aaronic Priesthood. Both priesthoods are found in The Church of Jesus Christ of Latter-day Saints.

Marilyn and I were interested and committed to serving the Lord and reaching our full potential as children of our Heavenly Father. We both felt called to serve. We felt refreshed by a priesthood that is bestowed by worthiness and a desire to serve as opposed to academic rigor. Although we can understand why the Catholic Church requires a comprehensive education for all priests (undergraduate and graduate studies), we have seen no evidence that this emphasis on education protects the Church from abuses or increases the quality of ministry. Protection and quality lies in choosing the best men, and such men are not necessarily the most highly educated.

Conversely, we have seen no evidences where lack of seminary-type religious education has hindered Latter-day Saint priesthood leaders—myself included. In fact, by virtue of the fact that Latter-day Saint priesthood holders have to work in the real world at regular jobs, are married, and are raising or have raised children, gives them an edge in being an effective leader, counselor, and minister. Whatever deficiencies, real or perceived, that are generated by lack of religious education, are more than made up for in the "school of hard knocks"—in other words, the school of life.

Long before our association with the Latter-day Saints, Marilyn expressed to me her feelings that the Catholic Church should give greater emphasis to spiritual gifts than to academic gifts in choosing its priests. Academic and spiritual gifts are not mutually exclusive, but the latter does not flow from the former: we knew of many good men, men who would have made fine priests but who could not endure the academic rigor and prerequisites of the Catholic priesthood, and so gave up. Likewise, we know of Catholic priests who felt a strong inclination towards marriage and left the priesthood to marry, including the pastor of the first parish where Marilyn served as a youth minister.

I am reminded of the admonition of Paul to the Corinthians that "God hath chosen the foolish things of the world to confound the wise; and God hath chosen the weak things of the world to confound the things which are mighty" (1 Corinthians 1:27). In this letter to Timothy Paul clearly details the requirements for a bishop: "A bishop then must be blameless, the husband of one wife, vigilant, sober, of good behavior, given to hospitality, apt to teach; Not given to wine, no striker; not greedy of filthy lucre; but patient, not a brawler, not covetous. One that ruleth well in his own house, having his children in subjection with all gravity. (For if a man know not how to rule his own house, how shall he take care of the church of God?)" (1 Timothy 3:2–5). Clearly, the Catholic priesthood is not in alignment with the counsel of Paul—especially with respect to being married and rearing a family.

A Latter-day Saint priesthood holder must be a "worthy male" and receive the priesthood from those with authority to grant it. This simplicity appears much more in line with what was intended in the Bible, providing spiritual and practical application. Although education can greatly enhance a person's ability to minister, having the companionship of the Holy Ghost is far more valuable than having an academic degree.

Marilyn and I have seen the strength of the Lord that comes with true authority, not by apostolic succession alone, but through the ordinances of the fulness of the gospel of Jesus Christ. Looking back on our experiences as Catholics, we have come to believe that the authority of the priesthood is absent from the Catholic Church through the apostasy, and that such an absence is the primary reason for the many problems that have plagued the Catholic Church for centuries to this very day.

Many wonderful and committed men hold the Catholic priesthood who serve diligently and are making a difference in the lives of Catholics around the world. Imagine, if you will, fifty to one hundred times more Catholic priests than there are today, with the majority being married and able to serve in a variety of roles. Imagine your home having the priesthood in it as a husband or father. What you are imagining is the priesthood of The Church of Jesus Christ of Latter-day Saints.

Priesthood Power—Healings and Blessings

The priesthood of Jesus Christ has power from God for the blessing of his children on earth. Certainly such power includes the power to heal and bless. Otherwise the priesthood is merely ceremonial, and not the power of God on earth.

As a Catholic I was never comfortable with the idea of hands being laid upon me or others to bring about healings or blessings. I had heard of "charismatic Catholics" who participated in such events, but I was not raised in that tradition. Marilyn had more of an open mind to charismatic matters, but she too was raised with a more conservative view of the priesthood. The exercise of laying one's hands on another seemed a bit fanatical to me and in the tradition of the TV evangelists who publicly heal people on national television.

The reason for my cynical view was that the mainstream Catholicism I grew up with did not practice or demonstrate a charismatic priesthood full of the Holy Spirit with the power to bless and heal. I grew up witnessing more reserved priesthood expressions, which were highly ceremonial and ritualistic. I never saw hands laid on anyone other than for the sacrament of confirmation.

In this section, we will examine the healing and blessing power of the priesthood and compare and contrast Catholic and Latter-day Saint doctrines on this dynamic form of ministry.

CATHOLIC DOCTRINE

Anointing of the sick is one of the Seven Sacraments, sometimes called the "sacrament of the dying." It is administered to a baptized individual who is in danger of death. The Church has designated that the most appropriate time for an individual to receive this sacrament is when the person is near death, even if the person had previously received an anointing and the sickness has merely become worse.

The purpose of the anointing is to provide "special grace of healing and comfort to the Christian who is suffering the infirmities of serious illness or old age, and the forgiving of the person's sins" (Catechism glossary).

The anointing of the sick can take place anywhere (home, hospital, battlefield, and so on) and should only be performed by a bishop or priest. The ordinance calls for the priest or bishop to lay hands upon the inflicted, to pray over them, and then to anoint the individual with oil that has been blessed by the bishop.

In the gravest of circumstances, under the inspiration of the authorized Catholic minister, conditional provisions have been given for the anointing of the sick to Christians who are not in full standing with the Catholic Church, if it is the person's desire to be anointed.

Catholic doctrine calls for the Church to rely upon the power of the Holy Spirit to continue the work of Jesus Christ, the great physician, in healing the members of his Church. The sacraments of Penance and the Anointing of the Sick have the express purpose of healing the faithful Christian by the power of priesthood.

There is no Catholic doctrine authorizing blessing and anointing those who are *not* gravely ill or injured.

See Catechism 1401, 1421, 1517, 1519, 1527–1530, and glossary.

LATTER-DAY SAINT DOCTRINE

Latter-day Saint doctrine on healing holds the premise that healing comes as a result of faith. Therefore, administering to the sick is always preceded by a request for the blessing by the person in need or an individual close to that person (parent, sibling, or other). In doing so the healing comes as an answer to exercised faith (Matthew 8:5–15).

As the power of God on earth, the priesthood has the authority and power to heal and bless the faithful. While those who hold the Melchizedek Priesthood are given the power to anoint the sick and perform blessings, there are some priesthood holders who are given the gift of healing the sick, a gift of the spirit. In all cases, holders of the priesthood are admonished to use their priesthood "by persuasion, by long-suffering, by gentleness and meekness, and by love unfeigned" (D&C 121:41).

The power to bless can come in the form of anointing the sick (in whatever state they may be) or to provide a blessing of guidance and comfort to an individual. The individual need not be gravely ill, but they must have faith that the Lord Jesus Christ (or an individual acting on faith in their behalf), acting through the priesthood, will heal them of their infirmity. Among the ordinances that include blessings that can take place through the priesthood are blessings of children, of comfort or guidance, and of healing. Some blessings take place during the ordinance of confirmation and others take place when individuals are set apart in callings. There are also patriarchal blessings, which provide guidance and encouragement, and blessings of homes and dedication of graves.

Priesthood blessings for healing are executed in two stages, typically begin with one priesthood holder anointing the head of the afflicted with consecrated oil. (Oil is consecrated by Melchizedek Priesthood holders in a separate ordinance.) After the anointing, the priesthood holder places his hands on the head of the afflicted, calls the person by his or her full name, states the authority of the priesthood, recites a simple prayer regarding the anointing, and closes in the name of Jesus Christ. This is all done audibly, not in silence.

A second Melchizedek Priesthood holder then places his hands with those of the first on the person's head and seals the anointing: he pronounces a blessing as dictated by the Holy Ghost, and then closes in the name of Jesus Christ. This too is done audibly. In an emergency, a single Melchizedek Priesthood holder can both anoint and seal.

A blessing of comfort is performed by a Melchizedek Priesthood holder by laying his hands upon the head of the individual, calling the person by his or her full name, stating the authority of the priesthood, providing a blessing as dictated by the Holy Ghost, and then closing in the name of Jesus Christ.

A priesthood holder should be in a state of worthiness when performing a blessing, with each blessing given in a reverent and dignified manner. He should realize that he is acting on behalf of the Savior Jesus Christ. In some cases a group of Melchizedek priesthood holders may perform the blessing. This is typically done with each priesthood holder having his right hand on the head of the individual being blessed and his left hand on the shoulder of the priesthood holder next to him, all forming a circle around the individual.

See *Gospel Principles*, 83 and 147; *Mormon Doctrine*, 22 and 345; and "Lesson 5: Performing Priesthood Ordinances," *Duties and Blessings of the Priesthood: Basic Manual for Priesthood Holders, Part B,* 41.

Thoughts and Commentary

During our investigation, Marilyn and I became more passionate about the priesthood representing God on earth and possessing the power of healing and blessing—despite our more conservative upbringing in

Catholicism. We witnessed during our investigation, and countless times since our baptism, the exercising of the priesthood by God working through a variety of men (young and old) in healing the sick, comforting the down-trodden—even rebuking the weather. Where I once thought such actions were borderline crazy, I came to embrace that such actions through the priesthood were the way Christ intended his priesthood to be (such as the blessing given to our son Jason when he was in the hospital as described in chapter one).

Such actions remind us of the scripture from John 14:12, which states: "Verily, verily, I say unto you, He that believeth on me, the works that I do shall he do also; and greater works than these shall he do." I cannot recall meeting anyone in the Catholic Church who took seriously this remarkable assurance offered by Jesus. The belief that the power of God could be exercised by men to do miracles, healings, and blessings of all kinds was certainly not widespread among the Catholics we knew. Perhaps many harbor this belief but may be too afraid or embarrassed to express it.

This discovery of the power of priesthood made a profound difference in our lives and the lives of our children, and it will continue to do so now and for all generations of our family throughout eternity. Christ meant for us to do great things in his name in building the Kingdom of God on earth. Why not then exercise a priesthood that actually puts that promise into action to bless the lives of the children of God?

Priesthood Marriage and Celibacy

Many years ago, and even today, there was on-going and heated debate among our Catholic friends about whether priests should marry. Older Catholics generally supported a celibate priesthood; while younger Catholics generally believed celibacy blocked many fine men from entering the priesthood and were in favor of a married priesthood. One of the primary reasons Marilyn left her vocation as a nun was that she had a strong desire to marry.

In this section we will examine Catholic and Latter-day Saint doctrine on marriage and the priesthood. Our examination will include a review of the history of the celibate priesthood in order to shed additional light on the evolution of this controversial topic.

CATHOLIC DOCTRINE

The Catholic doctrine on celibacy in the priesthood is historical, generally well known, and clearly defined: "In the Latin Church the sacrament of Holy Orders for the presbyterate is normally conferred only on candidates who are ready to embrace celibacy freely and who publicly manifest their intention of staying celibate for the love of God's kingdom and the service of men" (Catechism 1599).

Celibacy is defined in the Catechism as "the state or condition of those who have chosen to remain unmarried for the sake of the kingdom of heaven in order to give themselves entirely to God and to the service of his people" (Catechism glossary). Curiously, the definition of celibacy refers to marriage only, not to sex. Celibacy is highly celebrated in the Catholic Church as a means of proclaiming the "Reign of God" and consecrating one's self to God and to the Church.

See Catechism 1579, 1599, and glossary.

LATTER-DAY SAINT DOCTRINE

Both married and unmarried men are permitted to hold the priesthood in The Church of Jesus Christ of Latter-day Saints. Like all members of the Church, priesthood holders must live the law of chastity, which states: "We are to have sexual relations only with our spouse to whom we are legally married. No one, male or female, is to have sexual relations before marriage. After marriage, sexual relations are permitted only with a spouse."[4]

THOUGHTS AND COMMENTARY

Much has been written about celibacy in the Catholic Church. Many faithful members of Catholicism argue that allowing priests to marry would help the Church to prosper in a multitude of ways. Marilyn was extremely vexed by the staunch opposition of Catholic Church leaders to a married priesthood as she had firsthand experience of its negative effects in a variety of ways. When Marilyn and I discussed the history of celibacy and associated aberrations, we began to understand how a practice became a doctrine and found its way into the Catechism—despite scriptural evidence to the contrary. This backwards progression became another piece of evidence to further support the apostasy.

Proponents of a married priesthood generally point to the fact that Peter and several of the Apostles were married men, and this tradition continued into the second and third century when, it is widely believed, most priests in the Catholic Church were married. It was around this time that Gnosticism put forward the unfounded assertion that marriage had a negative impact on the lives of men and women alike.

For centuries after the Ascension of Christ, historical records indicate that priests, bishops, and as many as thirty-nine popes were married.[5] In AD 325, at the Council of Nicaea, a proclamation was put forth outlining that after their ordination, priests were not allowed to marry. It is reported that about sixty years later, around AD 385, Siricius severed relations with his wife in order to position himself to become pope.[6] As Pope, Siricius decreed that priests could no longer have sexual relations with their wives, moving one step closer to the celibate priesthood.

Although not substantiated, some hypothesize that the celibate priesthood came about due to issues of property in the Church. In the early church, if a priest died there were apparently questions as to whom the property of the priest belonged—the wife of the deceased priest, or the church.

Eusebius, a scholar born in AD 260, who was made Bishop of Caesarea in 314, provided valuable insights into the marriages of the Apostles and his concerns on the subject of celibacy in the Catholic Church. Eusebius was not in favor of a celibate priesthood and stated his concerns freely in several letters and writings.

In the book, *Full Pews and Empty Altars: Demographics of the Priest Shortage in United States Catholic Diocese*, the authors state that by the year 2005, the U.S. will have experienced a 40 percent decrease in the total number of priests from 1965 levels, while at the same time experiencing a 65 percent increase in the number of Catholics.[7] If these projections were correct, the doctrine of a celibate priesthood is likely one of the main reasons for this unfortunate lack of ministry and overworked priests in the Catholic Church.

One can see from this brief history that celibacy in the Catholic Church evolved over time. Elder Bruce R. McConkie infers that the requirement of celibacy is a part of the great apostasy, being contrary to such scriptures as Hebrews 13:4, Genesis 1:28, and 1 Timothy 4:1-3. Elder McConkie explains that many have used the writings of Paul to support the doctrine of celibacy, but that such justifications are distorted.[8]

The scriptural and historical support for a married priesthood is overwhelming. Furthermore, common spiritual sense about the role God gave to man in mortality suggests that celibacy, although a noble intention in showing commitment and sacrifice to the Lord, is incompatible with that role. Consider the scripture from Genesis 2:18: "It is not good that the man should be alone; I will make him an help meet for him."

Marilyn and I both believe that the freedom of priesthood holders to marry and raise families is vital to the well-being of the entire religious community. We also believe that this freedom could be detrimental to a typical Catholic parish without the same type of infrastructure as found in The Church of Jesus Christ of Latter-day Saints. With little or no priesthood support or layman help, the typical Catholic priest is asked to manage and minister to an entire parish. This task would be daunting if not impossible in the present Catholic priesthood organization. But if the priesthood were held by all worthy males in a parish, the labor of ministry could be shared joyously among many.

Paid Ministry

Should a priesthood holder or any minister be paid for his services to a community or congregation? This question can evoke a wide variety of emotions among members and clergy of various Christian sects. Some scriptural references suggest the answer is no, while others imply a limited form of compensation is acceptable. This section will explore the differences in philosophy between Catholics and Latter-day Saints with respect to compensation for priesthood service.

CATHOLIC DOCTRINE

We were unable to locate an official statement or doctrine concerning monetary compensation given to priests and others who minister in the Catholic Church. A passage from the Catechism of the Catholic Church suggests that one should not pursue wages in doing good (perhaps referring to the ministry), implying that wages should not be the reason that one would enter into the ministry:

> The practice of the moral life animated by charity gives to the Christian the spiritual freedom of the children of God. He no longer stands before God as a slave, in servile fear, or as a mercenary looking for wages, but as a son responding to the love of him who "first loved us": [St. Basil continues] If we turn away from evil out of fear of punishment, we are in the position of slaves. If we pursue the enticement of wages, . . . we resemble mercenaries. Finally if we obey for the sake of the good itself and out of love for him who commands . . . we are in the position of children. (Catechism 1828)

The Catholic priesthood is listed as a career in the 1998–99 Occupational Handbook, citing "the shortage of Roman Catholic priests is expected to continue, resulting in a very favorable job outlook through the year 2006." According to William P. Daly, Director of Research for the National Association of Church Personnel Administrators (NACPA), the median salary received by priests increased from $12,222 in 1966 to $15,483 in 1999 to $16,885 for 2001–02. During the same time period priests' median total taxable income and support likewise increased from $26,569 to $33,059. Priests can also be paid stipends for services such as marriages and other ceremonies.

In 2005 the average annual salary for full-time lay ministers (not priests or nuns) was $35,261 per year, up from the 1992 average of $13,000 to $20,000 per year.[9]

LATTER-DAY SAINT DOCTRINE

The Church of Jesus Christ of Latter-day Saints, like the Catholic Church, has no specific doctrine or official statement on wages or salary of priesthood holders. However, it is well-known that with the exception of selected worldwide Church leaders who are offered (and who often do not accept) a small stipend, the Church has an all-volunteer, unpaid lay ministry. This means that bishops, stake presidents, and other priesthood holders retain their professional careers and do not receive Church compensation of any kind to serve in their respective priesthood callings.

Elder Boyd K. Packer of the Quorum of the Twelve Apostles had this to say about this unpaid ministry:

> In The Church of Jesus Christ of Latter-day Saints there is no paid ministry, no professional clergy, as is common in other churches. More significant even than this is that there is no laity, no lay membership as such; men are eligible to hold the priesthood and to carry on the ministry of the Church, and both men and women serve in many auxiliary capacities. This responsibility comes to men whether they are rich or poor, and with this responsibility also comes the authority. There are many who would deny, and others who would disregard it; nevertheless, the measure of that authority does not depend on whether men sustain that authority, but rather depends on whether God will recognize and honor that authority.[10]

Elder Derek A. Cuthbert of the Seventy said:

> Over the years of my membership in The Church of Jesus Christ
> of Latter-day Saints, I have greatly appreciated the opportunities for
> service, for there is no paid ministry. Every worthy male member of the
> Church above the age of twelve may hold an office in the priesthood.
> Similarly, the girls and women of the Church receive many assignments
> to lead and teach and serve. Each family is visited monthly by priest-
> hood home teachers, who care for their needs, and by visiting teachers
> from the women's Relief Society, whose motto is "charity never fai-
> leth."[11]

THOUGHTS AND COMMENTARY

Like most people, I gave no thought as a Catholic to the payment of
priests for the services they perform in the Catholic Church. This practice
is widely—nearly universally—accepted and adhered to it without question or complaint. For instance, we provided a stipend to the priest who
performed our civil marriage ceremony in Houston, Texas, because we
knew that such an offering was common and expected.

Although we doubt that few, if any, Catholic priests enter into their
vocation with the purpose of becoming wealthy, we had seen the negative
effects of a paid ministry among the laity. As Associate Director of Youth
Ministry for the Houston-Galveston Diocese, Marilyn saw firsthand the
negative effects of a paid ministry. These effects are not isolated to the
Catholic Church; they can exist wherever there is a paid ministry.

Like the Catholic Church, of which my own mother worked for
many years as an accountant, The Church of Jesus Christ of Latter-day
Saints has paid employees, but these paid positions are limited to temporal operations and not ministry.

Several passages in the Bible warn against a paid ministry, or clearly
indicate the need to avoid compensation for religious service. In 1 Peter
5:2, Peter admonishes the priesthood to "feed the flock of God which is
among you, taking the oversight thereof, not by constraint, but willingly;
not for filthy lucre, but of a ready mind." Jesus confirmed this principle
when he said, "Freely ye have received, freely give" (Matthew 10:8). Other
such scriptures can be found in Luke 10:4; John 10:12; 1 Thessalonians
2:9; 2 Thessalonians 3:8; Titus 1:6, 11; and Acts 20:33.

Without stringent academic requirements for the priesthood or compensation of any kind, relying completely on the inspiration of the Lord

and the faith of Church members, the ministry of the Church changes lives, grows, and is astonishingly effective. I can't help but think this is exactly the way the early Church operated, where men such as the Apostles had to earn a living while fulfilling their ecclesiastical duties. If there was support rendered, it was merely that which sustained life and nothing more. Such a ministerial priesthood has been restored to the earth today.

NOTES

1. *Gospel Principles*, 81.
2. Ibid., 90.
3. Ibid., 91.
4. Ibid., 249.
5. Kelly, J. N. D. *Oxford Dictionary of Popes*. New York, Oxford Press. 1986.
6. Padovano, A. "Power, Sex, and Church Structures," Lecture presented at Call To Action, Chicago. 1994.
7. Schoenherr and Young, *Full Pews, Empty Altars* (University of Wisconsin Press, 1993).
8. *Mormon Doctrine*, 118–19.
9. David De Lambo, "Lay Parish Ministers," National Pastoral Life Center, as cited by www.futurechurch.org, "Lay Ecclesial Minsters in the Catholic Church."
10. Boyd K. Packer, "Follow the Brethren," *Liahona*, Sept. 1979, 53
11. Derek A. Cuthbert, "What's the Difference?" *Ensign*, Nov. 1985, 24.

10

Organization

Structure of the Church of Jesus Christ

For the Church of Jesus Christ to carry out the work of building the kingdom of God on earth and into the eternities it must be organized effectively. God is a God of order and his son Jesus Christ came to organize his Church on earth before his Ascension into heaven. While the Catholic Church and The Church of Jesus Christ of Latter-day Saints both claim to be the true church of Jesus Christ on earth, they have extremely different structures by which they are administering the Lord's work.

This chapter will examine the structural differences between the two churches, outlining the offices of the priesthood and other pertinent organizational dynamics that make up the ecclesiastical foundation of each.

CATHOLIC DOCTRINE

The structure of the Catholic Church is apostolic, meaning the foundation of the Church is built upon the principle that apostolic succession has come from the original Twelve Apostles (mainly Peter) to the present day Pope and the College of Bishops who govern the Church today.

The Church is usually locally organized into parishes, which are then grouped geographically into dioceses.

NOTE: My research on the hierarchy of the Catholic Church uncovered sometimes conflicting information on organizational structures and on how they interact in the Church. My brief descriptions are a synthesis from these various sources. Exceptions abound.

The Church hierarchy includes the following ten ecclesiastical components:

The Pope

The Pope is "head of the college of bishops, the Vicar of Christ and Pastor of the universal Church on earth" (Catechism 936). The Pope Ministers on behalf of Christ on earth to lead the Church as a shepherd would lead his flock. Other titles of the Pope include the Successor of Peter, the Bishop of Rome, and the Holy Roman Pontiff.

The College of Bishops

The College of Bishops is made up of all of the bishops of the Catholic Church. These bishops are the successors of the Twelve Apostles. The purpose of the College is to assist in the governance of the Catholic Church. As the leader of the College of Bishops, the Pope determines how the power of the College is to be employed, while having the authority to call or dismiss a council (in other words, a gathering of bishops to discuss doctrine or ecclesiastical matters) with the final approval of all decisions made by the council. Hence, the Council's authority is predicated upon its ability to be united with the Pope.

The College of Cardinals

Cardinals are appointed by the Pope but have no more ecclesiastical authority than that of bishops, although one might argue their political influence exceeds that of a bishop under specific circumstances related to their appointment. The College of Cardinals is made up of select bishops who are assigned a special status and position. The primary purpose of the College of Cardinals is to advise the Pope on select matters determined by him. Beginning in 1059 to the present, when the Pope passes away, the College of Cardinals elects a new Pope from among its ranks. Before that time, elections were conducted by the clergy and the people of the diocese of Rome.

Synod of Bishops

The Synod of Bishops can be thought of as a continuation of the Second Vatican Council, whereby the Synod meets in Rome as a scheduled advisory board to the Pope to consider selected issues and develop official Church teaching.

Magisterium

The Magisterium is the "keeper and preserver" of official Catholic Church teachings. The Magisterium is called upon to interpret the word of God, which may originate as scripture or tradition. The teachings of the Catholic Church adhere to the standards on faith and morals taught by the Apostles. The Magisterium guards this adherence.

Bishops

Appointed by the Pope, bishops preside over dioceses. A diocese is made up of a number of parishes in a given geographic region. A bishop may be appointed to the office of an archbishop, who presides over a territory that would be considered larger than average or be located in an area or city of significant importance. There is no difference in authority between an archbishop and a bishop.

Priests

Priests take a vow of obedience to the bishop and are typically assigned to a parish to minister to the people, exercise ecclesiastical authority over it, and manage its day-to-day operations.

Deacons

Deacons are ordained male assistants to bishops and priests. Deacons help by performing certain spiritual duties. These include the distribution of the Eucharist, proclaiming the gospel, assisting matrimonial services, baptizing, presiding over funerals, and other like ministerial activities. Deacons are not authorized to consecrate the Eucharist. There is no female equivalent to the position of a deacon.

Nuns and Brothers

A woman who feels a vocation to the religious life in the Catholic Church and is willing to take a vow of chastity, charity, obedience, and poverty for life can become a nun. Many different orders of sisterhood exist in the Catholic Church, each community having a set of rules approved by Rome.

Men who feel called to live a religious life, but not as a priest or deacon, can become a brother in various communities approved by Rome. A brother will take vows similar to those taken by nuns, including chastity and obedience.

Lay Ministers

Catholics who take an active role in Church service, but who do not choose the religious life, can become lay ministers. Lay ministers can occupy paid parish positions or can be volunteers. Their work is usually directed by the parish pastor or other authorized parish personnel. These lay ministers are "made to share in the priestly, prophetical, and kingly office of Christ; they have therefore, in the Church and in the world, their own assignment in the mission of the whole People of God" (Catechism 873).

See Catechism 873, 869, 936, and glossary. Also see www.catholic-pages.com, www.bible.ca/catholic-church-hierarchy-organization.htm, and Canon 336 and 338 of the 1983 Code of Canon Law.

LATTER-DAY SAINT DOCTRINE

The Church of Jesus Christ of Latter-day Saints is the restored church of Jesus Christ on earth, and as such, it is patterned after the church established by Jesus Christ during his public ministry.

The Restoration of the Church of Jesus Christ includes a full restoration of the structure of the Church, beginning with a restoration of the authority of the priesthood. In 1829 both the Aaronic and Melchizedek Priesthoods were restored to the earth, laying the ground work for this revelation given through the prophet Joseph Smith in April of 1830: "The rise of the Church of Christ in these last days, being one thousand eight hundred and thirty years since the coming of our Lord and Savior Jesus Christ in the flesh, it being regularly organized and established agreeable to the laws of our country, by the will and commandments of God" (D&C 20:1).

This revelation inspired the direction that the Church would be organized with the same offices as during the time of Christ's public ministry, including "Apostles, prophets, seventies, evangelists (patriarchs), pastors (presiding officers), high priests, elders, bishops, priests, teachers, and deacons."[1] Chapter 9 defines these offices of the priesthood in more detail. The commitment of the Church to restoring and maintaining the same ecclesiastical structure as during the time of Christ on earth is stated in the sixth article of faith: "We believe in the same organization that existed in the Primitive Church, namely, apostles, prophets, pastors, teachers, evangelists, and so forth."

The Church has grown and become more complex than it was in the early days—growing from six members in 1830 to over 13 million members world wide in 2007. The Lord has revealed the changes necessary to adapt to this growth and complexity. For example, local wards (similar to Catholic parishes) are now organized into stakes (akin to small Catholic dioceses). Stake presidents (akin to bishops in the Catholic Church) preside over these stakes. High councils, each consisting of twelve priesthood leaders answering to the stake president, have been established to provide a structure at the local level that echoes that of the Church as a whole with its twelve apostles answering to the Prophet. Each structural component comes about through revelation and mirrors the framework of the early church of Jesus Christ.

Missions have been established to teach the gospel across the world.

At the ward and stake levels, an array of positions necessary to carry the temporal and ecclesiastical duties common at these levels are filled by unpaid members of the Church. Church leaders at these levels are also unpaid.

Also, a number of unpaid auxiliaries exist at these and other levels of the Church. The auxiliaries include the Relief Society (one of the largest women's organizations in the world), Young Men organization, Young Women organization, Primary, Sunday School, and various other organizations.

Following is a brief description of these ward level organizations and positions. They are duplicated, sometimes with different titles, at the stake and worldwide levels to provide guidance and support.

Bishopric

The bishop calls two counselors to serve with him, forming the bishopric of a ward. All ward auxiliary functions are given guidance and leadership via the bishopric.

Priesthood

Each ward has an elders quorum and high priest group. In each organization there is a leader (elders quorum president and high priest group Leader) with two counselors. All adult men eighteen and older belong to either the elders quorum or high priest group and are assigned as home teachers.

Relief Society

The Relief Society organization is dedicated to teaching and ministering to the needs of women eighteen and older. Each Relief Society has a president, two counselors to the president, teachers, and other positions typical for the operation of a church organization.

Young Men and Young Women

The Young Men organization and Young Women organization are dedicated to teaching and ministering to the needs of youth ages twelve to eighteen years. In each organization (Young Men and Young Women separately) there is a president, two counselors, teachers, and advisors.

Primary

The Primary organization is dedicated to teaching and ministering to the needs of children eighteen months to twelve years. Each Primary has a president, two counselors, teachers, and other positions typical for the operation of a church organization.

Sunday School

The Sunday School organization is dedicated to teaching the Church curriculum to members ages twelve to adult. Each Sunday School has a president, two counselors, and teachers for each class—typically taught by age group.

Activities

The activities committee is dedicated to providing ward or stake activities, including socials, dances, and other social group events. Each activities committee is made up of a chair person and others as needed.

Mission

Each ward has a ward mission council that helps to coordinate missionary activities within the ward. Full-time missionaries are assigned to each ward to teach people interested in investigating the Church. Each ward mission council has a ward mission leader and an appropriate number of member missionaries, who are members of the ward. There is no mission organization at the stake level.

Others

There are other functions at the ward and stake level, including single adults, employment, music, library, public affairs, family history, and seminary. In addition there are priesthood committees that are organized to do things such as help people move into and out of their homes, conduct family history, preach the gospel, and other spiritual and temporal matters.

As time passes and the Church grows across the globe, there will undoubtedly be refinements in organization and function. Such refinements were made by the Twelve Apostles after the Ascension of Christ.

When the Apostles took up the matter of caring for widows, they directed that the saints should organize and assign this duty so that the Apostles could continue to focus on teaching, leading, and spreading the faith: "Wherefore, brethren, look ye out among you seven men of honest report, full of the Holy Ghost and wisdom, whom we may appoint over this business" (Acts 6:3).

Like the headquarters of the Catholic Church, The Church of Jesus Christ of Latter-day Saints has a large operational infrastructure that is staffed by salaried professionals, such as accountants, lawyers, and facilities managers. They accomplish their work through paid employees and workers.

See *Gospel Principles*, 109–112.

THOUGHTS AND COMMENTARY

The Catholic Church and The Church of Jesus Christ of Latter-day Saints are both hierarchical organizations. Both enjoy strong leadership that cascades down to the local level, where it is hoped that members embrace the direction and carry out the efforts of building the kingdom of God on earth, according to the will of God as given to his chosen servants.

However, the two churches differ markedly in the functions and relationships among entities in their hierarchies. The Catholic Church has evolved away from the original biblical structure, while The Church of Jesus Christ of Latter-day Saints has from its beginnings made a great effort to remain within the biblically outlined organizational structure. Jesus Christ established his church according to certain organizational principles (Luke 10:1; Luke 6:13–16; Mark 3:14), and his apostles reaffirmed these principles, as evidenced by such events and writings as the appointment of Matthias after the death of Judas (Acts 1:25–26) and the validation of church structure by Paul in his many letters (Ephesians 2:20; Ephesians 3:5; Ephesians 4:11; and 1 Corinthians 12:28).

Another stark difference is the virtually universal lay ministry of The Church of Jesus Christ of Latter-day Saints. Every ward and stake is staffed and managed entirely by unpaid members of the Church: men, women, and youth all hold positions of responsibility by way of being called, not volunteering. Latter-day Saints believe that everyone must have a meaningful part to play in running the Church and advancing the work of Christ on earth. This ecclesiastical principle keeps people engaged and feeling a sense of contributing to the building of the king-dom of God.

The opposite of this structure is a church in which people belong but have little to no involvement. When people are selectively involved in a church, they are not given the opportunity to feel a spiritual and temporal commitment to the gospel of Jesus Christ. Christianity was meant to be a participatory community, where people serve and minister to one another. Our experience in the Catholic Church was that there were many who were willing and desirous to be involved, but the lack of organization and infrastructure created gaps in opportunities and left many with only an occasional assignment to complete or volunteer for. Conversely, in The Church of Jesus Christ of Latter-day Saints, everyone has a calling, com-mitting everyone to the ministry.

Marilyn and I have come to fully recognize the wisdom in the resto-ration of the structure of the Church of Jesus Christ to its original form, augmented by the appropriate components to compensate for the growth of the Church in order to maintain an effective ministry. You need only examine the fruits of The Church of Jesus Christ of Latter-day Saints (see chapter 16) to know that its organization and structure are inspired. There is a tremendous comfort and confidence in having this organization on the earth, knowing that the same organization was established and sanctified by Jesus Christ himself.

Church Name

Growing up Catholic, I can't remember being too curious about what the term *catholic* meant, nor did I ponder why the church I attended was called by this name or its surname (Saint Lawrence, Christ the Good Shepherd, Saint Ignatius, and so on). I knew there were other churches, and I was proud to be a Catholic—a member of the one true church. When I came to understand that "catholic" meant *universal*, my under-standing of the Church's claim to be the one true church was broad-ened, and I became more thoughtful about what constituted a universal church.

During my investigation of The Church of Jesus Christ of Latter-day Saints, I became even more interested in how a church is named. I learned that a church name does far more than serve as an identifier on the outside of the building. It is not just what one calls one's self, it is that which boldly proclaims who you worship and whom you follow. This section addresses the question, "What's in a name." The answer we found was astonishing.

Catholic Doctrine

The term *catholic* comes from the Greek words *kata-holos*, meaning "according to the whole." It is thought that Ignatius in the second century first applied this word to the Church. His meaning was that the fledgling institution that was to become the Catholic Church was the single visible entity among other Christian entities that held claim to being Christ's church.

The Catechism expands upon the term *catholic*: "The Church is Catholic in a double sense. . . . First, the Church is catholic because Christ is present in her. . . . Secondly, the Church is catholic because she has been sent out by Christ on a mission to the whole of the human race" (Catechism 830 and 831).

The Catechism refers to the Church as being one, holy, catholic, and apostolic. And although the Catholic Church believes there can be elements of sanctification and truth found outside of the Catholic Church, it believes it is "the sole Church of Christ" (Catechism 870).

See Catechism 830, 831, and 866–870.

Latter-day Saint Doctrine

On April 26, 1838, eight years after the revelation on the organization and governance of the Church, came a revelation from the Lord that included what the name of the Church would be called: "Thus shall my church be called in the last days, even The Church of Jesus Christ of Latter-day Saints" (D&C 115:4).

Elder Russell M. Nelson of the Quorum of the Twelve Apostles wrote an article in 1990 in which he describes each phrase from the "Church of Jesus Christ of Latter-day Saints" to expound on their meaning. The following is a summary of that article:

The Church

The first two words of the name the Lord chose for His earthly organization . . . Note that the article *The* begins with a capital letter. This is an important part of the title, for the Church is the official organization of baptized believers who have taken upon themselves the name of Christ." (D&C 10:67–69; D&C 18:21–25.) The foundation of the Church is the reality that God is our Father and that His Only

Begotten Son, Jesus Christ, is the Savior of the world. The witness and inspiration of the Holy Ghost confirm those realities. The Church is the way by which the Master accomplishes His work and bestows His glory.

of Jesus Christ

By divine directive, the title of the Church bears the sacred name of Jesus Christ, whose church this is. (See D&C 115:3–4.) . . . We worship God the Eternal Father in the name of His Son by the power of the Holy Ghost. We know the premortal Jesus to be Jehovah . . . We know Him to be "the chief corner stone" upon which the organization of His Church is based. (Ephesians 2:20.) We know Him to be the Rock from whom revelation comes to His authorized agents (see 1 Moroni 10:4; Helaman 5:12) and to all who worthily seek Him (see D&C 88:63).

of Latter-day

It is true that scriptures foretell the final days of the earth's temporal existence as a telestial sphere. The earth will then be renewed and receive its paradisiacal, or terrestrial, glory. (A of F 1:10.) Ultimately, the earth will become celestialized. (See Revelation 21:1; D&C 77:1; D&C 88:25–26.) But its *last* days must be preceded by its *latter* days! We live in those latter days, and they are really remarkable. The Lord's Spirit is being poured out upon all inhabitants of the earth, precisely as the Prophet Joel foretold. His prophecy was of such significance that the angel Moroni reaffirmed it to the Prophet Joseph Smith. (See Joel 2:28–32; Joseph Smith—History 1:41.)

Saints

The word *Christian* appears in only three verses of the King James Version of the Bible. . . . In contrast, the term *saint* (or *saints*) appears in thirty-six verses of the Old Testament and in sixty-two verses of the New Testament. Paul addressed an epistle "to the saints which are at Ephesus, and to the faithful in Christ Jesus." (Ephesians 1:1.) To recent converts there he said, "Ye are no more strangers and foreigners, but fellow citizens with the saints, and of the household of God." (Ephesians 2:19; see also Ephesians 3:17–19.). In his epistle to the Ephesians, Paul used the word *saint* at least once in every chapter! . . . A saint is a believer in Christ and knows of His perfect love.[2]

Elder Nelson's explanation answers the question, "What's in a name?" We can see there is deep spiritual meaning in each element of the name, "The Church of Jesus Christ of Latter-day Saints," laying the groundwork for a meaningful spiritual association in communion and community with Christ and the faithful.

The Church is often referred to as "the Mormon Church" or "LDS Church." Both of these have been given to the Church by the media as nicknames. Church members have been counseled to use the full name of the Church as much as possible in order to convey the true meaning of the Lord's work on the earth and his Church in these latter days.

THOUGHTS AND COMMENTARY

When Marilyn and I came to seriously consider the significance of the name of the church of Jesus Christ, we were surprised to discover the power of a name. Being accustomed to the word *catholic,* which is a reference to a characteristic rather than to the underlying essence, we never really thought of how a church name might define a believer, or even define the community and who and what it worshipped. A scripture from the Book of Mormon sums the subject up thoughtfully, where Jesus Christ appears to the people of America and speaks about the naming of his church (3 Nephi 27:3–7):

> And they said unto him: Lord, we will that thou wouldst tell us the name whereby we shall call this church; for there are disputations among the people concerning this matter.
>
> And the Lord said unto them: Verily, verily, I say unto you, why is it that the people should murmur and dispute because of this thing?
>
> Have they not read the scriptures, which say ye must take upon you the name of Christ, which is my name? For by this name shall ye be called at the last day;
>
> And whoso taketh upon him my name, and endureth to the end, the same shall be saved at the last day.
>
> Therefore, whatsoever ye shall do, ye shall do it in my name; therefore ye shall call the church in my name; and ye shall call upon the Father in my name that he will bless the church for my sake.

There is nothing wrong with calling a church "catholic" to mean the universal church of Jesus Christ; however, there is so much more meaning in a name that reaffirms our taking upon us the name of Jesus Christ, becoming one of the saints of God, and being a part of His Church in these latter days. We have come to sincerely appreciate the meaningful nature of the name and how it shines forth as a beacon of hope and joy to all the world.

NOTES

1. *Gospel Principles,* 112.
2. Russell M. Nelson, "Thus Shall My Church Be Called," *Ensign*, May 1990, 16

11

Popes and Prophets

CHURCHES are often led by individuals who must bear the burden of spiritual and temporal leadership for their congregations. History records the lives of excellent and revered church leaders across many religions and sects, as well as the lives and misdeeds of churchmen who have been less than exemplary—even reprehensible. How an ecclesiastical leader lives, is perceived, and is revered in a religion can make a substantial difference in the effectiveness of that leader and in the quality of the members of the church he leads.

The leader of the Catholic Church is called "the Pope," while the leader of The Church of Jesus Christ of Latter-day Saints is called "the Prophet." This chapter will examine the differences between these two leaders and how their callings are structured and administered.

CATHOLIC DOCTRINE

The Pope is defined in the Catechism as "the successor of St. Peter as Bishop of Rome and Supreme Pontiff of the universal Catholic Church. The Pope exercises a *primacy* of authority as Vicar of Christ and shepherd of the whole Church; he receives the divine assistance promised by Christ to the Church when he defines *infallibly* a doctrine of faith or morals" (Catechism Glossary).

Catholics believe that through an unbroken line of succession from the Apostle Peter, and by divine association, the Pope holds "full, supreme, and universal power over the whole Church, a power which he can always exercise unhindered" (Catechism 882). Just as Christ gave Peter commission over all of the Church with the power to bind and loose on earth, this same commission rests upon the College of Bishops with the Pope as its leader.

With the authority of Christ, the gift of infallibility is given to the Pope in specific matters and doctrine relating to faith and morals. This same infallibility is with the body of bishops, when united with the Pope, as they "exercise supreme Magisterium, above all in an Ecumenical Council" (Catechism 891), including the interpretation of the Word of God (the Bible). Members of the Catholic Church are expected to support and follow their leaders.

Popes are selected according to a democratic voting process. Between fifteen and twenty days following the death of a Pope, the College of Cardinals meets in conclave to elect the new Pope. According to current statutes, 120 of the estimated 184 cardinals are allowed to vote in a very precise voting process. Once an individual, usually from among the cardinals, receives at least two-thirds plus one vote, they are appointed as the new Pope. When this happens white smoke rises from the Vatican, whereas black smoke rises when the voting fails to produce a new Pope.

See Catechism 100, 881 to 883, 890, 891, 937, 2034, and glossary.

LATTER-DAY SAINT DOCTRINE

The leader of The Church of Jesus Christ of Latter-day Saints is the Prophet and President who, with the First Presidency and Quorum of the Twelve Apostles, leads Christ's church on the earth with Jesus Christ at the head.

A prophet is a man called by God to be his representative on earth. When a prophet speaks for God, it is as if God were speaking. A prophet is also a special witness for Christ, testifying of His divinity and teaching His gospel. A prophet teaches truth and interprets the word of God. He calls the unrighteous to repentance. He receives revelations and directions from the Lord for our benefit. He may see into the future and foretell coming events so that the world may be warned.[1]

Only the prophet of the Church, who is the presiding high priest (D&C 107:65–67), can receive revelations for the Church, provide binding interpretations of scripture, or change the existing doctrines of the Church. The prophet holds the "keys to the kingdom" with the power to loose or bind in all temporal and spiritual matters of the Church (Matthew 16:19). Although other members of the First Presidency and the Quorum of the Twelve Apostles are themselves prophets, when the term

153

"prophet of the Church" is used, it means specifically the President and Prophet of the Church.

Prophets have been on the earth since the time of Adam and Eve (Amos 3:7), although often marginalized by church political leaders, persecuted, or murdered. A prophet is chosen by God and called to be a prophet through the proper priesthood authority. The profile of a prophet can vary tremendously in terms of age, level of education, work vocation, or family upbringing.

The Lord has established a pattern that the most senior member of the Quorum of the Twelve Apostles is to be the prophet of the Church. This pattern ensures there is continuity in leadership without political maneuvering or elections of any kind.

While many people on earth today revere and covenant to follow the prophets of the Old and New Testament, it is even more important that the people of the earth today follow the words of the living prophet. The prophet addresses the world during semi-annual conferences, regular firesides (topic-driven gatherings of a short duration, usually during the evening hours), weekly appearances across the world, and through frequent official Church magazine articles written by him. All of God's children, and most specifically the members of The Church of Jesus Christ of Latter-day Saints, are counseled to follow the inspired teachings of the prophet in order to avoid the snares of the world and enjoy the blessings of the gospel of Jesus Christ.

See *Gospel Principles,* 47 to 49, and 87.

THOUGHTS AND COMMENTARY

Marilyn has always had the greatest reverence for the Pope of the Catholic Church. I, like many others, also revere the Pope, but Marilyn having seen the Pope in Rome and even possessing a Papal blessing that was given to her years before, has had a special feeling about the Pontiff. In my own opinion, many of the men who have occupied the office of Pope have been among the most dedicated and humble people the world has ever known. For example, Pope John Paul II was a remarkable man, serving the world for twenty-six years as Pope, publishing sixteen major works (eleven books, two plays, and three works of poetry), and helping shape the world spiritually and politically in a direction that has benefited mankind. John Paul II inspired millions as he traveled extensively, using the ten languages he spoke fluently, and was an ecumenical example of peace and forgiveness in not only the Catholic world, but the Christian world at large. Few in history will achieve as much as he did.

Before understanding the differences between a Pope and a Prophet, we first must understand prophets in general. A fundamental question for us during our investigation was this: Did we believe in the existence of modern-day prophets, starting with Joseph Smith and proceeding to the present day? In earning her degree in Catholic theology, it was deeply ingrained into Marilyn that there were no more prophets after John the Baptist; therefore, the doctrine of modern-day prophets was particularly challenging for Marilyn.

An extensive review of the New Testament makes clear that prophets existed after the Ascension of Jesus Christ. Would the Lord have a reason to keep prophets from the earth after the Apostles passed on? Over time Marilyn and I couldn't think of a reason to deny, and in fact every reason to affirm, that prophets existed in our own time. We had no reason to suspect that the Lord would cease to provide us prophets to declare his word. Our comprehensive study of the Book of Mormon, an examination of the revelations given through the Prophet Joseph Smith, and our own personal prayers helped us achieve a sound testimony of modern-day prophets.

What stood out to me was the fact that the prophet of the Church is considered the "literal representative" for God on earth, given the power of revelation for the entire Church, and has the authority to speak for God on earth. In our studies of the papacy, we came to the conclusion that the Pope has similar ecclesiastical authority as the prophet, but on a more limited basis, especially in the area of revelation, where the Catholic Church does not believe in any further revelation (Catechism 73). Marilyn and I passionately believe the Lord has and will provide his children all of the direction and inspiration they require to return back to him, including a prophet on the earth who administers unfettered in that calling.

The final test for us was to see and hear the prophet speak. Since our baptism into The Church of Jesus Christ of Latter-day Saints, we have witnessed numerous talks given by the living prophets of our time, including Ezra Taft Benson, Howard W. Hunter, Gordon B. Hinckley, and Thomas S. Monson, along with talks given by past prophets of the Church. In each case we have felt the power and presence of the Holy Ghost, while receiving guidance and counsel that has helped us in our spiritual journey and in caring for our family. In comparison with what we have felt in the past in listening to the public talks made by Pope John Paul II, which are limited in availability, there was really no comparison. It was the Holy Ghost that revealed to us that although the Pope is a great and holy man, it is the prophet of The Church of Jesus Christ of Latter-day Saints that speaks for God to lead his children on earth. Of this we have absolutely no doubt in our minds. Our family has developed endearing testimonies of the prophet and has benefited spiritually and temporally as a result of those testimonies.

NOTE

1. *Gospel Principles,* 47.

12

Mary

As Christians we all grow up hearing the story of the Nativity at Christmastime and the role of Mary in the birth of Jesus. Although the stories of Mary's trials and joys are simple, much doctrine has been generated about her. This doctrine is worth exploring and understanding. There is no spiritual figure, other than Jesus himself, who is more revered among Catholics than Mary.

This chapter will examine the doctrine that has made Mary such a central figure in the Catholic Church, and how this doctrine compares to that of The Church of Jesus Christ of Latter-day Saints.

CATHOLIC DOCTRINE

Mary occupies a unique and honored position as the mother of Jesus. She is the "Mother of God," because Jesus Christ is the "Son of God made man, who is God himself" (Catechism 509).

From the moment of her conception, Mary was kept free from original sin in what is known as the Immaculate Conception. She remained free from personal sin throughout her mortal life—earning her the right to be referred to as "Full of Grace."

When the angel Gabriel told her of her mission, Mary, through her faith and obedience, cooperated, becoming the new Eve—mother of the living.

Saint Augustine wrote that Mary "remained a virgin in conceiving her Son, a virgin in giving birth to him, a virgin in carrying him, a virgin in nursing him at her breast, always a virgin."[1] Mary is referred to and honored as "ever-virgin" and the "Seat of Wisdom."

Upon her death Mary was taken up into heaven (referred to as the Assumption), where she shares the glory of Christ's Resurrection, while awaiting the Resurrection of all mankind in Christ and advocating for them in her maternal role.

The modern Catholic Church is passionately devoted to Mary and shows her great veneration, understanding that veneration is different from adoration and worship, which are reserved only for God. A common misconception is that the Catholics pray to Mary. This is not true from a doctrinal perspective, but can easily be misconstrued from the passion many Catholics have for Mary: "Because of Mary's singular cooperation with the action of the Holy Spirit, the Church loves to pray in communion with the Virgin Mary, to magnify with her the great things the Lord has done for her, and to entrust supplications and praises to her" (Catechism 2682).

The Catholic Church honors and recognizes Mary in a variety of ways throughout the year, showing regular devotion to her through liturgical feasts, the saying of the rosary, and the "Marian" celebrations.

See Catechism 508–511, 721, 971–975, 2682, and glossary.

LATTER-DAY SAINT DOCTRINE

The earliest scriptural reference to Mary can be found in Genesis, where the Lord speaks to the serpent in the Garden of Eden: "And I will put enmity between thee and the woman, and between thy seed and her seed; it shall bruise thy head, and thou shalt bruise his heel" (Genesis 3:15).

The woman referred in this scripture is Mary, her seed being Jesus Christ who would come to bruise the head of the serpent. Many centuries later, seven hundred years before the birth of Christ, Isaiah made reference to Mary saying: "Behold, a virgin shall conceive, and bear a son, and shall call his name Immanuel" (Isaiah 7:14).

Little is known about Mary's life before she spoke to the Angel Gabriel about the coming forth of Christ through her. The scriptures teach us that Mary was faithful in obeying the word of God, grateful for the blessings of the Lord, and wise in receiving counsel from God's chosen servants.

Mary being mortal, conceived Jesus Christ as a virgin, with the angel telling her beforehand, "The Holy Ghost shall come upon thee, and the power of the Highest shall overshadow thee: therefore also that holy thing which shall be born of thee shall be called the Son of God" (Luke 1:35).

Through this act God became the literal father of Jesus Christ. Jesus is the only individual on earth to be born of a mortal mother and an immortal father, making him "the only begotten son of God."

The Church of Jesus Christ of Latter-day Saints accepts that Mary gave birth to Jesus Christ as a virgin. However, the Church does not accept the doctrine of the Immaculate Conception, nor is it believed that Mary was "ever-virgin" or taken up into heaven to share in the glory of Christ's Resurrection.

THOUGHTS AND COMMENTARY

Attending Catholic preparatory school and Mass every Sunday, Marilyn and I were constantly being made aware of the importance of Mary, even saying the Hail Mary prayer on nearly a daily basis (I can still recite the prayer by heart). In her childhood, May was Marilyn's favorite time of year during which the church sang songs of Mary and crowned her with a crown of flowers.

However, we never took such veneration to an extreme so as to worship Mary. We knew of Catholics who went on pilgrimages to Medjugorje and were regularly captivated by appearances of Mary on buildings, objects, and so forth. Although the Catholic Church does not promote the worship of Mary, some Catholics still cross the line from veneration to worship without even realizing it.

When one ponders the remarkable Catholic doctrine regarding Mary and the reverence the church has for her, it is easy to understand how some Catholics get quite carried away with the subject of Mary and her purported place in the spirituality of the faithful. Conversely we were somewhat surprised at the lack of emphasis given Mary by The Church of Jesus Christ of Latter-day Saints. No doubt the key doctrines regarding the virgin birth of Jesus Christ and Mary's "blessed state" among women and in the eyes of God are clear components of Latter-day Saint doctrine. Still, as Catholics investigating the Mormon Church, we were simply accustomed to more doctrine and emphasis on Mary.

As we did on so many occasions during our investigation, Marilyn and I had to step back and study the three key differences that we felt were important: the Immaculate Conception, Mary's ever-virgin state, and the Assumption.

The Bible does not offer much detail on the life of Mary before or after the birth of Jesus Christ. Catholic doctrines about Mary came about long after the Ascension of Christ and not as a result of divine revelation (as the Catholic Church does not accept revelation after the Ascension of Christ); but rather through councils, debates, and spiritual pondering by Church leaders and theologians.

Immaculate Conception

The doctrine of the Immaculate Conception was defined by Pope Pius IX in what came to be known as the Ineffabilis Deus, published on December 8, 1854. Pope Sixtus IV from 1483 left Catholics free to make up their own minds as to whether Mary was subject to original sin—this freedom was verified at the Council of Trent. The doctrine argues that since Jesus became personified of the Virgin Mary, it was a requirement that Mary be totally free from sin to bear Christ.

Mary Ever-Virgin

From AD 107, under Ignatius of Antioch, to about AD 1555 at the Council of Trent, there was constant and spirited debate on the subject of Mary's perpetual virginity. It was at the Council of Trent on August 7, 1555, that the newly elected Pope Paul IV issued an Ecclesiastical Constitution called "Cum Quorundam," laying the foundation for the doctrine that Mary was a virgin before, during, and after the birth of Jesus Christ.

Mary's Assumption

The story of Mary's assumption dates back centuries, but did not become Catholic Church doctrine until Pope Pius XII in November of 1950 "dogmatically and infallibly defined" it in his Apostolic Constitution "Munificentissimus Deus." This led to the annual celebration of the Feast of the Assumption of Mary.

All three of these doctrines—the Immaculate Conception, Mary ever-virgin, and the Assumption, did not originate from the word of God, but rather through councils and papal proclamations. If the Catholic Church believed in further revelation such declarations may be more easily accepted. However, Catechism 73 clearly states that there will be no further revelation after Christ, and therefore these three points of doctrine concerning Mary have no divine origin and are therefore spiritually suspect.

I was more inclined to turn to the scriptures, and to discern through the Holy Ghost the truth of these matters. I could find scant biblical support for these three doctrines on Mary. In fact, there are *no less than six* scriptural references to Mary having other children. These are not scriptures that merely use the term "brother" in a general sense, but are more literal. For example Paul writes the following in his letter to the Galatians: "Then after three years I went up to Jerusalem to see Peter, and abode with him fifteen days. But other of the apostles saw I none, save James the Lord's brother" (Galatians 1:18–19).

Since all of the Apostles were men, and could be considered the Lord's brothers, why would James be singled out as "the Lord's brother"? Matthew 13:55 and Mark 6:3 further support that James was a brother of Jesus and that Jesus had brothers and sisters.

To explain away this biblical reference, some Catholic theologians argue that Joseph had a marriage prior to his with Mary and had children from that marriage. There is no historical evidence for this claim. In fact, Pope Boniface VIII was said to have denied the virginity of Mary following the birth of Christ.

Then there is the scripture from Matthew which states: "Then Joseph being raised from sleep did as the angel of the Lord had bidden him, and took unto him his wife: And knew her not till she had brought forth her firstborn son: and he called his name Jesus" (Matthew 1:24–25).

The term *knew* is generally associated in the scriptures with sexual intercourse for the purposes of procreation. For instance, in Genesis 4 we read that "Adam knew Eve his wife; and she conceived, and that Cain knew his wife; and she conceived" (Genesis 4:1, 17). Joseph didn't *know* Mary until after Jesus was born, thus the doctrine of the virgin birth of Jesus stands, but Mary being ever-virgin does not.

The value and importance the Catholic Church places on celibacy is well-known, and we believe that the doctrine of Mary being ever-virgin was an extension of that emphasis. The doctrines of the Immaculate Conception, Mary being ever-virgin, and the Assumption, are not central to Mary's character and the role she fulfilled as the Mother of Jesus Christ, therefore they are not critical to the canon. We feel no less about Mary as a result of embracing the Latter-day Saint doctrine, and in fact feel more aligned with the Bible in exploring the alternatives to the Catholic doctrines.

Latter-day Saints hold Mary in high esteem and recognize that she holds a "blessed state in the eyes of God." Mary is revered, venerated, and said to be a "pattern of righteousness for all Saints to follow." Latter-day

Saints place an appropriate emphasis on Mary and her profound contributions to all of Christianity, without adhering to proclamations that attribute to her characteristics that neither enhance nor diminish her spiritual role.

See Robert J. Matthews, "Mary and Joseph," *Ensign*, Dec. 1974, 13; *Mormon Doctrine*, 375; *Gospel Principle*, 63; Ezra Taft Benson, "Jesus Christ: Our Savior, Our God," *Ensign*, Apr. 1991, 2; and Susan Easton Black, "Mary, His Mother," *Liahona*, Dec. 1991, 7.

NOTE

1. St. Augustine, Serm. 186, 1: PL 38, 999.

13

The Seven Sacraments

THE Catholic Church has a time-honored doctrine surrounding seven ordinances that are commonly referred to as the Seven Sacraments. The Seven Sacraments permeate nearly every aspect of a Catholic's life and provide all that is required for complete spiritual fulfillment. Regarding these Seven Sacraments the Catechism says: "The seven sacraments touch all the stages and all the important moments of Christian life: they give birth and increase, healing and mission to the Christian's life of faith. There is thus a certain resemblance between the stages of natural life and the stages of the spiritual life" (Catechism 1210).

Although similar sacraments exist in The Church of Jesus Christ of Latter-day Saints, they are not referred to in the same way, nor do they have the same meaning. This chapter will explore the doctrine of all seven sacraments of the Catholic Church —Baptism, Reconciliation, Eucharist, Confirmation, Marriage, Holy Orders, and Last Rites—and compare and contrast them with similar ordinances of The Church of Jesus Christ of Latter-day Saints.

Baptism

Baptism is a traditional ordinance and ceremony in many Christian religions with various symbols and meanings associated with it. It is performed in rivers for some churches and over small in-church fonts at others. Some churches will baptize small children and others will only baptize adults. The doctrine of baptism is starkly different between Catholicism and The Church of Jesus Christ of Latter-day Saints, prompting a number of questions around the origins and meanings of baptism.

CATHOLIC DOCTRINE

In Catholicism, the process of Christian initiation involves three of the seven sacraments together: Baptism as a beginning, Confirmation as a strengthening, and the Eucharist as nourishment. Baptism can be symbolized as being born into a new life in Jesus Christ, marking the soul with a permanent spiritual sign which consecrates the baptized individual for Christian worship. One who is baptized is adopted into the family of God as a son or daughter, made a member of the body of Christ, and shares in Christ's priesthood. It is by baptism that an individual is made a temple of the Holy Spirit.

Baptism also has a more pragmatic purpose in forgiving the baptized person of original sin and of all personal sins up to that point in time. It is through reconciliation that all other sins after baptism will be forgiven. The sacrament of Baptism is necessary for salvation, although there are provisions for salvation for "those who die for the faith, those who are catechumens, and all those who, without knowing of the Church but acting under the inspiration of grace, seek God sincerely and strive to fulfill his will" (Catechism 1281).

Jesus Christ commissioned his Church to "go therefore and make disciples of all nations, baptizing them in the name of the Father and of the Son and of the Holy Spirit, teaching them to observe all that I have commanded you" (Matthew 28:19–20). The sacrament of baptism is performed by pouring water onto the head of the candidate or by immersing the candidate into water and calling upon the Father, the Son, and the Holy Spirit—the Most Holy Trinity. Bishops, priests, or deacons can perform the sacrament of baptism. In cases where a certain necessity arises, the Catholic Church allows for anyone to baptize another person provided water is poured upon the head of the individual and the words "I baptize you in the name of the Father, and of the Son, and of the Holy Spirit" are said.

Because of the permanent spiritual imprint that is left on the soul of a person when they are baptized, baptism can be performed only once in a lifetime for a given individual.

There are no age prerequisites for baptism, meaning infants can be baptized as well as seniors. The Catechism offers the following doctrine with respect to the baptism of children: "Since the earliest times, baptism has been administered to children, for it is a grace and a gift of God that does not presuppose any human merit; children are baptized in the faith of the Church. Entry into Christian life gives access to true freedom" (Catechism 1282).

Should a child die without having received the sacrament of baptism, the Catholic Church encourages the membership to pray for the child's salvation and put their trust in God's mercy.

See Catechism 1275–1284.

LATTER-DAY SAINT DOCTRINE

The fourth article of faith of The Church of Jesus Christ of Latter-day Saints states: "We believe that the first principles and ordinances of the Gospel are: first, Faith in the Lord Jesus Christ; second, Repentance; third, Baptism by immersion for the remission of sins; fourth, laying on of hands for the gift of the Holy Ghost."

This article provides a glimpse into the serial process by which an individual can be baptized and receive the Holy Ghost. When we exercise faith in Jesus Christ, repent of our sins, and are baptized, we are forgiven of our sins through the Atonement of Christ (see Chapter 8 on atonement) and can receive the Holy Ghost. This process is reminiscent of what Ananias told Paul following Paul's dramatic conversion: "Arise, and be baptized, and wash away thy sins" (Acts 22:16).

Before his Ascension Jesus told his Apostles to teach and baptize all nations (Matthew 29:19–20). Because baptism is a requirement for membership in the Church of Jesus Christ, this commission is as strong and applicable today as it was the day the Lord commanded it.

Baptism is a gateway through which blessings may flow when an individual exercises his or her agency (free will) to be baptized. It is after baptism that we are able to receive the gift of the Holy Ghost (Moses 6:52).

Baptism shows obedience and a willingness to follow Christ. When Jesus Christ was baptized he did so "to fulfill all righteousness" (Matthew 3:15). Jesus was baptized not because he was in need of forgiveness from his sins, but because he wanted to set the example for everyone to follow. The narrow path that Jesus wants us to follow leads to eternal life. The celestial kingdom is made possible through the ordinance of baptism.

Jesus told Nicodemus "Verily, verily, I say unto thee, Except a man be born of water and of the spirit, he cannot enter into the kingdom of God" (John 3:5). Jesus reinforced this doctrine while visiting the people of the

Americas after his Resurrection (and before his Ascension), but in a more blunt and urgent tone: "Whoso believeth in me, and is baptized . . . shall inherit the kingdom of God. And whoso believeth not in me, and is not baptized, shall be damned" (3 Nephi 11:33–34).

One of the most important aspects of baptism is the covenants we make with the Lord. Covenants are two-way promises, meaning that we promise to do certain things, and in return the Lord promises to do certain things. The covenants we make at baptism are the following:

> When we are baptized we make covenants with the Lord to: come into the fold of God; bear one another's burdens; stand as witnesses of God at all times and in all places; and serve God and keep his commandments. . . . When we are baptized and keep the covenants of baptism, the Lord promises to: forgive our sins; pour out his Spirit more abundantly upon us; give us daily guidance and the help of the Holy Ghost; let us come forth in the First Resurrection; and give us eternal life.[1]

We renew these covenants each Sunday when we partake of the Sacrament (bread and water). These covenants are mentioned in the sacrament prayer. This is discussed more fully in an upcoming section on the Eucharist and the sacrament.

Baptism is available to everyone who is at least eight years old, has a desire to be baptized, and has shown the ability to be responsible for their actions. Through modern-day revelation the Lord has revealed that the age of accountability is reached in eight years, and those who are at least eight years old are qualified to enter into the waters of baptism. Children younger than eight years old cannot be baptized.

Should a child die before the age of accountability, he or she is brought up into the celestial kingdom. Joseph Smith in a vision recorded the following: "And I also beheld that all children who die before they arrive at the year of accountability are saved in the celestial kingdom of heaven" (D&C 137:10).

Baptism can only be performed under the authority and direction of a bishop, and by those who hold the office of priest in the Aaronic Priesthood or those holding the Melchizedek Priesthood. Having two priesthood witnesses present, baptisms are performed by completely immersing the candidate into the water (all parts of the body including hair), and then bringing them out of the water. This process of immersion is to symbolize both death (being buried in the water), and life (coming out of the water in the likeness of the Resurrection)—see Romans 6:3–5 and D&C 20:73–74.

See *Gospel Principles,* 129 and 131–34.

Thoughts and Commentary

We were in the midst of our investigation of The Church of Jesus Christ of Latter-day Saints when we had our son Jason baptized into the Catholic Church. Marilyn and I went through the Catholic baptismal preparation classes and found ourselves questioning the doctrine and principles being taught to us during the classes. The comprehensive Catholic doctrine on baptism (extensively abbreviated for the purposes of this book) can be confusing. Our questions to the parish priest who directed the classes centered around three key areas:

1. Original Sin

We weren't comfortable with the concept of original sin. The second article of faith of The Church of Jesus Christ of Latter-day Saints states: "We believe that men will be punished for their own sins, and not for Adam's transgression." We both found it interesting that our parish priest explained that the baptism was more of a "welcome into the community" as opposed to the remission of original sin. Reviewing the Catholic doctrine in detail, I have come to believe that he had softened the doctrine beyond recognition. Catholic baptism is for remission of the sin of Adam and Eve, in other words, Original Sin (Catechism 1279).

We could not accept that a loving and just Father in Heaven would punish any of his children for the sin of another human being. The fall of Adam created consequences for us all, but not a sin for which we must be forgiven through baptism.

2. Age of Accountability and Repentance

The Bible is very clear that we are to repent and be baptized for the remission of sins. Consider the words of Peter: "Repent, and be baptized every one of you in the name of Jesus Christ for the remission of sins, and ye shall receive the gift of the Holy Ghost" (Acts 2:38).

The fourth article of faith is spiritually logical: the process begins with faith; faith leads to repentance, and baptism follows. Even Catholic doctrine suggests faith as a prerequisite for baptism.

Our son Jason at less than a year old was an infant and completely unable to comprehend faith in Christ or repentance. Furthermore, Catholic doctrine calls for any sin after baptism to be forgiven through the sacrament of reconciliation (or penance). Not only can an infant or young child not repent before baptism, but it is many years after baptism into the Catholic faith that they are able to participate in the sacrament of reconciliation, or even comprehend such an act. Would God really allow a child to live in sin for several years between baptism and reconciliation?

The age of accountability being eight as outlined in the Latter-day Saint doctrine is sound and aligns with biblical principles. We found it to be more consistent with the mercy and justice of a loving Heavenly Father; thus, we gained a testimony that infant baptism in Catholicism was a wonderful occasion for families and spiritually uplifting. However, it is inconsistent with the doctrine of Jesus Christ and is therefore unable to have the desired effect upon the soul of the baptized.

3. Method of Baptism

During our investigation of the Church, we were part of a fairly progressive Catholic community. The baptismal font was located in the front of the church (literally a little in-ground pool of sorts). We were told our son Jason was to be baptized in the font in the arms of a deacon, who would dip him in the water as prescribed in the Catholic doctrine. We clearly understood that our son could not be fully submersed under the water without risk to his health—he being an infant.

In reviewing the biblical accounts of baptism by immersion, we were further convinced not only that immersion was the right way physically and spiritually, but also that this method would require the individual to be much older, thus further validating the age of accountability requirement among Latter-day Saints.

Beyond these three points above, Marilyn and I discussed the Latter-day Saint doctrine of baptism and found the concept of there being a "baptismal covenant" between the Lord and the individual to be magnificent. To consider baptism as a promise by the Lord to provide blessings, predicated upon our own righteousness, was the real essence of the gospel of Jesus Christ. And then to learn that this baptismal covenant that each of us makes is renewed each Sunday during our partaking of the sacrament made us even more confident and joyous of the doctrine.

Another more subtle, yet significantly important aspect of baptism is that it be performed by those holding the authority of the priesthood.

Marilyn, and to a lesser degree me, at first struggled with the fact that we were baptized as Catholics and didn't feel we needed to be baptized again. The true doctrine of baptism discussed here helped us understand the way baptism was meant to be administered. Once we grasped the importance of the authority of the priesthood, we gained a stronger understanding of why we needed to be baptized again by the proper authority.

To see all three of our children prepare themselves for baptism by accepting through their own free will the challenge to repent and make a covenant with the Lord was marvelous. It gave Marilyn and me great joy to witness this. For me to be able to hold the priesthood and baptize my own children was an added delight and memory that I will treasure for all eternity. Having now studied and lived the doctrines of baptism, we have an unwavering testimony of the truthfulness of the Latter-day Saint doctrine on baptism.

Penance, Reconciliation, and Repentance

The primary mission of the earthly ministry of Jesus Christ was to sacrifice himself in order to make reconciliation with God possible. The modern-day Christian process of forgiveness focuses entirely on the Atonement of Christ; however, when examining the method by which repentance is administered there are meaningful differences between the churches illuminating formality and comprehensiveness.

CATHOLIC DOCTRINE

Sins committed after baptism are forgiven through the sacrament of penance, also known as confession or reconciliation. Jesus Christ gave to his apostles the authority to forgive sins: "Whose soever sins ye remit, they are remitted unto them; and whose soever sins ye retain, they are retained" (John 20:23). This same authority is in place today through apostolic succession.

Sin in any form has the stunning effect of impairing God's love, damaging human dignity as a child of God, and injuring the well-being of the Church. The consequences of sin are felt by the faithful individual, the Church on the whole, and individual sinners.

Sins can be measured in terms of their effects, the degree in which they wound the individual soul and the entire Church. There are two major categories of sin: Mortal Sin and Capital Sin, with venial sin being a subcategory of Mortal Sin: "Mortal sin destroys charity in the heart of man by a grave violation of God's law; it turns man away from God, who is his ultimate end and his beatitude, by preferring an inferior good to him" (Catechism 1855).

Mortal sins are not committed accidentally and are done with full knowledge and consent of the sinner. Mortal sins are described as "grave matters" and may include those sins mentioned by Paul in his letter to the Galatians, including adultery, fornication, uncleanness, lasciviousness, idolatry, witchcraft, hatred, variance, emulations, wrath, strife, seditions, heresies, envyings, murders, drunkenness, and revellings (Galatians 5:19–21). When a mortal sin is committed without the consent or knowledge of the sinner it is a venial sin. "Venial sin allows charity to subsist, even though it offends and wounds it" (Catechism 1855).

Capital Sins are those "which engender other sins and vices. They are traditionally numbered as seven: pride, covetousness, envy, anger, gluttony, lust, and sloth" (Catechism glossary). These sins are commonly referred to as the seven deadly sins, those from which all of the sins of commission and omission flow.

We lose our communion with God through sin, but can regain our communion through reconciliation—but only if we ask for it for ourselves and for others. In finding forgiveness one must first achieve conversion and repentance through sorrow for the sins committed with a firm resolve to not commit such sins in the future. This process of conversion encompasses the past and future, being strengthened by the hope that God's mercy will heal the wounds of sin.

The actual sacrament of penance includes three distinct actions of the individual seeking absolution, along with the priest granting absolution to the individual. The three actions of the individual include "repentance, confession or disclosure of sins to the priest, and the intention to make reparation and do works of reparation" (Catechism 1491).

Repentance, which is also known as contrition, is ideally motivated by one's faith and love for God, making it a perfect contrition; otherwise, it will be imperfect contrition as it comes from other less perfect motivations.

Confession involves the admitting the sin and taking responsibility for it, thus freeing oneself from spiritual decline, opening up to God, and bringing hope to the future. Confession is often done in a confessional booth within a church (this is the most common), but can also be done face-to-face with the priest.

Upon hearing a confession, the priest will prescribe specific actions that are to be performed by the confessing individual in order to heal the damage caused by sin and to enter into habits that are consistent with being a disciple of Christ. This is often a set of particular prayers and other such actions. The prescription of such actions and the authority to forgive sins is given only to priests, who have received such authority from the Catholic Church.

The final step of reparation involves making public or private amends for the wrong committed. This may involve such acts as the returning of stolen goods, or repairing the damage of gossip by communicating to others and the offended.

The sacrament of penance is first administered just before an individual's first communion. The youngest age at which an individual can participate in penance was outlined in a letter sent to the world's bishops by the Vatican Congregations for the Sacraments and Divine Worship and for the Clergy, March 31, 1977, reinforcing the 1910 decree of Pope Pius X, "Quam Singulari": "The age of discretion both for confession and for communion is the age in which the child begins to reason, i.e. around the seventh year, either before or after. From that time begins the obligation of satisfying both the precept of confession and of communion."

Catholics are "bound by an obligation faithfully to confess serious sins at least once a year" (Catechism 1457). Catholics are encouraged to regularly participate in penance, even for venial sins (everyday faults), in order to resist evil, develop a healthy conscious, and take full advantage of the healing powers of Christ. Frequency of one's participation in penance is linked to how merciful one can become—emulating the mercy of the Father. Catholics are urged to abstain from communion if they have committed a mortal sin and have not received absolution through the sacrament of penance.

Another form of penance is the process of indulgences, whereby an individual can obtain a diminution of temporal punishment as a consequence of sin—for themselves, as well as for the souls in Purgatory. Only the Pope can grant indulgences to the faithful of the Catholic Church.

Penance is critical in the spiritual life of every Catholic, as without it the penitent cannot be reconciled to God, cannot be reconciled to the Church, and will be subject to eternal and temporal punishment as a result of sin. Through penance, Catholics can achieve peace of mind and conscious, spiritual comfort, and the enabling spiritual power they need to cope with life's challenges with the adversary.

See Catechism 1455–1458, 1485–1498, 1854, 1855, and glossary.

LATTER-DAY SAINT DOCTRINE

During our time on earth, where we are expected to progress and grow in mortality, we are likely to sin. Sin comes about because of our weaknesses, our disobedience, and sometimes through ignorance. John describes sin as "all unrighteousness" (1 John 5:17). Sin hampers our spiritual progress. Knowing this, God set a path by which we could be forgiven of our sins—this path is repentance, made possible through the Atonement of Jesus Christ.

Before the time of Christ, the Jews were instructed to sacrifice specific animals in a specific way in order to receive absolution from specific sins. In the ultimate act of love, Jesus Christ was sacrificed by God the Father in payment for the sins of all mankind. This great Atonement for all sin brings forgiveness to the children of God, through repentance, and allows the repentant to get back on a spiritual track.

The process of repentance has been in place since the first man and woman were on the earth. Adam was instructed by the Lord on the subject of repentance: "Wherefore teach it unto your children, that all men, everywhere, must repent, or they can in nowise inherit the kingdom of God, for no unclean thing can dwell there, or dwell in his presence" (Moses 6:57).

True repentance puts a person into a state of humility and Godly sorrow, requiring the repentant to possess particular spiritual strength to adequately carry out the full process. The prelude to and process of repentance may be accompanied by tears, fervent prayers, and a feeling of sorrow. Elder Spencer W. Kimball said: "There is no royal road to repentance, no privileged path to forgiveness. Every man must follow the same course whether he be rich or poor, educated or untrained, tall or short, prince or pauper, king or commoner. . . . There is only one way. It is a long road spiked with thorns and briars and pitfalls and problems."[2]

The process of repentance involves seven key steps.

1. We must recognize the sin that was committed.
2. We must feel sorrow for having committed the sin, recognizing the transgression against the Lord and the pain that accompanies such a transgression.

3. We must forsake that sin and commit in our hearts to refrain from engaging in that sin again.

4. We must confess our sin to the Lord, and if the sin is serious, we also confess it to the proper priesthood authority (typically starting with the bishop) . If the sin has affected another person, confession must be made to that person as well. For less serious sins, private acknowledgement to the Lord is the most appropriate path of confession.

5. We must make restitution as appropriate and necessary. This means doing all we can to right that which was wrong as a consequence of the sin. For instance, stolen goods should be returned to the victim and gossip should be rectified with all of the individuals involved.

6. We must forgive others so that the Lord will forgive us. The process of our forgiving others allows us to be cleansed of the negative feelings and characteristics that can be harbored when we fail to forgive others.

7. We must pledge and do all we can to keep the commandments of God.

Through these seven steps of repentance, we can fully enjoy the forgiving and enabling aspects of the Atonement of Jesus Christ. We can enjoy the freedom that comes from being clean from sin and feel joy in our lives.

Church members are encouraged to make repentance a regular part of their daily lives—morning and night. In our personal prayers and thoughts we are able to recall our actions and identify those specific actions that are out of harmony with the gospel of Jesus Christ. There will be sins of commission (things we did that we should not have done) and sins of omission (things we should have done but did not). By identifying these types of sins in our lives, and repenting of those sins, we can bring to our souls the sweet solace of forgiveness and joy that only the Atonement of Christ can bring.

See *Gospel Principles*, 122—27.

THOUGHTS AND COMMENTARY

Marilyn and I both recall going regularly to confession during our Catholic grammar school days. We would stand in line with the other children and wait our turn to enter into the darkened closet to confess to the priest whatever sins we may have committed since our last confession. After doing so we would return to the pews and typically say a number of Hail Marys or Our Fathers as assigned by the priest. The level of anxiety before and during confession was directly related to the sin that needed to be confessed. I often wondered how many details to share and if the priest really cared about such details.

This regular ritual of confession became less of a habit as we became older—not because we sinned less, but because to us confession to a priest for minor infractions seemed too formal and staged, while the counsel offered and prayers required for forgiveness seemed trivial. We believed in the power of forgiveness through Christ, but we simply had issues with the method being prescribed by the Catholic Church.

We noticed first in our examination of the Latter-day Saint doctrine of repentance that it was taken very seriously—perhaps more seriously than any other Church doctrine. To this day, it is a source of focus from the Prophet of the Church to local leaders. In our experiences The Church of Jesus Christ of Latter-day Saints puts far more emphasis on the process of repentance than the Catholic Church.

A large part of this emphasis is the aforementioned seven steps, which are frequently discussed in sacrament meetings, Sunday School, priesthood, and Relief Society lessons. While the Catholic doctrine includes three of the seven steps, Marilyn and I came to realize that the other four steps omitted by the Catholic Church were critical in the process of full repentance. Such attention to detail in principle and practice gives deeper meaning to the repentance process, while also providing additional guidance on how to become clean before the Lord through the Atonement of Christ.

The next thing we noticed was the absence of the need to confess minor sins to clergy. We were very comfortable with the principle of allowing each individual to exercise agency in deciding what is serious and what is not, and allowing us to fully utilize the companionship of the Holy Ghost given to all baptized members of the Church. Such a practice personalizes the repentance process and encourages prayer and communion with our Heavenly Father in the pursuit of forgiveness. At the same time, the Church provides clear guidance as to what constitutes a serious sin, when confession to an ecclesiastical leader may be necessary.

The last and most important thing that Marilyn and I noticed in the

Latter-day Saint doctrine on repentance is the relentless focus on Jesus Christ and his Atonement as the key to forgiveness. When one examines the Catholic doctrine, there is a stark absence of Atonement-related content and discussion. Forgiveness is all about the Atonement of Christ, and therefore, anything less than a relentless focus on the Atonement with respect to repentance reflects a misunderstanding of the source from which forgiveness comes.

My family and I understand the Latter-day Saint doctrine on repentance, making its application more possible in our lives. Through this doctrine we can be released from the bondage of sin and appreciate more the Atonement of Christ.

Eucharist or the Sacrament

You will be hard pressed to find anything more sacred in Catholicism than the Eucharist, and in the Latter-day Saint religion than the sacrament. Both are the focus of Sunday worship for each religion embodying the sacrifice of Jesus Christ; however, the differences in doctrine are large and generally separated by the scriptural interpretation of the word *remembrance*.

CATHOLIC DOCTRINE

Jesus said, "I am the living bread which came down from heaven: if any man eat of this bread, he shall live for ever: and the bread that I will give is my flesh, which I will give for the life of the world. . . . Whoso eateth my flesh, and drinketh my blood, hath eternal life; and I will raise him up at the last day. . . . He that eateth my flesh, and drinketh my blood, dwelleth in me, and I in him" (John 6:51, 54, 56).

The Catholic Church takes these words of Christ very seriously, and literally, through the sacrament of the Eucharist (or communion). The Eucharist is at the core of the life of the Church, as within the Eucharist, Christ manifests and links his Church and its membership with his atoning sacrifice to his Father, freely offering the "graces of salvation on his Body which is the Church" (Catechism 1407). The Eucharist commemorates the Passover of Christ, encompassing the life, death, and Resurrection of Christ made manifest during the liturgy.

The Eucharist, which consists of wine and bread made from pure wheaten flour, is celebrated through an integrated act of worship that includes the consecration of bread and wine that transubstantiates the bread and wine into the body and blood of Christ. As a consecrated host,

"Christ himself, living and glorious, is present in a true, real, and substantial manner: his Body and his Blood, with his soul and his divinity."[3] (The Eucharistic sacrifice is offered by Christ himself, acting by way of proxy through the celebrating priest(s), while at the same time being present in the bread and wine.

Presiding at the Eucharist, often referred to as consecrating the bread and wine into the body and blood of Christ, can only be performed by ordained priests or bishops. Deacons cannot perform the act of consecration. To celebrate the Eucharist, the priest takes the bread and wine, invoking the blessing of the Holy Spirit, and proclaims the words of consecration in a similar manner to that which was done by Christ at the Last Supper: "This is my body which is given for you. . . . This cup is the new testament in my blood, which is shed for you." (Luke 22:19–20).

In addition to fulfilling the admonition of Christ as a sacrament, the Eucharist is given as a recompense for sin for both the living and the dead "and to obtain spiritual or temporal benefits from God" (Catechism 1414). The Eucharist strengthens the union with God, brings about forgiveness for venial sins, and can even preserve the receiver from more serious sin. In strengthening the individual, the unity of the Church is strengthened as the body of Christ: "Christ gives us in the Eucharist the pledge of glory with him. Participation in the Holy Sacrifice identifies us with his Heart, sustains our strength along the pilgrimage of this life, makes us long for eternal life, and unites us even now to the Church in heaven, the Blessed Virgin Mary, and all the saints" (Catechism 1419).

Catholics typically receive their first communion, along with the sacrament of penance, at around the age of seven. The Catholic Church counsels its members to be in a "state of grace," being free from mortal sins through the sacrament of penance in order to receive the Eucharist. The church recommends that the Eucharist be received at least once a year—weekly, even daily for some, is the more preferred frequency.

See Catechism 1406–1419

LATTER-DAY SAINT DOCTRINE

Catholic Church uses the term "sacrament" to mean any one of the Seven Sacraments. What the Catholic Church calls "sacraments," the Latter-day Saints call "ordinances." One of the Latter-day Saint ordinances is the sacrament, the ordinance that is similar to the Eucharist in the Catholic Church—meaning the bread and water taken during a

Church service in reverence to and remembrance of Jesus Christ.

Before his Ascension, Jesus Christ had a great desire for us to remember his atoning sacrifice and to remain true in keeping his commandments. To accomplish this, Jesus brought together his Apostles before his crucifixion to partake of the Passover supper. The Apostles did not understand that Christ would die soon in the great Atonement, and Jesus wanted to instruct them on the sacrament so they would remember him and remain faithful to their covenants.

During the supper Jesus broke bread into pieces and recited the stirring words that amazed the Apostles: "This is my body which is given for you: this do in remembrance of me" (Luke 22:19). The Joseph Smith Translation of the Bible brings even greater clarity to this scripture: "Take, eat this is in remembrance of my body which I give a ransom for you" (Joseph Smith Translation, Matthew 26:22).

After the supper Christ took a cup of wine, blessed it in a like manner, and spoke the words: "This cup is the new testament in my blood, which is shed for you" (Luke 22:20). Once again the Joseph Smith Translation offers a more distinguishable rendering of the same event: "Drink ye all of it. For this is in remembrance of my blood . . . , which is shed for as many as shall believe on my name, for the remission of their sins" (Joseph Smith Translation, Matthew 26:23–24).

By providing this astounding instruction, Christ instituted the Sacrament—bread and wine (later changed to water) that are blessed by the holy priesthood and consumed by them and all other worthy members of the Church. The bread and water of the sacrament are to help us remember the flesh and blood of Jesus Christ given up as a sacrifice in atonement for our sins.

Members of the Church are called to meet each Sunday (the Sabbath day) for worship services and to receive the sacrament. Before receiving the sacrament, it is blessed by a priest in the Aaronic Priesthood, or an individual holding the Melchizedek Priesthood. The bread of the sacrament is administered by the priesthood by breaking the bread into small pieces and then reciting on bended knee these words:

> O God, the Eternal Father, we ask thee in the name of thy Son, Jesus Christ, to bless and sanctify this bread to the souls of all those who partake of it, that they may eat in remembrance of the body of thy Son, and witness unto thee, O God, the Eternal Father, that they are

willing to take upon them the name of thy Son, and always remember him and keep his commandments which he has given them; that they may always have his Spirit to be with them. Amen. (D&C 20:77)

The water of the sacrament (previously wine) is placed in small disposable cups in elegant trays. A holder of the priesthood, typically a priest, on bended knee says these words:

> O God, the Eternal Father, we ask thee in the name of thy Son, Jesus Christ, to bless and sanctify this wine [water] to the souls of all those who drink of it, that they may do it in remembrance of the blood of thy Son, which was shed for them; that they may witness unto thee, O God, the Eternal Father, that they do always remember him, that they may have his Spirit to be with them. Amen. (D&C 20:79)

After the bread and water are blessed, they are passed reverently to the congregation by a deacon or other priesthood holder. The blessing and passing of the bread and water is done separately so as to create a time of reflection in-between receiving each.

Spiritual preparation to partake of the sacrament is important, along with ensuring we are in a state of worthiness (void of serious sin and with a repentant heart). Perfection is not required to partake of the sacrament, nor is membership in The Church of Jesus Christ of Latter-day Saints— only a desire to love and serve the Lord and to receive his blessings.

For Latter-day Saints, the sacrament includes renewal of the covenants with the Lord made at baptism. As the sacrament prayer so eloquently states (Moroni 4:3), we covenant to "take upon [us] the name of thy Son, and always remember him and keep his commandments which he has given [us]." In return we are promised that we "may always have his Spirit to be with [us]." By keeping these covenants we will have the Spirit of the Lord and be given "knowledge, faith, power, and righteousness to gain eternal life."[4]

See *Gospel Principles,* 151 and 153–55.

THOUGHTS AND COMMENTARY

To Catholics, the doctrine of the Eucharist is extremely sacred, as is the Mass in which it is fulfilled. We feel a similar sacredness when we partake of the sacrament in The Church of Jesus Christ of Latter-day Saints.

Marilyn as a Catholic felt especially strongly about the Eucharist, while I felt more of a mystery surrounding the partaking. We both had similar feelings that we were celebrating the sacrifice of Christ and participating in a holy and sacred ordinance. Neither of us were passionate about the doctrine of transubstantiation, as we didn't feel such an event was required to support the faith and belief we had in the Eucharist. We did not consider seriously whether we were partaking of the literal body and blood of Jesus Christ, but rather we focused on the act of faith in the Holy Communion itself as it related to Jesus Christ.

There is indeed scriptural support for the sacramental eating and drinking of the literal flesh and blood of Christ, although the Prophet Joseph Smith in an inspired translation of the Bible believed there was an omission of the word *remembrance*. The transubstantiation doctrine is supported by some early church fathers, such as St. Ignatius of Antioch and Justin Martyr who believed in it.

There is a great deal of interpretation that must take place on both sides. Was Christ speaking metaphorically about his flesh and blood with respect to the Eucharist? Did he mean the act to be a remembrance of his atoning sacrifice, or did he mean there was a transformation of wafers and wine into his literal body and blood?

As a Catholic, Marilyn had a number of very sacred experiences in the liturgy, mainly centered on the Eucharist. Those experiences were not tied to the transubstantiation, but rather her own faith on the Atonement of Christ and the relationship she had with the Savior. It wasn't about whether the Eucharist was the literal flesh and blood of Christ; it was about the spirituality that Marilyn strived for as a Christian. Even the pomp and circumstance of the liturgy made the Eucharist seem especially sacred. Those hallowed experiences are important and vital to Marilyn's lifelong spiritual journey and something she still cherishes.

For me, the Eucharist was something I looked forward to and revered in a powerful way. So much so that when my childhood parish began allowing lay ministers to administer communion, I always stood in whatever line the priest was distributing the Eucharist, feeling the Eucharist was far too holy to be trusted to a lay minister. Furthermore, when the practice of allowing the members to hold out their hand to accept the Eucharist came into being, I always chose to take the Eucharist in my mouth, never touching what I believed to be the holy wafer. I, like Marilyn, did not focus on the transubstantiation, but rather the sacrament itself and how I used those experiences as a means to become closer to Christ.

Our Eucharistic experiences were perfect preparation for the Latter-day Saint doctrine of the sacrament that we came to accept and love. Since our baptism we have experienced the sacrament hundreds of times over a twenty-year period in The Church of Jesus Christ of Latter-day Saints. We have come to experience and understand in a deeply spiritual way that both the Eucharist in the Catholic Church and the sacrament in The Church of Jesus Christ of Latter-day Saints are sacred weekly events where there is a remembrance of the Atonement of Jesus Christ.

However, as Latter-day Saints, we have come to understand more fully the covenants associated with partaking of the sacrament each week as opposed to what we experienced as Catholics. There are no formal covenants associated with the Eucharist, making it more of a symbolic ritual of great spiritual significance.

Each week when we partake of the bread and water in remembrance of the Atonement of Jesus Christ, we understand and renew those covenants we made at our baptism. This dynamic has made a tremendous difference and has given special meaning to the sacrament we partake of each week. Furthermore, to experience the sacred preparation, blessing, and passing of the sacrament by the young Aaronic Priesthood holders (ages twelve through eighteen) brings an additional special meaning to the weekly experience—especially seeing our sons perform these sacred duties.

Marilyn and I are extremely grateful for the Latter-day Saint doctrine of the sacrament and how it has enriched our spiritual lives, bringing us closer to Heavenly Father and Jesus Christ while deepening our understanding and appreciation of the Atonement and Resurrection of our redeemer.

Confirmation and Gifts of the Spirit

Some of the most inspiring stories of the New Testament involve the receiving of the Holy Spirit, or Holy Ghost. Each recorded instance is exciting and powerful, often resulting in miraculous events. Bestowing the Holy Spirit today is done much in the same way among Catholics and Latter-day Saints; however, the end result of what is given to the receiver is extremely different as one will see in this section.

CATHOLIC DOCTRINE

In chapter 6 we outlined in detail the role and mission of the Holy Spirit as a key member of the Holy Trinity. Not covered in chapter 6 are the details of the method in which Catholics receive the Holy Spirit. The New Testament is rich with stories and testimony of the faithful receiving the Holy Spirit: "Now when the apostles at Jerusalem heard that Samaria had received the word of God, they sent to them Peter and John, who came down and prayed for them that they might receive the Holy Spirit; for it had not yet fallen on any of them, but they had only been baptized in the name of the Lord Jesus. Then they laid their hands on them and they received the Holy Spirit" (Acts 8:14–17).

Catholics receive the Holy Spirit through the sacrament of confirmation. Like baptism, confirmation imparts a permanent spiritual imprint on the soul of the confirmed, helping them become more deeply rooted in Christ, more perfectly fortified in their bond with his Church, and endowed with the strength to testify of Christianity in both word and deed.

In the Roman Catholic Church the sacrament of Confirmation is administered when an individual has reached the age of reason (the time at which a person becomes morally responsible—about seven years old). However, starting in July 2002 the Vatican approved the U.S. bishops' decision to establish an age range for conferring Confirmation as being between the ages of seven and approximately sixteen. At that time, in a communication by Bishop Joseph A. Fiorenza of Galveston-Houston, president of the U.S. Conference of Catholic Bishops, bishops were given authority to set more specific policy in their own dioceses.

In addition to the age requirements, a candidate for Confirmation must also "profess the faith, be in the state of grace, have the intention of receiving the sacrament, and be prepared to assume the role of disciple and witness to Christ, both within the ecclesial community and in temporal affairs" (Catechism 1319).

Confirmation is performed by a bishop by anointing the forehead of the candidate with oil (sacred chrism), accompanied with the laying on of the bishop's hand with the words "Be sealed with the Gift of the Holy Spirit." Although a bishop may delegate the conferring of the sacrament of Confirmation to a priest, this is typically not done, thus allowing a priest to celebrate Baptism and a bishop to celebrate Confirmation. Despite such separation between Baptism and Confirmation, there is still a clear and distinctive connection between the two sacraments, starting with the renewal of baptismal promises. This connection is strengthened with the sacrament of the Eucharist, highlighting the harmony between these sacraments of Christian initiation.

It is also most appropriate in discussing the sacrament of Confirmation to discuss the gifts of the Holy Spirit, which are defined as: "Permanent dispositions that make us docile to follow the promptings of the Holy Spirit. The traditional list of seven gifts of the Spirit is derived from Isaiah 11:1–3: wisdom, understanding, knowledge, counsel, piety, fortitude, and fear of the Lord" (Catechism glossary).

These seven gifts of the Holy Spirit are received through sanctifying grace, when the life of God penetrates us. Such an infusion can happen when one of the Seven Sacraments is received in a state of worthiness, helping us to live a Christian life.

Proceeding from the Holy Spirit are the fruits of the Spirit that are formed within us as the "first fruits of eternal glory" (Catechism 1832). There are twelve fruits of the Spirit: "charity, joy, peace, patience, kindness, goodness, generosity, gentleness, faithfulness, modesty, self-control, chastity" (Galatians 5:22–23). These fruits of the Holy Spirit are the qualities fashioned in our lives when we employ the Gifts of the Holy Spirit and remain faithful in Christ.

See Catechism 1313–1321, 1832, and glossary.

LATTER-DAY SAINT DOCTRINE

Latter-day Saint confirmation is an ordinance by which individuals become a member of the Church and receive the gift of the Holy Ghost.

Children of record (under the age of eight years old) are shown on the rolls of the Church. However, it is only at their confirmation (eight years old an above) that they become full members of the Church, formally sustaining the covenants they made at their baptism. New converts are likewise confirmed following their baptism.

The second key aspect of confirmation is the bestowing upon the individual the gift of the Holy Ghost. While all individuals are able to experience the influence of the Holy Ghost, sometimes referred to as the "Spirit of Christ" (John 1:4–9), only those who are confirmed members of The Church of Jesus Christ of Latter-day Saints have the continual Gift of the Holy Ghost, often referred to as the constant companionship of the Holy Ghost. There is a distinct difference between the two as explained by President James E. Faust:

> The Prophet Joseph Smith taught, "There is a difference between the Holy Ghost and the gift of the Holy Ghost." Many outside the

Church have received revelation by the power of the Holy Ghost, convincing them of the truth of the gospel. Through this power sincere investigators acquire a testimony of the Book of Mormon and the principles of the gospel before baptism. However, administrations of the Holy Ghost are limited without receiving the gift of the Holy Ghost. Those who possess the gift of the Holy Ghost after baptism and confirmation can receive more light and testimony. This is because the gift of the Holy Ghost is "a permanent witness and higher endowment than the ordinary manifestation of the Holy Spirit." It is the higher endowment because the gift of the Holy Ghost can act as "a cleansing agent to purify a person and sanctify him from all sin."[5]

The gift of the Holy Ghost is given as a privilege to those individuals who have exercised faith in Jesus Christ, entered into the waters of baptism, and been confirmed as members of The Church of Jesus Christ of Latter-day Saints. With the gift of the Holy Ghost, a person can receive continual guidance and inspiration from the Holy Ghost, a member of the Godhead.

Confirmation is performed following baptism through the laying on of hands by those who are worthy in holding the Melchizedek Priesthood. The Lord by revelation through the prophet Joseph Smith said: "Whoso having faith you shall confirm in my church, by the laying on of the hands, and I will bestow the gift of the Holy Ghost upon them" (D&C 33:15).

Although the gift of the Holy Ghost is bestowed upon a person, there are no guarantees that the person will receive all of the benefits associated with constant guidance from the Holy Ghost. Each individual confirmed must "receive" the Holy Ghost. Elder Bruce R. McConkie offers the following: "The gift of the Holy Ghost is the *right* to have the constant companionship of the Spirit; the actual *enjoyment* of the gift, the *actual receipt of the companionship* of the Spirit, is based on personal righteousness; it does not come unless and until the person is worthy to receive it."[6]

Such worthiness comes through the sincere pursuit of keeping the commandments of God and keeping our thoughts and actions uncorrupted. In doing so, we can have not only the constant companionship of the Holy Ghost, but also the gifts of the spirit. These gifts, which are mentioned in several biblical passages (1 Corinthians 12:4–10; Mark 16:16–18; and Isaiah 11:1–3), give to us specific spiritual powers to be able to bless the lives of others and help lead us back to live with our

Father in Heaven. The Bible, the Book of Mormon, and the Doctrine and Covenants provide detail on these gifts.

Although certain gifts of the Spirit are defined in scripture, there are many others, "endless in number and infinite in variety."[7] Each gift is given for the benefit of the receiver and for those whom he serves, directly and indirectly. Gifts of the spirit include, but are not limited to, faith, healing (to heal and to be healed), exhortation, preaching, speaking in tongues, the interpretation of tongues, translation, wisdom, knowledge, teaching, knowing Jesus Christ is the son of God, believing the testimony of others, prophecy, and working miracles.

Latter-day Saint leaders encourage members to seek and understand the gifts with which the Lord has endowed us. We develop these gifts through prayer, fasting, and worship. Furthermore, we are urged to seek after the "best gifts" (D&C 46:8). At the same time, we are warned that Satan has the power to imitate the gifts of the spirit in an attempt to mislead us. Moses encountered such trickery among the sorcerers and magicians of the Pharaoh as they performed counterfeit miracles (Exodus 7:8–22).

See *Gospel Principles,* 137–39, 141–45, and 147–49.

THOUGHTS AND COMMENTARY

Marilyn and I were both confirmed in the Catholic Church, being anointed with oil, having hands laid upon us to be sealed with the gift of the Holy Spirit, and given a more mature status in our respective Catholic communities. These were wonderful and memorable experiences which laid a foundation for our spiritual future.

Many years later, we were both confirmed in The Church of Jesus Christ of Latter-day Saints. This took place directly after our baptism. Hands were laid upon our heads. We were confirmed as members of the Church and received the gift of the Holy Ghost as a constant companion.

One might consider both of these ceremonies and conclude they seem somewhat, if not entirely, identical. For us, however, there was a major difference in the two ceremonies. When we were confirmed as Latter-day Saints were given the gift of the Holy Ghost as a constant companion. We have come to understand there is a monumental difference between being *sealed* with the gift of the Holy Spirit (or Holy Ghost) and *receiving* the gift of the Holy Ghost (or Holy Spirit). For some it may be semantics, but for us it was a night and day difference. Where in our Catholic confirmation we had access to the Holy Ghost, in our Latter-day Saint confirmation we had the Holy Ghost as a constant companion.

Consider the events surrounding the bestowal of the Holy Spirit by the Apostles as recording in Acts 8:17: "Then laid they their hands on them, and they *received* the Holy Ghost" (emphasis added). This scripture is plain and unspectacular, although the event itself was a miracle to those who received the Holy Ghost. Nearly two decades ago, hands were placed on Marilyn and me, just like the Apostles of old, and we received the Holy Ghost—more specifically the gift of the Holy Ghost. The ceremony and doctrine behind our Latter-day Saint confirmation is another example of the Restoration.

Catholics and Latter-day Saints believe in gifts of the spirit. As a Catholic, I heard very little about these gifts in sermons, religious education, and other related events. The Catholic Church acknowledges the gifts of the spirit, but does not emphasize those gifts on a regular basis. Latter-day Saints, on the other hand, not only acknowledge these gifts, but expands the list provided in the Catechism to more align with the teachings of Paul and the experiences of the early Apostles in the New Testament. These gifts of the Spirit demonstrate the revelation of the Lord and personify the passion that Latter-day Saints have for the Spirit in all things. Marilyn and I see these gifts of the Spirit exercised on a regular basis.

The power of the Holy Ghost and the gifts of the Spirit cannot be overemphasized and are critical to the spiritual development of all Christians and the building up of the kingdom of God on earth. The Catholic Church provided us with a framework of confirmation and an introduction to the Holy Spirit. The Church of Jesus Christ of Latter-day Saints helped us build upon that framework and introduction with a complete immersion to the Holy Ghost and on-going "how–to" teachings and encouragement on using the gifts of the Spirit. How wonderful it has been to understand and be instructed on how to use one of the most powerful spiritual gifts given to us while travailing through the challenges of mortality.

Matrimony, Marriage

While the institution of marriage is respected and revered among Catholics and Latter-day Saints, the question is whether marriage lasts for life only or forever beyond the grave. Can a marriage remain in force in heaven? This section will answer this all-important question while addressing the historical practice of polygamy.

CATHOLIC DOCTRINE

Marriage is a lifelong covenant made between a man and woman for their mutual benefit and for the procreation and rearing of children. When a valid marriage takes place between two individuals who have been baptized into the Catholic faith, the marriage is considered a sacrament.

The scriptures abound with passages acknowledging that men and women were created for each other for the purposes of marriage: "It is not good that the man should be alone" (Genesis 2:18); "For this cause a man shall leave his father and his mother, and shall cleave to his wife; and they shall become one flesh" (Genesis 2:24). Paul counseled the men of the church to "love your wives, even as Christ loved the church and handed himself over for her" (Ephesians 5:25).

Those who engage in the marriage covenant must do so of their own free will and not by constraint or law (ecclesiastical or otherwise). Should there be any such constraints, or a lack of consent between the spouses, the marriage is void as they are unable to achieve the binding to "become one flesh."

Because of the seriousness of the marriage covenant, and in the spirit of creating a lasting bond between man and wife, marriage preparation is critical. While education in the family is of primary importance, the Church provides formal training and education to prospective spouses. For instance, Marilyn and I were assigned an experienced Catholic sponsor couple and participated in nearly six months of regular sessions with formal exercises, discussions, and sharing between ourselves, under the guidance of our sponsor couple, and occasionally our parish priest.

The sacrament of marriage is performed in the Catholic Church as part of a public liturgical celebration. The liturgy and marriage ceremony is performed by a priest, or Church-authorized witness, and attended by friends and family, who also are also witnesses of the ceremony. The celebrating priest receives the collective consents of the soon-to-be married couple in the name of the Church, and pronounces upon them the blessing of the Church. The sacrament of marriage is binding until the spouses are parted by death.

Once married, the couple is encouraged to share in one another's sexuality as part of "the conjugal love of man and woman . . . [where] physical intimacy of the spouses becomes a sign and pledge of spiritual communion. Marriage bonds between baptized persons are sanctified by the sacrament" (Catechism 2360). By procreating and having children, married couples are able to participate in God's fatherhood.

The Catholic Church does not prohibit the marrying of couples in the Catholic Church where one of the spouses is not Catholic. However, there is specific Canon Law governing such marriages:

> 1) the Catholic party is to declare that he or she is prepared to remove dangers of defecting from the faith and is to make a sincere promise to do all in his or her power so that all offspring are baptized and brought up in the Catholic Church; 2) the other party is to be informed at an appropriate time about the promises which the Catholic party is to make, in such a way that it is certain that he or she is truly aware of the promise and obligation of the Catholic party. (Code of Canon Law, canon 1125)

Even with the provisions of canon 1125, the Catholic Church discourages such mixed marriages, feeling there is a strong potential for strife and separation as a result of disunity in religion. Should a divorce take place between two living individuals married in the Catholic Church, they can continue to be members of the Catholic faith in leading a Christian life, but are counseled to refrain from receiving the Eucharist depending on the circumstances.

See Catechism 1605, 1625–1627, 1630, 1632, 1634, 1659, 1660, 1663–1665, 2360, 2398, and 2400.

LATTER-DAY SAINT DOCTRINE

Marriage is one of the most important ordinances that we as children of God will ever receive during our time in mortality—perhaps for all eternity. Not only does our exaltation depend on entering into the covenant of marriage, but also our happiness in earthly life and throughout the eternities. The prophet Joseph Smith taught: "In the celestial glory there are three heavens or degrees; And in order to obtain the highest, a man must enter into this order of the priesthood [meaning the new and everlasting covenant of marriage]; And if he does not, he cannot obtain it" (D&C 131:1–3).

Marriage is ordained of God (D&C 49:15) and is "the most sacred relationship that can exist between a man and woman."[8] Marriage has been a key component of the gospel since the beginning and is so sacred and important that the Lord has provided a way for marriages to last forever and not just until "death do you part."

For a marriage to be for time and all eternity, it must be performed in the holy temple by a Melchizedek priesthood holder who holds the sealing power. Just as Christ gave Peter the power to bind on earth and in heaven (Matthew 18:18), so are specific priesthood holders given this same power today (D&C 132:19).

The marriage sealing is a simple ceremony where a couple kneels at the altar of the temple, surrounded by friends and family and two specific witnesses. The man and woman covenant to one another before God. The presiding sealer, acting under the direction of the Lord, promises the couple being married wonderful blessings, including exaltation, reminding the couple that such blessings are predicated on their living righteous lives in keeping the commandments of God. When the ceremony is complete, the couple is declared to be husband and wife for time and all eternity.

Only Latter-day Saints who hold a temple recommend can be married in the temple—there are no exceptions. Civil marriage ceremonies can be conducted for Latter-day Saints who do not wish to, or who cannot, be married in the temple. As with all marriages that are not sealed in the temple, they are for life (time only) and cannot be maintained beyond temporal death. Consequently, they will have no claim on each other in the afterlife, nor will they have claim to any of their children (who can be sealed to them in the temple). See chapter 17 for more details on the temple.

An eternal marriage is the pinnacle of a Latter-day Saint's spiritual and temporal life and should be taught, discussed, and planned for from the very earliest age. President Spencer W. Kimball taught: "Marriage is perhaps the most vital of all the decisions and has the most far-reaching effects. . . . It affects not only the two people involved, but their children and . . . their children's children. . . . Of all the decisions, this one must not be wrong."[9]

See *Gospel Principles*, 241–42, and 244.

THOUGHTS AND COMMENTARY

When it comes to marriage and The Church of Jesus Christ of Latter-day Saints the first question on everyone's mind is, "What about plural marriage?" Some people are under the false impression that plural marriage in the Church still exists. Before diving into the doctrine of eternal marriage, Marilyn and I spent some time before and after our baptism understanding plural marriage.

At various times throughout biblical history, the Lord has commanded or allowed men of faith to practice plural marriage. Abraham, Isaac, Jacob, Moses, David, and Solomon were such men. When sanctioned by the Lord, plural marriage was a righteous practice; however, we can also find instances of abuse of plural marriage.

In the early years of The Church of Jesus Christ of Latter-day Saints, members of the Church endured periods of hardship. The Lord desired to quickly build his Church using righteous souls. One way of addressing both dynamics was to call specific individuals to plural marriage. Such a practice was meant to proliferate families and ensure precious souls were born to righteous families to be raised in the gospel of Jesus Christ.

The revelation relating to the new and everlasting covenant, including eternal marriage and the plurality of wives, was given in 1843 and recorded in section 132 of the Doctrine and Covenants. Historical records suggest that the doctrines and principles involved with the revelation were known to the Prophet Joseph Smith as far back as 1831. It is said that Joseph was greatly troubled by the principle of plural marriage and spent a great deal of time praying and pondering the principle in hopes of greater understanding.

After the public announcement of plural marriage in 1852, only a few righteous priesthood holders were called to practice plural marriage. Joseph Smith and other Church leaders he knew well, including Brigham Young and Heber C. Kimball, were given and challenged by this command and eventually sealed to multiple wives. Less than 5 percent of the men in the Church were allowed to enter into plural marriage.

The practice of plural marriage was highly regulated to prevent potential abuses of the doctrine. Despite the efforts, history suggests there may have been abuses of the practice, even among Church leaders. Such abuses have been highly publicized, with attempts made to judge those of the nineteenth century by the standards and practices of the twenty-first century—a dangerous and questionable practice. The Bible provides examples of spiritual giants who fell into serious sin and were still given sizeable responsibilities in the kingdom. David committed adultery with Bathsheeba and facilitated the murder of her husband Uriah, but was still allowed to author the Psalms and provide the lineage for Jesus Christ. His son Solomon became an idol worshiper, but a portion of his writings were still included as part of the Old Testament. Paul (as the Pharisee Saul) was a persecutor of Christians, likely sending many to their death, before he was converted and given the honor of authoring part of the New Testament. These cases demonstrate the pitfalls of judging past religious figures with modern-day perspectives.

In 1882 the Edmunds Act was passed in the Senate, and ratified in the House in 1887, which made it illegal for anyone practicing, or suspected of practicing polygamy to vote. This was a difficult time for the Saints. The twelfth article of faith of the Church, written in 1842, states, "We believe in being subject to kings, presidents, rulers, and magistrates, in obeying, honoring, and sustaining the law." With the passage of the aforementioned federal laws, there was a clear conflict in the laws of the land and the laws of God.

Latter-day Saints continued practicing polygamy and as a result were sorely persecuted by surrounding communities and the federal government. Men who were law abiding citizens and leaders of the Church, having entered into the covenant of plural marriage, were forced to go into hiding.

During this period, the state of Utah struggled to be admitted into the union. Admittance for Utah was important for economic and political reasons, but more important so that the Saints could finally settle to build the Lord's Church in peace and without the persecution they had experienced in all of their previous settlings. For many years they struggled, until the Church ended its support of plural marriage in 1890. At that time President Wilford Woodruff issued the manifesto ending plural marriage. In 1896 Utah was admitted into the union and given statehood.

In 1998, President Gordon B. Hinckley made the following statement about the Church's position on plural marriage: "This Church has nothing whatsoever to do with those practicing polygamy. They are not members of this Church. . . . If any of our members are found to be practicing plural marriage, they are excommunicated, the most serious penalty the Church can impose. Not only are those so involved in direct violation of the civil law, they are in violation of the law of this Church."[10]

Anyone who is critical of the Church and its practice of plural marriage need only ask themselves why such a practice would be instituted by the Lord, and why men would embrace it (albeit reluctantly). Opponents of the Church quickly jump to the conclusion that it was sex and lust that drove the institution of plural marriage. But this begs the question, why would a man, who could easily obtain extra-marital sex at almost no cost to himself, suffer the economic anguish of raising multiple families; be responsible for emotionally and physically taking care of more than one woman; and risk loss of property, fines, and long imprisonment for his trouble? This seems to be a lot of responsibility for merely satisfying a lust to have sex with multiple women.

Isaiah 4:1 suggests plural marriage may return during the Millennium. Speaking of the latter days, Isaiah says, "And in that day seven women shall take hold of one man, saying, We will eat our own bread, and wear our own apparel: only let us be called by thy name, to take away our reproach." Marilyn and I have shared with each other various thoughts on this matter, but we don't burden ourselves with pondering this possibility, for if the Lord requires something of us we know he will give us the means of providing it. In the meantime, a person can expect to be excommunicated immediately should he or she enter into plural marriage. It is simply forbidden.

After considering the history and dynamics of plural marriage, we are satisfied that it involved a spiritual struggle that is reminiscent of other biblical struggles, such as the allowance of divorce by the Lord in Deuteronomy 24:1–3, and then the rebuke of divorce by Jesus in Matthew 19:7. The Lord will do as he pleases, when he pleases. As written in the book of Isaiah (the Lord speaking): "For my thoughts are not your thoughts, neither are your ways my ways, saith the Lord. For as the heavens are higher than the earth, so are my ways higher than your ways, and my thoughts than your thoughts" (Isaiah 55:8–9).

With the subject of plural marriage resolved, we turned our attention toward the more important doctrines of marriage in the present day. When we learned about the possibility of our marriage being an eternal bond, we were overcome with joy and amazement. Joy because we truly wanted to be together forever; and amazement because we had written our own vows for our marriage in the Catholic Church and included in the verbiage that we would be together for all eternity and never part. At that time we had no detailed knowledge of the Latter-day Saint doctrine on marriage and were completely unaware of any doctrine that would bring such a blessing.

We probed a little deeper into the doctrine, being aware of the scripture from Matthew 22 where the Sadducees challenge Jesus on the subject of marriage in the Resurrection. Jesus answered, "For in the Resurrection they neither marry, nor are given in marriage, but are as the angels of God in heaven" (Matthew 22:30). This scripture could be interpreted to mean eternal marriage is not to be. However, we came to understand that there will indeed be no marrying in the Resurrection, but rather all such matters are taken care of in the holy temples of the Lord on earth before the Resurrection. Thus the importance of sealing marriages in the temple today! The opportunity to have an eternal family was the primary driving factor for our becoming baptized into The Church of Jesus Christ of Latter-day Saints.

The results of temple marriage? The average divorce rate among Catholics is 21 percent according to a 1999 Barna Research Group study. If one was to add annulments the number may be higher. The *Los Angeles Times* reported the findings of Brigham Young University professor Daniel K. Judd in April of 2000 who estimated that only 6 percent of Latter-day Saints who marry in a temple ceremony subsequently experience divorce.[11]

In November of 1987, Marilyn and I were married at Christ the Good Shepherd Catholic Church in Houston, Texas, in a civil ceremony conducted by a priest who held the authority of binding us together during our earthly life—till death do us part.

In July of 1990, Marilyn and I were married in the Dallas Texas Temple of The Church of Jesus Christ of Latter-day Saints in an ordinance conducted by a Melchizedek Priesthood holder who held the authority of binding us together for all time and all eternity—both here on earth and beyond the veil (after death).

Our marriage in the Catholic Church will always be remembered as one of the most wonderful days of our lives. We still reminisce about the joy and happiness we felt declaring our love before God, friends, and family—not to mention the fun we had during the reception. Imagine our having doubled that joy by being sealed in the holy temple knowing our union will last forever. How grateful we are to have been prepared for this blessing through our civil union in the Catholic Church.

As we ponder marriage, Marilyn and I feel our Father in Heaven would not bring us together for a life time of love, challenges, and togetherness, only to see make us part for all eternity after our death. We have a strong and vibrant testimony that the Lord intends marriages and families to live beyond the grave, and therefore has made a way for that to happen on earth through the sealing powers of the priesthood in holy temples.

Holy Orders

The sacrament of Holy Orders in the Catholic Church is defined as the following: "Holy Orders is the sacrament through which the mission entrusted by Christ to his apostles continues to be exercised in the Church until the end of time: thus, it is the sacrament of apostolic ministry. It includes three degrees: episcopate, presbyterate, and diaconate" (Catechism 1536).

Chapter 9 of this book provides a comprehensive review of the priesthood, including the key points of the doctrine of Holy Orders in the Catholic Church, along with the equivalent doctrine in The Church of Jesus Christ of Latter-day Saints.

Anointing of the Sick

The sacrament of Anointing of the Sick in the Catholic Church is defined as the following:

> One of the seven sacraments, also known as the 'sacrament of the dying,' administered by a priest to a baptized person who begins to be in danger of death because of illness or old age, through prayer and the anointing of the body with the oil of the sick. The proper effects of the sacrament include a special grace of healing and comfort to the Christian who is suffering the infirmities of serious illness or old age, and the forgiving of the person's sins. (Catechism glossary)

Chapter 9 of this book provides a comprehensive review of the priesthood, including the key points of the doctrine of anointing of the sick in the Catholic Church and in The Church of Jesus Christ of Latter-day Saints.

NOTES

1. *Gospel Principles*, 133–34.

2. Spencer W. Kimball, *The Miracle of Forgiveness* (Salt Lake City: Deseret Book, 1999), 149.

3. cf. Council of Trent: DS 1640, 1651.

4. *Gospel Principles*, 155.

5. James E. Faust, "Born Again," *Ensign,* May 2001, 54.

6. Bruce R. McConkie, *Mormon Doctrine,* 313.

7. Bruce R. McConkie, *A New Witness for the Articles of Faith* (Salt Lake City: Deseret Book, 1985), 371.

8. *Gospel Principles*, 241.

9. Spencer W. Kimball, "The Matter of Marriage," Devotional Address, Salt Lake Institute of Religion, 22 Oct. 1976.

10. Gordon B. Hinckley, "What Are People Asking about Us?" *Ensign,* Nov. 1998, 70.

11. William Lobdell, "Holy matrimony: In era of divorce, Mormon Temple weddings are built to last," *Los Angeles Times,* 8 Apr. 2000. See http://www.adherents.com. Mirrored at http://www.divorcereform.org/.

14

Life after Death

THE subject of life after death has kept theologians, philosophers, paranormal enthusiasts, and even the most casual thinkers busy for centuries. All discuss and theorize about what takes place after our heart stops beating. Is there life after death, and if so what is that life like? What is heaven and how does one gain entrance into this place, if it is a place? Is there really a hell, and what transgressions must an individual commit to be relegated to this place, if it is a place?

The theology of life after death can become extremely broad if one considers non-Christian religions. Doctrines on reincarnation would have to be understood and contemplated. The list of possibilities seems limited only by imagination.

I will limit myself to Christian concepts and doctrines, particularly those of the Catholic Church and The Church of Jesus Christ of Latter-day Saints. Still, I think you may find new food for thought no matter what your level of knowledge is today.

Particular or Partial Judgment

One of the most serious misperceptions in Christianity is that when we die in the Lord, with faith in Jesus Christ, our spirits go directly to heaven. This is not necessarily correct according to the doctrines of either the Catholic Church or The Church of Jesus Christ of Latter-day Saints. A few will pass directly to heaven (or the celestial kingdom, as it is referred to by Latter-day Saints) immediately after death, but the vast majority of us will go through a particular (or partial) judgment that begins the life-after-death process.

CATHOLIC DOCTRINE

After an individual dies in mortality, they are subject to a particular judgment, which is, "The eternal retribution received by each soul at the moment of death, in accordance with that person's faith and works" (Catechism glossary).

During one's life on earth, there is the opportunity to accept or reject Jesus Christ and the grace that his Atonement offers. Upon death that opportunity ends. Although the Bible speaks of a judgment that is focused on the final meeting with Christ after his Second Coming, numerous passages speak of an immediate reward upon death based upon an individual's faith and works (for example Luke 16:20–25 and Luke 23:43). It is clear through these scriptures and others that the resulting consequences after death can greatly differ from one individual to the next, each person receiving this particular judgment immediately upon death.

The possible outcomes of particular judgment are three: immediate entrance into heaven; entrance into purgatory to be purified before entering heaven; or entrance into hell to face damnation—each of which will be discussed in later sections of this chapter. While faith and works are most often mentioned as the basis on which we are judged, it is more fundamentally our love, encompassing both faith and works, on which we will be judged.

See Catechism 1021, 1022, 1055, and glossary.

LATTER-DAY SAINT DOCTRINE

The Book of Mormon prophet Alma taught that there is a "state of the soul between death and the resurrection" (Alma 40:11). This state is in the spirit world where all will await the resurrection in one of three different places within the spirit world. Assignment to one of these three interim states is the result of the partial judgment. "Then shall the dust return to the earth as it was: and the spirit shall return unto God who gave it" (Ecclesiastes 12:7).

See *Gospel Principles*, 295.

THOUGHTS AND COMMENTARY

Marilyn and I understood the subject of judgment conceptually during our investigation, but neither one of us had considered two judgments (partial and final), and therefore the doctrine of a partial (or particular) judgment was new to us. To understand the differences between the two churches requires little study as both churches teach very similar theology. The basic teaching is that immediately upon death, everyone will be judged and assigned a state of being according to their works and faith prior to the Second Coming and their own resurrection. There are small nuances in the doctrines of both churches that are worth considering.

The Catholic Church

Upon death we will be judged and rewarded immediately with entrance into heaven, entrance into purgatory for further purification, or entrance into hell to be punished. The circumstances that will decide where one goes is a question and not fully answered in the Catechism of the Catholic Church; however, it is my understanding through my own personal study that those who die in a state void of serious sin will go to heaven; those who die in a state of venial sin will go to purgatory; and those who die in a state of mortal sin will go to hell.

If this is correct, what is the effect of deathbed penance (or repentance)? This question was posed by Rusticus, Bishop of Gallia Narbonensis to Leo the Great and answered by Leo in Letter 167:

> Question: "Concerning those who on their deathbed promise repentance and die before receiving communion."
>
> Reply: Their cause is reserved for the judgment of God, in whose hand it was that their death was put off until the very time of communion. But we cannot be in communion with those, when dead, with whom when alive we were not in communion.[1]

The Church of Jesus Christ of Latter-day Saints

Upon death we will be judged and rewarded with either a place in paradise, a place in the spirit prison, or a place in temporary hell. This judgment and reward will be based on faith and works.

About deathbed repentance, Elder Bruce R. McConkie offers the following explanation: "This life is the time that is given for men to repent and prepare to meet God. Those who have opportunity in this life to accept the truth are obligated to take it; otherwise, full salvation will be denied them. Hopes of reward through so-called *death-bed repentance* are vain."[2]

Purgatory, Limbo, and the Spirit World

Where do the judged go after the partial (or particular) judgment? The consequences stemming from the partial judgment lead to entrance into a spiritual existence somewhere between death and the resurrection. For Catholics this includes the states of heaven, purgatory, hell, and perhaps limbo; for Latter-day Saints this includes the spirit world, of which there are three divisions—paradise, spirit prison, or temporary hell

CATHOLIC DOCTRINE

Upon death the soul separates from the body, leaving the temporal body to decay while the soul goes on to meet God in anticipation of being reunited with a glorified body in the Resurrection before the final judgment. Souls who are in "God's grace and friendship, but still imperfectly purified," although guaranteed of eternal salvation, must undertake further purification, being cleansed of mortal imperfection prior to their entrance into "the joy of heaven" (Catechism 1030). The place where this purification takes place is called purgatory.

Purgatory should not be confused with hell or the punishments that are associated with damnation; rather, it is a place of cleansing or purifying. The theology of purgatory originated as dogma at the Council of Basel-Ferrara-Florence (1431–1445), and as a decree at the twenty-fifth session of the Council of Trent (1545–1563). While there are some sins that will be forgiven in the next world through the fire of purification in purgatory, there will be others that will not be forgiven—for instance see the scripture regarding blasphemy against the Holy Spirit in Matthew 12:32.

The Catholic Church teaches that souls in purgatory can benefit from prayers and other offerings from those still living in mortality. Such a practice is supported in scripture, as in 2 Maccabees 12:46, which states (speaking of Judas Maccabeus), "Thus he made atonement for the dead that they might be freed from this sin." This is further exemplified by the example of Job, whose sons were purified by Job's sacrifice. In honor of the memory of the dead, the Catholic Church approves of the offering of prayers, alms, indulgences, and works of penance. The hope is that those in purgatory, with the help of our prayers and offerings, will be purified sufficient to "attain the beatific vision of God" (Catechism 1032).

While these prayers and offerings can be made on behalf of deceased persons, it is important to note that the Catholic Church teaches that "there is no repentance for men after death" (Catechism 393).

See pg 20 for

A third possible spiritual existence after death is limbo. Under pre-Vatican II Catholic doctrine, limbo was defined as a state of eternal happiness set apart for un-baptized infants and children who die before the age of reason. The 1992 version of the Catechism does not mention limbo, but does raise a question concerning the eternal destiny of these infants and children. In a 1984 interview with Vittorio Messori, then-Cardinal Joseph Ratzinger, head of the Congregation for the Doctrine of the Faith (now Pope Benedict XVI), said limbo "has never been a definitive truth of faith." A little over twenty years later, Pope Benedict XVI in another interview is quoted as saying, "Let it drop, since it has always been only a theological hypothesis."[3]

In 2005 the International Theological Commission, an arm of the Congregation for the Doctrine of Faith, discussed a church movement toward abolishing limbo.[4] Despite this news report, it must be understood that the International Theological Commission is only an advisory body to the Congregation for the Doctrine of the Faith; therefore such conclusions as those reached on limbo have no official standing as Catholic doctrine.

See Catechism 393, 997, 1030-1032, 1498, and glossary.

LATTER-DAY SAINT DOCTRINE

Latter-day Saints refer to all states in the afterlife before heaven as the spirit world. The spirit world is a place where our spirits will exist after death and before the Resurrection. In this place, we will wait, learn, work, and rest from our labors on the earth. In the spirit world, we prepare for our resurrection where our spirits will unite with our mortal bodies to be judged and given a place in the eternities among the three levels of heaven or outer darkness (both will be explained in a later section).

Our spirits are able to progress in the spirit world in the same shape and form as humans (only in a spirit form), including the same attitudes, thought patterns, desires, and appetites as we had on earth. If we die with a certain attitude towards righteousness or wickedness, we will have that same attitude in the spirit world.

A common question is what form will spirits have in the spirit world? The answer is given by the prophet Joseph F. Smith, who taught that all spirits are in adult form, having been in adult form before their mortal existence, and being in an adult form after their death—regardless of how old they are at death.[5]

The spirit world is divided into two main parts, with one of those parts being subdivided into two parts—a total of three parts, or divisions. The Book of Mormon prophet Alma defined paradise as one part, and the spirit prison as another. After partial judgment, spirits who died with a degree of purity, having been obedient to the commandments of the Lord and the will of God on earth, will go to paradise (Luke 23:43). Those who die with a lesser degree of purity and obedience will go to the spirit prison (1 Peter 3:19). There is a separation between the righteous and wicked in paradise and the spirit prison (Luke 16:26); however, as spirits progress and learn gospel principles they may move from one state to another.

Paradise is described by the prophet Alma as being a place where righteous spirits are able to find rest from their earthly trials. This rest includes the opportunity to be engaged in service to the Lord. This vision of service was seen by way of revelation through Joseph F. Smith. He records having seen Jesus Christ, after his death, appointing individuals in Paradise to "carry the light of the gospel to them that were in darkness, even to all the spirits of men" (D&C 138:30).

Spirit prison is a term used by the Apostle Peter in his first epistle. He wrote of Jesus after his burial: "By which also he went and preached unto the spirits in prison" (1 Peter 3:19). These spirits in prison have not received the gospel for one reason or another and therefore remain subject to temptation. All have agency (free will) to choose good and evil. They are taught and guided by those in Paradise. If they accept the gospel and the ordinances performed for them in the holy temples on earth (see chapter 17 on temples), they can depart from the spirit prison to enter paradise.

The spirit prison is divided between those who have not yet received the gospel and those who rejected the gospel while living on the earth. Those who rejected the gospel are in a state of suffering "in a condition known as hell,"[6] which is really a temporary hell before the resurrection. These individuals in hell are unable to experience the mercy of Jesus Christ, having separated themselves according to their own agency. Their time in hell will be temporary, as outlined in Acts 2:27: "Because thou wilt not leave my soul in hell." Following this period of suffering, these individuals will take part in the second resurrection (to be discussed in a later section of this chapter) and be allowed entrance into the telestial kingdom, the least of the kingdoms of God following the final judgment. The telestial kingdom can be referred to as the lowest level of heaven (to be discussed in a later section).

From the time that Jesus descended into the spirit prison until the present day, the Church of Christ operates in the spirit world. The teachings of President Wilford Woodruff testify to this fact: "The same Priesthood exists on the other side of the veil. . . . Every Apostle, every Seventy, every Elder, etc., who has died in the faith as soon as he passes to the other side of the veil, enters into the work of the ministry."[7]

Likewise families are organized in the Spirit World. President Jedediah M. Grant, a counselor in the First Presidency under Brigham Young, was said to have seen a vision of the Spirit World. He described this to Heber C. Kimball, who wrote: "He said that the people he there saw were organized in family capacities."[8]

The location of the spirit world is physically the same realm as that in which we live in today. Referring to the spirits of righteous people who have died and entered into the spirit world, the prophet Joseph Smith said they "are not far from us, and know and understand our thoughts, feelings, and motions, and are often pained therewith."[9] On this matter President Ezra Taft Benson said, "Sometimes the veil between this life and the life beyond becomes very thin. Our loved ones who have passed on are not far from us."[10] President Brigham Young left little ambiguity when he commented, "Where is the spirit world? It is right here."[11]

THOUGHTS AND COMMENTARY

The Catholic Church and Church of Jesus Christ of Latter-day Saints have similar doctrines on the afterlife before the Resurrection with respect to structure, but are vastly different in terms of the specifics. Catholics believe there are three post-death/pre-resurrection states: heaven, purgatory, and hell. Latter-day Saints also believe there are three states: paradise, spirit prison, and temporary hell. Catholicism at one time added limbo as yet a fourth state; however, it appears that this hypothetical is largely ignored today.

Understanding the Catholic doctrine to some degree before our investigation allowed us to more easily accept the Latter-day Saint doctrine. However, after further personal study I found the Latter-day Saint doctrine on the spirit world to be comprehensive and mapped exceptionally well with biblical scripture, whereas the Catholic doctrine was not necessarily biblically based. The Latter-day Saint doctrine describes the afterlife as more of a continuum rather than finalities, which makes far more sense given the place of the final judgment long after death.

The Church of Jesus Christ of Latter-day Saints teaches that unbaptized children under the age of eight go directly to the celestial kingdom when they die (see the section on baptism in chapter 13). In Catholicism these un-baptized souls go to a state in which they rely on our prayers and God's mercy and judgment for admittance into heaven. We felt the Latter-day Saint doctrine in this regard shows more mercy and justice for children who are unfortunate enough to meet this fate in mortality.

Latter-day Saint doctrine defines the physical nature of spirits. This description concurs with those of many people who have seen visions of ancestors and loved ones. The Catholic doctrine does not attempt to describe the physical nature of spirits, leaving the subject matter open to interpretation.

The qualifications for entrance into each state of the spirit world are laid out with great clarity in Latter-day Saint doctrine. This doctrine provides a more tangible and meaningful definition of paradise. Paradise is likened to the "blessedness of Heaven" in the Catholic faith: Souls there obtain a sort of rest. Latter-day Saint doctrine holds that those in paradise will teach the spirits in the spirit prison. This more fully concurs with what Christ did after his death and before his Resurrection according to scripture. There is work to do in spirit prison and many souls are needed to carry it out.

The bold Latter-day Saint assertion that the spirit world occupies an earthly realm is exceptionally illuminating and fits with the physical nature of spirits. Furthermore, this assertion is completely consistent with scripture and the numerous sightings of spirits over the centuries. If God should decide that someone should see a particular spirit for one reason or another (an ancestor, for example), he, the creator of all, certainly has the power to enable a living person to see the spirit form of one who has died. This perfectly explains the visions of many over the centuries who have seen spirits of the dead.

However, it should be noted that Latter-day Saint leaders do not emphasize such visitations, and urge members not to publicize them idly. Such visitations are usually personal, private, and sacred—and should be kept so. They are communicated only when some clear good would come from the communication. The Church of Jesus Christ of Latter-day Saints is not a church of pop clairvoyants and psychics.

The organization of the spirit world in Latter-day Saint doctrine explains a great deal about the gospel of Jesus Christ and encourages us to be righteous and worthy on earth so that we are prepared for our work in the afterlife. This teaching about the spirit world is a powerful motivator in this world.

These fantastic and enlightening doctrines are wonderful examples of how The Church of Jesus Christ of Latter-day Saints is the restored gospel in its fulness on earth. It provides wealth of biblically sound and divinely inspired doctrine on the spirit world. This doctrine not only gives valuable insights about the afterlife, it also provides spiritual motivation for living a Christ-centered life on earth, driven by the love of God and our neighbor. It offers much more than fear of hell to move us toward eternal life in the eternities.

The Second Coming

For Christians, the Second Coming of Jesus Christ is the most anticipated of all human events. This future event generates a host of questions with few answers. This section examines what we know and speculates about the Second Coming of Christ, while identifying significantly different Catholic and Latter-day Saint doctrines about it.

CATHOLIC DOCTRINE

At the end of time Christ will appear to judge the living and the dead. Creation will have been fully realized. This is called the *parousia*.

> At the end of time, the Kingdom of God will come in its fulness. After the universal judgment, the righteous will reign for ever with Christ, glorified in body and soul. The universe itself will be renewed: The Church . . . will receive her perfection only in the glory of heaven, when will come the time of the renewal of all things. At that time, together with the human race, the universe itself, which is so closely related to man and which attains its destiny through him, will be perfectly re-established in Christ (Catechism 1042).

Heaven and earth will be in Christ according to the statutes of God. The events of this time are described in compassionate detail by John the Revelator from the Book of Revelation in the New Testament:

> I also saw the holy city, a new Jerusalem, coming down out of heaven from God, prepared as a bride adorned for her husband. I heard a loud voice from the throne saying, "Behold, God's dwelling is with the human race. He will dwell with them and they will be his people

and God himself will always be with them (as their God). He will wipe every tear from their eyes, and there shall be no more death or mourning, wailing or pain, (for) the old order has passed away (Revelation 21:2–4).

At the time of the parousia, there will be a community of people who are redeemed and unified with Christ and who will symbolically be "the wife of the Lamb" (Revelation 21:9) and remain unharmed from that point forward. They will witness the beatific vision: the eternal and intimate knowledge of God, resulting in extraordinary happiness or blessedness. The physical universe will be restored and glorified to its original state, without any possibility of future blemish, and be subject to the service of the redeemed. This new earth will be a dwelling place for the righteous. There will be unparalleled happiness, and the framework of a new human family will be raised—all under the blessings and influence of the Holy Trinity.

The time and manner in which the parousia will take place is unknown to all on the earth. It is worth noting that while some Christian sects ascribe to the theology of a Millennium (a thousand year reign of Christ at the time of the resurrection before the final judgment), the Catholic Church does not.

See Catechism 1042–1045, 1047–1050, and glossary.

LATTER-DAY SAINT DOCTRINE

The Church of Jesus Christ of Latter-day Saints teaches that the Second Coming of Jesus Christ will usher in a period known as the millennium. Taken from the Latin word *mille* (a thousand) and *annum* (year), the millennium reign of Jesus Christ will be one thousand years of peace, joy, and love preceded by the First Resurrection, and followed by the Second Resurrection and final judgment.

At the Second Coming of Christ, the spirits in paradise will be resurrected and take part in the Millennium. Those living righteously upon the earth at the time of the Second Coming will "be changed in the twinkling of an eye from mortality to immortality" (3 Nephi 28:8). Those taking part will be righteous people who have lived lives worthy of the opportunity and will gain entrance into the terrestrial or celestial kingdom (second and highest level of heaven, respectively) following the final judgment. Brigham Young taught that there will be members of various religions and sects taking part in the Millennium, all of whom will retain their agency.[12]

The tenth article of faith confirms that during the Millennium "Christ will reign personally upon the earth; and, that the earth will be renewed and receive its paradisiacal glory." Many details of the millennium have yet to be revealed. Joseph Smith taught that Jesus would not likely live on the earth during the millennium, but rather appear as necessary to help govern.[13]

During the Millennium, members of the Church will be involved in missionary work and temple work. Missionary work will involve teaching the gospel to those on earth who lack the understanding of the fulness of truth. Temple work will involve participating in the ordinances of salvation and exaltation including baptisms, endowments, marriages, and sealings (see the section on temples in chapter 17). There will be no disease or death (D&C 63:51; D&C 101:29–31), due to the righteousness of those on earth. In the midst of these important spiritual activities will be much of life as we know it today (see Isaiah 65:21), except everything will be done and be governed on the principles of righteousness.[14]

As stated in the tenth article of faith, the earth will be renewed and it will resemble the Garden of Eden during the time of Adam and Eve. All land masses will be joined together as one continent (D&C 133:23–24).

There will be universal peace during the millennium, as Satan will be bound during the thousand years and will have no power over the children of God (Revelation 20:2–3; D&C 101:28). There will be no wars on the earth and harmony will reign throughout the land. The Prophet Isaiah had a vision of this period when he wrote, "They shall beat their swords into plowshares, and their spears into pruninghooks: nation shall not lift up sword against nation, neither shall they learn war any more" (Isaiah 2:4). Likewise the animal kingdom will be at peace (Isaiah 11:6–7).

There will be no separation of Church and state, as Christ will lead both the Church and the government as the religious and political leader. The government will be firmly established on principles of righteousness, with liberty and freedom for all people, with a capital in America and another in Jerusalem.[15]

The Millennium will also be a time when many gospel truths that are not known today will be revealed to the entire world. The prophet Joseph Smith received the following revelation: "Yea, verily I say unto you, in that day when the Lord shall come, he shall reveal all things—Things which have passed, and hidden things which no man knew, things of the earth, by which it was made, and the purpose and the end thereof—Things most precious, things that are above, and things that are beneath, things that are in the earth, and upon the earth, and in heaven" (D&C 101:32–34).

At the end of the Millennium, before the final judgment, there will be one final conflict that will engulf the entire earth as a final test. The Book of Revelation outlines this struggle in which Satan is set free for a short season (Revelation 20:7–8). Satan will gather his armies, while Michael will gather his, for one final battle for the souls of men. At this time there will be some who will exercise their agency contrary to the commandments of God. Following this final conflict, Satan and his followers will be cast out from among the children of God forever. This will be immediately followed by the final judgment and entrance into one of the three kingdoms.

See *Gospel Principles*, 282–85.

THOUGHTS AND COMMENTARY

In our experiences as Catholics, we don't remember spending much time discussing the Second Coming of Jesus Christ, outside of usual mention during the regular liturgy. We never discussed the time leading up to the Second Coming, what would happen during the Second Coming, or what would happen after. Thus, the Second Coming to us was something far removed and of little interest during our Catholic years.

The general description of the Second Coming of Jesus Christ differs little between the two churches. However, Latter-day Saint doctrine provides exquisite detail that motivates and excites. These details were enlightening and uplifting to Marilyn and me. We read from the Book of Revelation that there would be a thousand year period after the Second Coming of Christ, but we didn't understand the complete purpose or what would take place. Consider the following scripture from Revelation 20:2–7:

> And he laid hold on the dragon, that old serpent, which is the Devil, and Satan, and bound him a thousand years,
> And cast him into the bottomless pit, and shut him up, and set a seal upon him, that he should deceive the nations no more, till the thousand years should be fulfilled: and after that he must be loosed a little season.
> And I saw thrones, and they sat upon them, and judgment was

given unto them: and I saw the souls of them that were beheaded for the witness of Jesus, and for the word of God, and which had not worshipped the beast, neither his image, neither had received his mark upon their foreheads, or in their hands; and they lived and reigned with Christ a thousand years.

But the rest of the dead lived not again until the thousand years were finished. This is the first resurrection.

Blessed and holy is he that hath part in the first resurrection: on such the second death hath no power, but they shall be priests of God and of Christ, and shall reign with him a thousand years.

And when the thousand years are expired, Satan shall be loosed out of his prison.

Upon review of this extraordinary scripture, especially when pieced together with other Latter-day Saint doctrine, we gained a powerful testimony of the truthfulness of the Latter-day Saint doctrine. In particular the thousand-year millennial reign of Christ, the fact that Satan would be bound and then loosed, and that there would be two distinctly separate resurrections of the dead. How could one get anything different from reading this scripture from the Book of Revelation?

Scriptures from the Book of Mormon and the Doctrine and Covenants only added to our testimony of the doctrine on the Second Coming—once again demonstrating to us that by becoming Latter-day Saints we wouldn't be losing anything, but rather adding significantly to what we already had through the Restoration of the gospel.

The Church of Jesus Christ of Latter-day Saints teaches extensively on the Second Coming of Jesus Christ. Perhaps more important, the Church teaches about the events that will lead up to the Second Coming in order to prepare everyone for the signs. The Church doesn't emphasize the Second Coming from an apocalyptic or doomsday point of view, but rather as a way to warn everyone to get their spiritual lives in order and to prepare for the coming of Christ. With this enhanced understanding of the Second Coming, Marilyn and I believe that it is a key responsibility of the Church of Jesus Christ on earth to prepare members for life in the eternities and to help our family prepare for the Second Coming of Christ.

The Resurrection

Before, during, and after the time of Christ, there were vigorous debates between the Pharisees and Sadducees regarding the resurrection. The Pharisees believed in the resurrection and the Sadducees did not. The Resurrection is a difficult theological concept to grasp for Christians in that it calls on us to believe in a process of life to death to life again for a single organism, a process outside our human intellect.

This section will explore the resurrection doctrine of both churches, revealing significant differences that are important to understand at both a micro and macro level as part of the plan of salvation.

CATHOLIC DOCTRINE

When a person dies, the soul separates from the body—the body is laid to rest and the soul moves on to encounter God. By the power of Christ's resurrection, all who have died will experience their souls reuniting with their bodies in the resurrection.

"The raising of the righteous, who will live forever with the risen Christ, on the last day. The eleventh article of the Christian creed states, 'I believe in the resurrection of the body.' The resurrection of the body means not only that the immortal soul will live on after death, but that even our 'mortal bodies' (Romans 8:11) will come to life again" (Catechism glossary).

Christ spoke of the resurrection, leaving little doubt as to the truthfulness of the doctrine. The Apostle Paul was an avid defender of the doctrine of the Resurrection. In his first letter to the Corinthians (verses 12–14), Paul admonishes the saints who question the resurrection: "How can some of you say that there is no resurrection of the dead? But if there is no resurrection of the dead, then Christ has not been raised; if Christ has not been raised, then our preaching is in vain and your faith is in vain."

Preceding the final judgment at the "last day, at the end of the world" in close proximity to Christ's Parousia, the resurrection will come to all who have died, regardless of their state, "the righteous and the unrighteous" (Acts 24:15). This event is described in John 5:28–29: "The hour when all who are in the tombs will hear [the Son of man's] voice and come forth, those who have done good, to the resurrection of life, and those who have done evil, to the resurrection of judgment."

The bodies in which we will be resurrected in are the same that we have today. The doctrine affirming this concept comes from the Second Council of Lyon (the Fourteenth Ecumenical Council of the Roman

Catholic Church from 1272 to 1274), which yielded the statement: "We believe in the true resurrection of this flesh that we now possess."[16] The doctrine of being resurrected to our own body is further supported by Paul, who wrote, "We sow a corruptible body in the tomb, but he raises up an incorruptible body, a 'spiritual body' " (1 Corinthians 15:42–44).

Explaining the "how" of the resurrection is beyond human understanding, but will be the work of the Holy Trinity. Those with great faith may be given the ability to do so, while the Eucharist provides a glimpse of our own transfiguration as a proxy to the resurrection. Additionally, the sacraments of baptism and confirmation provide symbolic representations of the resurrection by being buried in the water as death, and rising out of the water in life, being touched by the Holy Spirit.

The resurrection and life of the risen Christ brings hope that we too will rise up in the resurrection at the last day and live with Christ forever. This is made possible as we allow God to dwell inside of us enabling Him to raise our mortal bodies. Through our participation in the Eucharist we are already unified to the Body of Christ, and through the resurrection we will "also will appear with him in glory" (Colossians 3:4).

See Catechism 989–991, 997–1003, 1015, 1017, 1038, and glossary.

Latter-day Saint Doctrine

Throughout the ages, death has brought about feelings of finality and despair. In the minds of many, death is the end leaving no hope for the future. The faithful know that Jesus Christ has "broken the bands of death" (Mosiah 16:7), and by doing so "death is swallowed up in victory" (1 Corinthians 15:54). This victory over death comes through the Atonement and Resurrection of Jesus Christ.

There are numerous scriptures that provide detailed accounts of Christ's resurrection, while providing a clear understanding of the future resurrection of all people who have lived and died in mortality upon the earth. Jesus exclaimed, "Because I live, ye shall live also" (John 14:19), referring to our own resurrection.

In death, our bodies and spirits are separated; in the resurrection during the Second Coming, our bodies and spirits are reunited in a perfected state. The Book of Mormon prophet Alma recorded these words from the prophet Amulek: "The spirit and the body shall be reunited again in its perfect form; both limb and joint shall be restored to its proper frame, even as we now are at this time. . . . Now, this restoration shall come to all, both old and young, both bond and free, both male and female, both the wicked and the righteous; and even there shall not so much as a hair of their heads be lost; but every thing shall be restored to its perfect frame (Alma 11:42–44).

The resurrection not only restores life, but ushers in a new phase in our eternal progression. The Apostle Dallin H. Oaks wrote, "In our eternal journey, the resurrection is the mighty milepost that signifies the end of mortality and the beginning of immortality."[17] Without the resurrection we could not achieve immortality, nor could we experience a "fulness of joy" (D&C 93:33–34). Paul understanding the hopelessness that would result from the absence of the resurrection wrote, "If there be no resurrection of the dead, then . . . is our preaching vain, and your faith is also vain" (1 Corinthians 15:13–14).

Our knowledge of the resurrection gives hope and understanding that death is not the end, but rather a gateway to the eternities. Our testimony of the resurrection helps us put into perspective our trials in mortality, while providing us motivation to live our lives in accordance with the commandments of God.

It behooves us to prepare ourselves for the resurrection by living a righteous life on earth, including taking care of the body we have now. The resurrection will not cleanse us from sin or magically change our souls from one state to another. In his letter to the Corinthians Paul was quite clear that those who are void of righteousness in mortality will not be raised in righteousness in the resurrection (1 Corinthians 15:35–44). To this end Alma counsels men that "this life is the time for men to prepare to meet God" (Alma 34:32).

Unique to Latter-day Saint doctrine is the principle of families being together forever through the sealing powers of priesthood in the holy temple. Applying this doctrine to the resurrection means that we have the opportunity to be resurrected with family members and to live together in the eternities. Not only is such doctrine a motivation to live a righteous life while on earth, but it gives hope in times where temporal death separates loved ones.

Elder Bruce R. McConkie points out that there are two distinctly different resurrections that are approximately one thousand years apart: "Two great resurrections await the inhabitants of the earth: one is the first resurrection, the resurrection of life, the resurrection of the just; the other is the second resurrection, the resurrection of damnation, the resurrection of the unjust."[18] Elder McConkie goes on to explain that the First Resurrection will happen at the Second Coming and have a morning (for those who will meet Christ at his Second Coming—celestial bodies) and an afternoon (for those who come forth right after the Second Coming—terrestrial bodies). See 1 Corinthians 15:40 for biblical references to celestial and terrestrial bodies, as well as the final section in this chapter. Following the thousand year millennial reign of Christ, the Second Resurrection will take place. Those coming forth first in the Second Resurrection will have telestial bodies, and those coming forth last in the Second Resurrection will be cast into outer darkness, both with and without bodies including those who gave up their first estate (Satan and his followers will not have a body and therefore, technically not resurrected) and the sons of perdition (those whose sins are unforgivable).

THOUGHTS AND COMMENTARY

I remember growing up celebrating Easter and the scant references to the Resurrection of Jesus Christ as being the reason we celebrated Easter. I can likewise remember various Catechism lessons and sermons that may have briefly mentioned the resurrection of Jesus Christ. However, I cannot remember any discussions or teachings about the resurrection of our own bodies. Marilyn's degree in Catholic theology gave her a more robust background on the resurrection, but even then there was little emphasis placed on our own resurrection. Like the Second Coming, Marilyn and I knew it was there, but we didn't discuss details of the resurrection of mankind in the liturgy or religious education, nor did we fully comprehend the resurrection from a spiritual or physical standpoint as part of Catholic doctrine.

After reviewing the Latter-day Saint doctrine on the resurrection, we became very interested in the chain of events as part of the afterlife concept. If we were to be resurrected, we wanted to understand how that would be done for us personally, and how that would be done for all of mankind.

The first thing that we had to do was begin referring to ourselves in the afterlife as "spirits," as opposed to the Catholic doctrinal concept of "souls." We read Elder Bruce R. McConkie's description of the relationship between spirits and souls:

> Spirit beings are *souls*; the two terms are synonymous. . . . After the spirit leaves the body and goes into the spirit world to await the

211

day of the resurrection, it is still designated as a soul. A mortal soul, however, consists of a body and spirit united in a temporary or mortal union. An *immortal soul* . . . is a resurrected personage, one who has been raised from mortality into immortality, one for whom body and spirit have become inseparably connected.[19]

Both Catholic and Latter-day Saint doctrines claim the resurrection of perfect and glorious bodies, and during our investigation, we took comfort in this. We found it very intriguing that The Church of Jesus Christ of Latter-day Saints puts a strong emphasis on taking care of one's body as the temple of God in relation to the resurrection. (See the Word of Wisdom in D&C 89.)

Adding to this, Latter-day Saint leaders discourage cremation driven by an overriding belief that "the body is good and as a creation of God is to be respected" and that "nothing should be done which is destructive to the body."[20] Marilyn and I, as strong believers in the sanctity of the body, found the doctrine and practice of keeping one's body healthy to have profound spiritual implications, with excellent practical application in life.

The concept of two resurrections was new to us, but we quickly resolved and adopted it through our reading about the two resurrections in Revelation 20:5–6, John 5:29, and Acts 24:15. Neither of us had previously taken notice of there being two resurrections before that time. Our new-found knowledge of the two resurrections documented in the Bible made it simple for us to comprehend the Latter-day Saint doctrine and correlated nicely given the nature of the judgment and how everyone will be rewarded accordingly.

The final doctrinal component that struck Marilyn and me was the emphasis on the family in the resurrection. Although as Catholics we felt we would see family again in heaven, the Latter-day Saint doctrine calls for the *joining* of families in the celestial kingdom after the resurrection and final judgment. This will be discussed in more detail in chapter 15. We wanted our family to be together forever, and Latter-day Saint doctrine made it clear that we could have this privilege. Once again we felt as if we were going from having a *little* information on a very important subject as Catholics, to having a *great deal* of information on a topic that would have eternal consequences to us and our family.

Final Judgment

Throughout the ages, there have been countless stories, jokes, metaphors, and cartoons depicting the final judgment. Typically the setting is God looking down upon an individual at the gates of heaven, or the "pearly gates" as they are often referred to as. The mighty Lord standing inside of the gates renders a deserving verdict based upon the individual's life on earth.

Nearly all Christian religions agree that there will be a final judgment following the resurrection. All mankind will be given a final reward based upon their faith and/or works upon the earth, some sects claiming a judgment more based on faith than works. This section will explore the doctrines of the final judgment, examining some small but meaningful differences between the Catholic Church and The Church of Jesus Christ of Latter-day Saints.

CATHOLIC DOCTRINE

The Catechism defines the "Last Judgment" as the following: "The 'Last Judgment' is God's triumph over the revolt of evil, after the final cosmic upheaval of this passing world. Preceded by the resurrection of the dead, it will coincide with the Second Coming of Christ in glory at the end of time, disclose good and evil, and reveal the meaning of salvation history and the providence of God by which justice has triumphed over evil" (Catechism glossary).

At the Second Council of Lyons, the declaration was made that "The holy Roman Church firmly believes and confesses that on the Day of Judgment all men will appear in their own bodies before Christ's tribunal to render an account of their own deeds."[21]

The New Testament beautifully describes, with no ambiguity, the scene that will take place at the final judgment, "When the Son of Man comes in his glory, and all the angels with him, he will sit upon his glorious throne, and all the nations will be assembled before him. And he will separate them one from another, as a shepherd separates the sheep from the goats" (Matthew 25:31–32).

Matthew goes on to describe how the sheep will be on Jesus's right and the goats on his left, and he will say to those on his right, "Come, you who are blessed by my Father. Inherit the kingdom prepared for you from the foundation of the world" (Matthew 25:34). He then explains to those on his right why they are being given such a wonderful reward: "For

I was hungry and you gave me food, I was thirsty and you gave me drink, a stranger and you welcomed me, naked and you clothed me, ill and you cared for me, in prison and you visited me" (Matthew 25:35–36).

Then Christ will look to those on his left and boldly pronounce judgment upon them by saying, "Depart from me, you accursed, into the eternal fire prepared for the devil and his angels. For I was hungry and you gave me no food, I was thirsty and you gave me no drink, a stranger and you gave me no welcome, naked and you gave me no clothing, ill and in prison, and you did not care for me" (Matthew 25:41–43). Christ will then explain the reasons for such a judgment and finalize the verdict with the words, "And these will go off to eternal punishment, but the righteous to eternal life" (Matthew 25:46).

In this scriptural account we are witnesses to the fact that each man (and woman) individually will be brought before Christ, who is "the way and the truth and the life" (John 14:6), and each person's bond with God and actions on earth will be made known to all. Upon that knowledge, the Last Judgment will be rendered to its fullest consequences—both good and bad—according to the earthly life that person led.

One's life on earth will have many aspects to it that will be exposed during the Last Judgment. That which was secret will be revealed; where love was rejected there will be a judgment rendered; those who felt the sacrifice of Jesus Christ was meaningless will be smitten for their rejection as they will have judged themselves; and those who mistreated and abused their neighbors will be held accountable as if they did those very things to Christ himself —"as you did it to one of the least of these my brethren, you did it to me" (Matthew 25:40). God's justice will reign over all injustices, and his love will conquer all death during the Last Judgment.

The time of the Last Judgment is only to God the Father. The Catholic Church expends all of its efforts and prays that not a single person would be lost during the Last Judgment. We know that should it be true that "no one can save himself," that it is likewise true that God "desires all men to be saved" (1 Timothy 2:4), and that for him "all things are possible" (Matthew 19:26; Catechism 1058).

See Catechism 678–682, 1021, 1038–1040, 1056, 1058, 1059, and glossary.

LATTER-DAY SAINT DOCTRINE

The scriptures abound with passages that clearly indicate we will be judged at the end times according to our works. Consider the following scripture from the book of Revelation: "And I saw the dead, small and great, stand before God; and the books were opened: and another book was opened, which is the book of life: and the dead were judged out of those things which were written in the books, according to their works" (Revelation 20:12).

There are many New Testament scriptures that directly correlate the reward that people will receive from their works on earth (such as Matthew 16:27; 1 Corinthians 3:14; 2 Timothy 4:14), each referring to the final judgment. The final judgment is the last and ultimate in a succession of judgments starting with premortal life, then earthly life, and concluding with resurrection. Not to be confused with the Partial Judgment that takes place immediately after our death, the final judgment takes place after our resurrection and the millennial reign of Christ.

The works on which we will be judged will include our words, thoughts, and actions. With respect to words, Jesus Christ taught his disciples, "Every idle word that men shall speak, they shall give account thereof in the day of judgment. For by thy words thou shalt be justified, and by thy words thou shalt be condemned" (Matthew 12:36–37). With respect to our thoughts, the prophet Alma taught, "Our thoughts will also condemn us" (Alma 12:14).

Our works are written in the books referred to in the scripture from Revelation 20:12. Joseph Smith taught that this scriptural reference was true in that we will be judged based upon records kept on earth. Joseph Fielding Smith said, "We are going to be judged out of the things written in books, out of the revelations of God, out of the temple records, out of those things which the Lord has commanded us to keep. . . . There will be the record in heaven which is a perfect record."[22]

The Apostle Paul taught about being judged out of records, but a different record—that which is written in our hearts. Paul wrote to the Romans, "Which shew the work of the law written in their hearts, their conscience also bearing witness, and their thoughts the mean while accusing or else excusing one another" (Romans 2:15). He likewise wrote to the Corinthians, "Ye are our epistle written in our hearts, known and read of all men: Forasmuch as ye are manifestly declared to be the epistle of Christ ministered by us, written not with ink, but with the Spirit of the living God; not in tables of stone, but in fleshy tables of the heart" (2 Corinthians 3:2–3).

These records written in our hearts will be made known during the final judgment and be used to render the verdict upon us. President John Taylor reinforced this principle when he said, "[The individual] tells the story himself, and bears witness against himself. . . . That record that is written by the man himself in the tablets of his own mind—that record that cannot lie—will in that day be unfolded before God and angels, and those who sit as judges."[23]

We will be judged not only by the Lord Jesus Christ in all his glory, but by those to whom Christ delegates the power and authority to judge. God the Father will not judge anyone, but will delegate that power and authority to the Savior (John 5:22). Likewise, this same delegation of judgment will take place as Christ assigns the original Twelve Apostles the power to judge: "That ye which have followed me, in the regeneration when the Son of man shall sit in the throne of his glory, ye also shall sit upon twelve thrones, judging the twelve tribes of Israel" (Matthew 19:28 and Luke 22:30). There will be others appointed as well by the hand Christ who will be given the power and authority to judge righteously.

The result of the final judgment will see everyone assigned to four possible places to dwell for all eternity: "the celestial kingdom (the highest degree of glory), the terrestrial kingdom (the second degree), the telestial kingdom (the lowest degree), . . . outer darkness (the kingdom of the devil—not a degree of glory)."[24] Doctrine and Covenants 76 describes each of these places in detail and discusses the choices we make and their effects on our assignment to the appropriate place—regardless of religious affiliation.

"We speak, think, and act according to celestial, terrestrial, or telestial law. Our faith in Jesus Christ, as shown by our daily actions, determines which kingdom we will inherit."[25] The Church urges all members to be faithful in mortality to take full advantage of the atoning power of Christ through repentance everyday, so that we will remain worthy and prepared for the final judgment. If we do this, we can return to live with our Heavenly Father in the celestial kingdom.

See *Gospel Principles*, 294–98.

THOUGHTS AND COMMENTARY

Although the concept of the final judgment has similarities between the two churches, there are important differences which shed light on ambiguous biblical scriptures, providing incremental insights into the final judgment.

Latter-day Saint doctrine outlines how the judgment will take place and the fact that although Jesus Christ will oversee the final judgment, many others will be involved in the actual execution of judgment. This is in complete agreement with the Bible and with other Latter-day Saint scriptures.

Latter-day Saint doctrine provides more detail on the things for which we will be judged and the processes of judgment. This detail gives valuable insights that help us view our own specific actions on earth in a broader perspective, generating a greater appreciation for the importance of self-control while living in mortality.

The Church of Jesus Christ of Latter-day Saints' doctrine on the final judgment fits extremely well with the greater picture of how the afterlife will unfold for each of us. Marilyn and I now have a vastly expanded appreciation for the events that are to take place after our time on the earth, allowing us to unfold that mystery to our children and help motivate them to keep the commandments and live a righteous life on earth in Jesus Christ. We were able to take that which we learned as Catholics and fill in many of the blanks that were once called mysterious. Like so many other subjects we studied, it was like a painting that needed those final brush strokes to make it complete.

Hell

The word *hell* conjures up a multitude of thoughts and visions—both spiritual and metaphorical. In the *Divine Comedy*, Dante depicts hell as a complex and haunting place. Hell is often synonymous with fire, torture, demons, and death, a place of eternal punishment.

Hell is often misunderstood, hence the many definitions and descriptions of hell from any number of religions.

This section will examine the doctrines of hell, an undesirable state in the afterlife, and compare some surprising differences in doctrine between both churches.

CATHOLIC DOCTRINE

The Catechism defines hell as "the state of definitive self-exclusion from communion with God and the blessed, reserved for those who refuse by their own free choice to believe and be converted from sin, even to the end of their lives" (Catechism Glossary).

The Catholic Church is explicit in that hell is a real place that will last for all eternity. Those who die with unresolved mortal sin will be judged accordingly and be relegated to spending all eternity in hell where they will suffer the punishments of endless torment. John the Baptist describes the state of hell as "unquenchable fire" (Luke 3:17), as did Jesus when he spoke of "Gehenna . . . the unquenchable fire" (Mark 9:43), a place set aside for those who reject faith in Christ. In the final judgment Jesus will "send his angels, and they will collect out of his kingdom all who cause others to sin and all evildoers. They will throw them into the fiery furnace, where there will be wailing and grinding of teeth" (Matthew 13:41–42).

Although the metaphors of fire and burning overwhelm the scriptural depiction of hell, the key suffering of hell will be the evil doers "eternal separation from God, in whom alone man can possess the life and happiness for which he was created and for which he longs" (Catechism 1035). One can literally translate this to there being no possibility for happiness in hell, and thus the relentless emphasis on suffering.

None of God's children are predestined to hell, but are rather assigned to the torment of hell through the continual exercising of free will in rejection of God until the end of life. It is impossible to become united with God without our electing to love God ourselves. The scriptures admonish man to accept the grace of God, to turn away from sin, to experience conversion, and walk in the path of righteousness toward eternal life. The Catholic Church entreats the mercy of God, through the celebration of the liturgy and prayers of its members, in hopes of being spared from final damnation (the living and the dead) and to have peace in this life and the next.

See Catechism, 1033–1037, 1055, 1058, and glossary.

LATTER-DAY SAINT DOCTRINE

The scriptures outline the existence of two different states of hell: one is temporary before the resurrection, and the other is eternal after the final judgment.

The Temporary State of Hell

This book's section on the spirit world identifies a division of the spirit prison called hell, or temporary hell. Those who die in a serious state of sin, without a testimony of Jesus Christ, will be relegated to spending their time in temporary hell until the second resurrection (of the unjust) at the end of the Millennium (John 5:28–29). In a revelation given to the

Prophet Joseph Smith the Lord said, "These are they who are cast down to hell and suffer the wrath of Almighty God, until the fulness of times, when Christ shall have subdued all enemies under his feet, and shall have perfected his work" (D&C 76:106).

The Lord describes these individuals as "liars, and sorcerers, and adulterers, and whoremongers, and whosoever loves and makes a lie" (D&C 76:103). These spirits will be resurrected, and because of God's infinite mercy, they will inherit the telestial kingdom (the third [lowest] level of heaven), be saved, and experience the presence of the Holy Ghost and the ministering of angels—but not the presence of God nor of Jesus Christ (D&C 76:88). They are damned because they can progress no further.

The Hell That Has No End

The second state of hell is the one most popularly thought of among Christians—the hell that has no end. It is the hell that involves endless torment and separation from God, a place eternally without hope. This hell is also referred to as outer darkness. There is no mercy attending to these spirits because they are lost as the "sons of perdition" (John 17:12). The Book of Mormon prophet Nephi further describes these sons of perdition and their grievous states and sins, and even those who become "like" the sons of perdition (3 Nephi 27:32 and 3 Nephi 29:7).

"Lucifer is Perdition. He became such by open rebellion against the truth, a rebellion in the face of light and knowledge. . . . In rebellion with him were one-third of the spirit hosts of heaven. These all were thus *followers* (or in other words *sons*) of perdition. They were denied bodies, were cast out onto the earth, and thus came the devil and his angels—a great host of *sons of perdition*."[26]

There are three degrees of glory that will be explained in the next section regarding heaven, each one being assigned following the final judgment. There will be those who will *not* receive any degree of glory (D&C 88:24). "And they shall go away into everlasting punishment, which is endless punishment, which is eternal punishment, to reign with the devil and his angels in eternity, where their worm dieth not, and the fire is not quenched, which is their torment—And the end thereof, neither the place thereof, nor their torment, no man knows" (D&C 76:44–45).

Besides the sons of perdition, these are individuals who have "sinned against the Holy Ghost" (Matthew 12:32), making it impossible to "renew them again unto repentance; seeing they crucify to themselves the Son of God afresh, and put him to an open shame" (Hebrews 6:6).

Joseph Fielding Smith taught, "How fortunate it is that in the mercy of God there will be comparatively few who will partake of this awful misery and eternal darkness."[27]

See H. Donl Peterson, professor of Ancient Scripture at Brigham Young University in an article titled "I Have a Question," *Ensign*, Apr. 1986, 36; Joseph Fielding Smith, *Doctrines of Salvation*, comp. Bruce R. McConkie, 3 vols. (Salt Lake City: Bookcraft, 1954–56), 1:47–49.

THOUGHTS AND COMMENTARY

When we investigated The Church of Jesus Christ of Latter-day Saints, we really didn't pay any particular attention to the differences in the doctrines on hell between the two churches. To us hell was hell—it was a bad place, and we knew that we should do all we could to avoid it in the afterlife.

Many years later, we learned that very few would end up in the eternal hell we were most familiar with, and instead many would end up in the terrestrial and telestial kingdoms. We came to realize that although the laws of mercy and justice must be satisfied in the final judgment of all mankind, that our Father in Heaven desires that none of his children would suffer for all eternity, and will provide a way for them, even to the last, to avoid eternal suffering. Even then, God himself cannot break his own laws and therefore there will always be suffering for sin.

The first big "ah-ha" for us was understanding the term *damnation*, which means "to be condemned." *Damnation* literally means to have no more progression, or to be damned in the same sense that water is held back by a dam. We as children of a loving Heavenly Father want to progress and return to live with him in heaven, and therefore our progression must include having faith in Jesus Christ, receiving the ordinances of salvation, and living a righteous life on earth. If we fail to one degree or another, we will be held back—or damned. This was an important realization to Marilyn and me because we had been taught as Catholics that hell was the punishment following an "all-or-nothing" judgment and that damnation meant eternal suffering in hell—period, end of story! The rest of Christendom could learn from the truth of this doctrine of damnation.

Understanding the concept of damnation, we have been able to grasp the doctrine that there is a temporary state of hell that exists immediately after death in the spirit world to punish those who have lived unrighteous lives on earth; and a permanent state of hell (outer darkness) that exists for those whom our Father in Heaven designates as deserving an eternity of suffering and pain following the final judgment (the sons of perdition). This concept of two states of hell is consistent with the scriptures and the knowledge that our Father in Heaven is all-loving, all-powerful, and desires not to lose even one soul to the adversary. In the end there will be many who will not choose the right and will place themselves outside of God's presence—but not necessarily a place of endless suffering. This is because God is a loving, compassionate, and merciful father as Jesus described, while at the same time being the jealous God described in the Old Testament.

If we use the Catholic definition of hell as being separation from God, then many will be in a state of damnation, or a hell-like state where they are separated from God. These are they who are assigned to the terrestrial kingdom, the telestial kingdom, and outer darkness. We will discuss these kingdoms in more detail in the next section. In general, however, these will not experience the glory of God the Father, but rather the glory of Jesus Christ in the terrestrial kingdom and the glory of the Holy Ghost in the telestial kingdom.

In reviewing the Catholic doctrine more fully for this book, I found myself intrigued as to what happens to people who are placed into hell at the particular judgment during and after the resurrection. Since the just and unjust are to be resurrected (according to Catholic doctrine), those who are relegated to hell at the particular judgment must be resurrected. After being resurrected, they will then be judged as all men must be. After the final judgment, are they sent back to hell? Are those in hell not resurrected at all? I personally found this to be a bit ambiguous and likely something that is not necessarily explained in detail by the Catholic Church. If not, the explanation may have escaped me during my research.

Heaven

Our final stop, in this chapter and our lives, I hope, is heaven.

While hell is depicted as a place of fire and torment, heaven is depicted as calm, peaceful, often buzzing softly with floating harp-playing angels passing slowly by. Like the few additional surprises the reader might have experienced in the preceding section on hell, a few surprises abound regarding heaven as well.

CATHOLIC DOCTRINE

The Catechism defines heaven as "Eternal life with God; communion of life and love with the Trinity and all the blessed. Heaven is the state of supreme and definitive happiness, the goal of the deepest longings of humanity" (Catechism glossary).

Following the final judgment, the righteous in a perfectly purified state of grace and friendship with God will be rewarded entrance into heaven. In heaven these faithful individuals will rule with Christ forever in a universe transformed, clothed in resurrected bodies that are glorified and perfected. In this glorious state, "we shall be like him [God], for we shall see him as he is" (1 John 3:2). This ability to see and be like God is not possible unless God reveals himself more fully to the understanding of man, as will be the case in heaven. This revealing is called "the beatific vision," in which God will be "all in all" (1 Corinthians 15:28). Imagine the happiness that will exist because of these wondrous events, and sharing immortality in heaven with "the righteous and God's friends" (Catechism 1028).

We cannot imagine what it will be like to be united with God in heaven. Although the scriptures provide anecdotal descriptions, still the understanding is beyond our reach. Paul gives counsel on this predicament when he tells the Corinthians, "no eye has seen, nor ear heard, nor the heart of man conceived, what God has prepared for those who love him" (1 Corinthians 2:9). Those blessed to be in heaven will not only reign with Christ, but will continue in a state of happiness fulfilling God's will along with others and the rest of creation.

See Catechism 1023–1029, 1060, and glossary.

LATTER-DAY SAINT DOCTRINE

The Latter-day Saint doctrine of heaven is established through key scriptures from the Bible, with additional detail found in modern-day scriptures. The biblical scriptures introduce and outline the existence of three levels of heaven, while the revelations given in the Doctrine and Covenants describe in detail the various glories in heaven that can be expected by those who will enter after the final judgment.

The Savior told his disciples, "In my Father's house are many mansions: if it were not so, I would have told you. I go to prepare a place for you" (John 14:2). This scripture is joined by two letters written by the Apostle Paul to the Corinthians. Paul wrote about a man who had been "caught up to the third heaven" (2 Corinthians 12:2), while mentioning and briefly describing two states in the resurrection—the celestial and the terrestrial—and alluding to a third (1 Corinthians 15:40–42).

Doctrine and Covenants sections 76 and 131 complete the missing parts of the scriptural puzzle by clearly describing three kingdoms of heaven following the final judgment, with the highest kingdom (celestial) having three degrees of glory within itself. There is also a fourth place called outer darkness, which is the eternal hell spoken of in an earlier section of this chapter.

Jesus spoke of "preparing" a place in the house of his father. This same type of preparation takes place for each of us on earth as we prepare ourselves for the kingdom into which we choose to enter. Our faith in Christ and works, exercised in the choices we have made on earth, will decide which kingdom (place or state) we are prepared to live in following the final judgment.

The Celestial Kingdom

The celestial kingdom is considered the highest of all of the levels of heaven (the third heaven that Paul spoke of). This is the kingdom Paul described as being the "glory of the sun" (1 Corinthians 15:41), in which Jesus Christ and our Heavenly Father will dwell. The happiness of those who will enter the celestial kingdom, and the beauty of the physical surroundings, will be far beyond our current ability to imagine.

Those who will enter the celestial kingdom are those who love and have chosen (and will continue to choose) to obey Jesus Christ and our Heavenly Father. These individuals have repented of their sins, committed their lives to Jesus Christ as their Savior, have entered the waters of baptism, have received the gift of the Holy Ghost, and have exercised faith sufficient to triumph over the world through the perfection of the Atonement of Jesus Christ.

The Lord has made a provision for other individuals to enter into the celestial kingdom as well. Those who die in mortality lacking a knowledge of the gospel but "would have received it with all their hearts" (D&C 137:7–9) are allowed entrance into the celestial kingdom, as are those children who "die before they arrive at the years of accountability [age eight]" (D&C 137:10)—including those who have been aborted.

Within the celestial kingdom is a place set aside for those who will be exalted—enabled to continue to grow their eternal families. To achieve this magnificent blessing, an individual must be married in the temple for time and all eternity and have made and kept sacred temple covenants. These individuals will become like Heavenly Father and receive all that he has, including the ability to have spirit children and to make new worlds; that is, they will inherit from Heavenly Father his creative ability. Jesus alluded to this great blessing in the parable of the talents when he said, "Well done, thou good and faithful servant; thou hast been faithful over a few things, I will make thee ruler over many things: enter thou into the joy of thy lord" (Matthew 25:23). The use of the word *ruler* is clearly intentional, signifying something greater than simply existing with God in heaven (although it is impossible to truly comprehend this in our mortal state).

Doctrine and Covenants 76:50–70 gives a detailed scriptural account of the celestial kingdom.

The Terrestrial Kingdom

The terrestrial kingdom is considered the second highest of the levels of heaven. This is the kingdom Paul described as being the "glory of the moon" (1 Corinthians 15:41), in which Jesus Christ will dwell on a frequent basis.

Those who will enter into the terrestrial kingdom are those who rejected the gospel of Jesus Christ on earth but received it in the spirit world. These are individuals who are honorable but were blinded by the craftiness of men, and thus, they were not valiant in their testimony of Jesus.

Those who dwell in the terrestrial kingdom will not have claim to their family in the eternities. Although not close to the happiness of those who will dwell in the celestial kingdom, our Father in Heaven will grant to these terrestrial bodies the happiness they will be ready and are prepared to receive.

Doctrine and Covenants 76:71–80 gives a detailed scriptural account of the terrestrial kingdom.

The Telestial Kingdom

The telestial kingdom is the lowest level of heaven. This is the kingdom Paul described as being the "glory of the stars" (1 Corinthians 15:41), in which the influence of the Holy Ghost will reside and angels will minister.

Those who will enter into the telestial kingdom are those who rejected the gospel and testimony of Jesus Christ on earth and in the spirit world. These individuals are described in the scriptures as liars, sorcerers, adulterers, whoremongers, and those who make and love lies. These individuals will be last to be resurrected after suffering for their earthly sins in the spirit world until the end of the millennium.

Those who dwell in the terrestrial kingdom will be without their family and will live on their own for all eternity. Although not close to the happiness of those who will dwell in the celestial or terrestrial kingdom, our Father in Heaven will grant to these terrestrial bodies the happiness they will be ready and are prepared to receive. Many will dwell in the telestial kingdom following the final judgment.

Doctrine and Covenants 76:81–89 gives a detailed scriptural account of the telestial kingdom.

Outer Darkness

Described in the proceeding section on hell, outer darkness is the eternal hell where the devil and those who follow him, including the sons of perdition, will be relegated to live for all eternity. Those who will dwell in outer darkness will have made their own choices to follow Satan and will not be forgiven. These people will suffer in darkness and sorrow forever.

Doctrine and Covenants 76:32–49 gives a detailed scriptural account of outer darkness.

The gospel of Jesus Christ imparts to all of God's children everything we need to know and understand to receive the blessings of the celestial kingdom. By learning and following the principles of the gospel, we can know our Heavenly Father, develop a personal relationship with our Savior Jesus Christ, and learn to live the life that God our father desires us to live—the life that will lead us back to him.

See "Chapter 35: Life after Death," *Gospel Fundamentals*, 195, and "Lesson 8: The Three Kingdoms of Glory," *Preparing for Exaltation: Teacher's Manual*, 38.

THOUGHTS AND COMMENTARY

One of the key stumbling blocks for Marilyn and me as we investigated

The Church of Jesus Christ of Latter-day Saints was the concept of there being three heavens and our becoming gods in the eternities. When we first heard this, we were shocked and unable to accept the doctrine. The main reason for our reluctance was having such an entrenched concept of heaven as being a single place where we lived with God. Our understanding as Catholics was simple and straightforward, while the Latter-day Saint doctrine seemed unnecessarily complicated, even fanciful.

To overcome this stumbling block, Marilyn and I had to engage ourselves in earnest biblical study, which continued for me long after our baptism given my interest in writing on the subject. The following is a rough outline of how we came to understand and accept the Latter-day Saint doctrine—a doctrine and way of life that we fully embrace today and about which we have a firm and unshakable testimony.

Varying Degrees of Reward for Varying Degrees of Righteousness

People live their lives on earth in varying degrees of righteousness. Some want to be close to God and his son Jesus Christ and work hard to achieve that. Others are lukewarm and do the minimum amount necessary to stay in touch with God. Others make terrible choices on earth (for various reasons) and live far away from God. With varying degrees of righteousness on earth, why would there not be varying degrees of glory and reward in the eternities?

Three Degrees of Glory

We reviewed the scriptures from John 14:2 (many mansions), 2 Corinthians 12:29 (a third heaven), and 1 Corinthians 15:40–42 (sun, moon, and stars, with the celestial and terrestrial being mentioned by name). There is a solid biblical foundation for their being three levels of heaven, or three degrees of glory in the eternities. This is further substantiated in Latter-day Saint scriptures in vivid and spectacular detail.

Becoming Gods

The concept of becoming gods (lowercase *g*) was strange to us, but even Catholic doctrine states, "Those who die in God's grace and friendship and are perfectly purified live for ever with Christ. They are like God for ever, for they 'see him as he is, face to face' (Catechism 1023). There are numerous scriptures from the Bible that substantiate exaltation (Luke 13:11; Galatians 4:7; Colossians 3; 2 Timothy 2–4; 2 Thessalonians 2:14;

Hebrews 6:1; James 1:4, 12; 1 Peter 5:4, 6; 2 Peter 2: 6, 9; 1 John 3:2; Romans 8:16–18; and Matthew 25). Although we had never thought of our reward in heaven as becoming gods, it was clear that exaltation—becoming a perfected resurrected being like God (or a god)—was part of God's plan and something well documented in the Bible.

Marriage as a Requirement

Marilyn didn't marry me until she was thirty-three years old. Until that time, she wasn't sure she would find anyone to marry and therefore contemplated a single life. When she heard the Latter-day Saint doctrine requiring entering into the everlasting covenant of marriage to gain entrance into the highest level of the celestial kingdom, she was not convinced. Marilyn understood the blessings of marriage but didn't feel a single life should be an inhibitor to anyone in the eternities. After several years of marriage and having children, both Marilyn and I have come to a deep realization of the value of the experiences of marriage and parenthood in the eternities. Given the nature of living in the highest level of the celestial kingdom, the experiences of marriage and parenthood are an absolute necessity.

We Choose the Heaven We Deserve (Even Desire)

At first glance one might conclude that there are a few winners (celestial kingdom dwellers) and a lot of losers (terrestrial and telestial kingdom dwellers). A natural thought is that many are going to be disappointed by not being in the terrestrial kingdom (if they are in the telestial kingdom) or by not being in the celestial kingdom (if they are in the terrestrial kingdom). However, at second glance this will surely not be the case. If someone didn't feel comfortable or able to live the laws of God on earth and do what it takes to be a righteous and loving individual in a life of service and sacrifice, why would they change in the eternities? An analogy would be taking someone who wants to work at McDonald's their whole life and trying to convince them to go to Harvard Medical School and work for Mayo Clinic instead. Most will simply not want to put the effort into changing their life to do that. Such will be the case in the eternities—God will put us into not only the kingdom we deserve, but it will be the kingdom in which we will feel most comfortable. That doesn't mean there won't be disappointment in not being in the presence of our Heavenly Father—there likely will be (see the explanation of the concept of damnation earlier in the chapter).

After extensive study and pondering Marilyn and I have come to enthusiastically embrace the Latter-day Saint doctrine of heaven, including all of its intricacies. We have come to understand that God's plan is simple and merciful, while satisfying the laws of justice in perfect harmony. We desire our entire family to be in the celestial kingdom together and will do all we can on earth, and beyond, to make that happen. Like the wedding vows we wrote that proclaimed we would be together forever long before we ever knew about the Church of Jesus Christ of Latter-day Saints, we came home to the doctrine that was not only scripturally sound, but that which was in our hearts.

There is a doctrine in The Church of Jesus Christ of Latter-day Saints called Lord's Plan for Happiness. This plan puts together all of the pieces of the plan we have discussed to this point. Once Marilyn and I saw the entire plan mapped out from our premortal life to entrance into the three kingdoms, the Holy Ghost bore witness to us that the plan was real and that we knew where we came from, where we wanted to go, and how to get there. Although I will not cover the plan in this book, the reader is encouraged to seek out that plan for further study and pondering—it is truly a remarkable culmination of many doctrines that cannot be overstated.

NOTES

1. "The Early Church Fathers and Other Works" originally published by Wm. B. Eerdmans Pub. Co. in English in Edinburgh, Scotland, beginning in 1867, (LNPF II/XII, Schaff and Wace).
2. Bruce R. McConkie, *Mormon Doctrine*, 631.
3. Richard Owen, "Pope to Demolish Limbo, Halfway House Between Heaven and Hell," *London Times,* 30 November 2005.
4. Michael Browning, "Catholic Church likely to abolish state of Limbo," (Cox News Service, 2 December, 2005).
5. *Gospel Doctrine*, 455.
6. Ibid., 292.
7. Brigham Young, *Journal of Discourses*, 22:333–34.
8. Heber C. Kimball, *Journal of Discourses*, 4:135–36.
9. Joseph F. Smith, *Teachings of the Prophet Joseph Smith* (Salt Lake City: Deseret Book, 1977), 326.
10. Ezra Taft Benson, "Life Is Eternal," *Ensign*, Jun. 1971, 32.
11. Widtsoe, John A. *Discourses of Brigham Young* (Salt Lake City: Deseret Book 1951), 367.

12. Daniel H. Ludlow, ed., *Latter-day Prophets Speak* (Salt Lake City: Book-craft, 1948), 261–62.
13. Joseph F. Smith, *Teachings of the Prophet,* 268.
14. *Journal of Discourses,* 115.
15. Joseph Fielding Smith, *Doctrines of Salvation,* 3:66–72.
16. Council of Lyons II: DS 854.
17. Dallin H. Oaks, "Resurrection," *Ensign,* May 2000, 14.
18. Bruce R. McConkie, *Mormon Doctrine,* 640.
19. Ibid., 748.
20. Val Hale, "I Have a Question," *Ensign,* Aug. 1991, 61.
21. Council of Lyons II [1274]: DS 859; cf. DS 1549.
22. Joseph Fielding Smith, *Doctrines of Salvation,* 2:200.
23. Daniel H. Ludlow, ed., *Latter-day Prophets Speak,* 56–57.
24. *Gospel Principles,* 297.
25. Ibid., 298.
26. Bruce R. McConkie, *Mormon Doctrine,* 746.
27. Joseph Fielding Smith, *Doctrines of Salvation,* 1:49.

15
Earthly and Eternal Families

THE family is the central unit in God's plan for his children on earth. In families, children are reared, principles of the gospel taught and learned, relationships formed, and linkages to generations created. A key and central doctrine of The Church of Jesus Christ of Latter-day Saints is the blessing that families can be together forever through the principles and ordinances of the gospel of Jesus Christ ministered through the holy priesthood in the temple.

Although we'll find the Catholic Church does not embrace the doctrines of the eternal family in the same way, there are meaningful parallels that will be explored to help the reader understand how Marilyn and I moved to the next level by embracing this wonderful principle of eternal families.

The Earthly Family

Each of us was born to a family here on earth. That family can take on a variety of forms from a single mother to something more elaborate and traditional. While earthly families come in all shapes and sizes, there is one common denominator: a mortal mother and father—it takes both to bring a child into the world.

This section will examine the ideal family as a model. We will examine doctrine relating to fathers, mothers, and children as the key components of a family, with the ideal scenario of a family having all three together. From this model, forms and methods can be adapted to less ideal circumstances.

CATHOLIC DOCTRINE

The family is at the core of social and spiritual life as the institution in which married couples are to offer themselves in love and the procreation of life. The family is the basic social unit in which children being reared can learn the values of morality, the fear and love of God, and the most appropriate use of agency.

The Catholic Church defines family in this way: "A man and a woman united in marriage, together with their children, form a family. This institution is prior to any recognition by public authority, which has an obligation to recognize it. It should be considered the normal reference point by which the different forms of family relationship are to be evaluated" (Catechism 2202).

More specifically, the Christian family is a spiritual union of parents and siblings in the likeness of the Trinity between the Father, Son, and Holy Spirit. The procreation and edification of children reflects the same love, devotion, and work of the Father toward us. Families are called to accept and worship Jesus Christ, to pray and read the scriptures daily, and to preach the gospel. The faith of children will be sown and grow within the homes of the faithful, dubbing the family home the "domestic church" where Christ, communion with God, the qualities of human life, and Christian love and kindness are taught and practiced. The importance of the family is so great that it prompts the Church to exclaim: "The well-being of the individual person and of human and Christian society is intimately linked with the healthy condition of that community produced by marriage and family."[1]

Responsibilities for the well-being of the family rest upon three key components that influence the health of the family: the parents, the children, and society.

Parents' Responsibilities

Parents are obliged to look upon their children as children of God, to teach them God's law, to encourage them to fulfill God's law, and esteem their children respectfully as human beings. Parents bear the primary responsibility for their children's education in all things, including the virtues, which are best facilitated in establishing a home where "tenderness, forgiveness, respect, fidelity, and disinterested service are the rule" (Catechism 2223). For parents to accomplish this they must educate themselves and practice self-denial, righteous judgment, and self-control, while teaching their children to cling or put spiritual matters above those which are material and prone to one's instincts.

A child's education in the gospel should begin as early as possible with the parents in the primary role of teacher, but also including other family members. Parents should instruct their children in prayer with a key purpose of identifying their profession and purpose as children of God. Such vocations should be respected and encouraged by parents while imparting an understanding that a Christian's primary vocation is to love and follow Jesus Christ. Parents must also help children avoid the debasing pressures that endanger our communities and families today.

Admitting their own imperfections and weaknesses before their children, parents have the solemn responsibility of being examples of Christianity to their children so that correction and guidance may be more effectively accepted and absorbed. The Catholic Church follows the admonition of Sirach who wrote: "He who loves his son chastises him often, that he may be his joy when he grows up. He who disciplines his son will benefit from him, and boast of him among his intimates" (Sirach 30:1–2). Some translations use the phrase, "He who loves his son will not spare the rod."

Children's Responsibilities

The fourth commandment admonishes children to "Honor your father and your mother, that you may have a long life in the land which the Lord, your God, is giving you" (Exodus 20:12). By developing a disposition of gratitude toward parents, children can develop "filial piety" (respect and love for one's parents), enabling them to progress in "wisdom and grace" (Catechism 2215). Sirach urges Children to "Remember, of these parents you were born; what can you give them for all they gave you?" (Sir 7:28). Parents are owed by their children obedience, appreciation, respect, and help—such actions bring about love and harmony in the home and among family.

Society's Responsibilities

The government of society is called upon to respect human rights and to facilitate the exercising of free will by individuals and families. The Catholic parish is at the core of the spiritual life of Christian families and a place of religious learning for families, in addition to being the Eucharistic community.

Strong families make for a strong community, and therefore, society bares a specific responsibility to sustain and fortify families, including marriages which are at the center of family living. The Church calls on civil authorities to take seriously its duty "to acknowledge the true nature of marriage and the family, to protect and foster them, to safeguard public morality, and promote domestic prosperity" (Catechism 2210).

The Church urges families to take responsibility for all of its members: young and old, sick and healthy, rich and poor, and the able and disabled. James stated this commission best when he wrote: "Religion that is pure and undefiled before God and the Father is this: to visit orphans and widows in their affliction and to keep oneself unstained from the world" (James 1:27).

On November 22, 1981, Pope John Paul II published *The Apostolic Exhortation Familiaris Consortio (The Christian Family in the Modern World)*. The document addresses in-depth the issues most affecting families today, including spiritual, physical and social aspects of life. The document is 34,138 words, constituting approximately 64 pages (12 point Times Roman font and 1" margins).

See Catechism 1666, 2202, 2205, 2207, 2208, 2210, 2215, 2222 to 2224, 2226, 2248, 2250, 2251, 2253, 2254, and 2685.

LATTER-DAY SAINT DOCTRINE

The Lord has commanded all of his children to "Organize yourselves; prepare every needful thing; and establish a house, even a house of prayer, a house of fasting, a house of faith, a house of learning, a house of glory, a house of order, a house of God" (D&C 88:119).

The family is the most important entity in the Church of Jesus Christ and one that can last forever in the eternities. The main purpose of the Church is to assist families in achieving this goal, to obtain eternal blessings, and to enter into exaltation. The Church as its organization, leadership, programs, and activities are intended to strengthen families and their members and support this purpose and mission for all families on earth.

Since the time of Adam and Eve, where the commandment was given to "be fruitful, and multiply, and replenish the earth" (Genesis 1:28), Heavenly Father has willed that married parents provide tabernacles of flesh for his spirit children. Once in the world, God's children are then to be raised by parents in a family in collaboration with Heavenly Father in order to bring to pass his purposes and plan.

To reach its full potential in the Lord, a family operates with each member carrying out a set of temporal and spiritual responsibilities. These responsibilities include those given to a father and mother individually, parents together, and children.

A father should fully assume his patriarchal role as the head of the family by exercising his priesthood and taking serious all of the responsibilities associated with these callings with "long-suffering, by gentleness and meekness, and by love unfeigned" (D&C 121:41). Fathers are to lead by example. Fathers lead the family in prayer, scripture reading, attending church meetings, and other activities as prescribed by the Church. It is the father's responsibility to support the family in all of their temporal needs. This is often accomplished by the father as being the primary provider of the home, or at least being a steady and strong contributor of income in conjunction with the mother or others under certain circumstances.

A mother will not only bring children into the world physically in partnership with God, but is called to teach and care for children in a special and specific role separate from that of the father. President David O. McKay taught:

> The noblest calling in the world is motherhood. True motherhood is the most beautiful of all arts, the greatest of all professions. She who can paint a masterpiece, or who can write a book that will influence millions, deserves the admiration and plaudits of mankind; but she who rears successfully a family of healthy, beautiful sons and daughters, whose immortal souls will exert an influence throughout the ages long after paintings shall have faded, and books and statues shall have decayed or have been destroyed, deserves the highest honor that man can give, and the choicest blessings of God.[2]

Mothers teach the gospel to children through work and play, helping children comprehend life and the world they live in. Mothers are the primary homemakers in creating a loving and nurturing environment within the home, while helping children build strong and appropriate feelings of self-esteem.

As parents, both fathers and mothers can do many things within the family together as "equal partners . . . to provide for the spiritual, emotional, intellectual, and physical needs of the family."[3] Parents lead and teach their children by example starting with love, thoughtfulness, and kindness toward each other to demonstrate the joys of marriage. Parents together are given serious charge to teach their children the gospel—failing to do so will bring grave consequences upon the heads of the parents (D&C 68:25). Parents are to teach siblings to love one another and to abstain from arguing and quarrelling and to "teach them to walk in the ways of truth and soberness . . . to love one another, and to serve one another" (Mosiah 4:14–15). Parents should be kind, loving, and respectful of children, but with a spirit of firmness and diligent resolve.

A child should share the vision and responsibility of their parents to create a healthy and joyful home. Children should obey all of the commandments of God and contribute to the harmony in a home through cooperation, love, and work. An important commandment for children of all ages is to "Honor thy father and thy mother" (Exodus 20:12). To honor means to love, respect, and obey. Paul told the Ephesians, "Obey your parents in the Lord: for this is right" (Ephesians 6:1).

The family is under constant attack. Satan is well aware of the importance of families and the impact they can have on thwarting his plan of evil. Satan desires to destroy families through a variety of means that include temptation, contention, and pride. To remain strong the General Authorities of the Church urge families to pray together daily, have family scripture study daily, hold weekly family home evenings, serve one another, and spend time together in wholesome activities that bring family members together.

On September 23, 1995, the First Presidency and the Quorum of the Twelve Apostles of The Church of Jesus Christ of Latter-day Saints published *The Family, A Proclamation to the World*. The document is 634 words, constituting 1.25 pages (12 point Times Roman font and 1" margins), with the Church distributed version being 1 page long.

See *Gospel Principles*, 231, 232, 234, 236–239, Conference Report, Apr. 1976, 5; or *Ensign*, May 1976, 5, and *The Family: A Proclamation to the World*.

THOUGHTS AND COMMENTARY

As Catholics, even with Marilyn in a leadership position at the diocesan level, we were never made aware of any official Catholic doctrines on the family, including the *Familiaris Consortio*. In researching this book, I was amazed at the depth of family-related doctrine from the Catechism and the spectacular content in the *Consortio*. I feel somewhat cheated that we never knew about this document as Catholics. Even so, the Catholic Church is generally family oriented; however, we personally did not experience an emphasis on the family to the degree outlined in Catholic doctrine, and certainly not to the extent we found in The Church of Jesus Christ of Latter-day Saints.

The Catholic doctrine on the family may be the Church's best kept secret. Catholics could benefit from study and rigorous application of this doctrine. However, the Catholic doctrine on the family can only make a difference in the lives of its members if the Church itself focuses on the doctrine so as to put it into daily practice. For instance, a document on the family that is sixty-four pages long (*Familiaris Consortio*) is not practical for daily reading or even occasional reference. It cannot be displayed on a wall as a reminder. It cannot, for all practical purposes, be used.

Conversely, "The Family: A Proclamation to the World" is printed on a single page and distributed throughout the Church. It is framed and displayed in nearly every Latter-day Saint home worldwide; often in more than one room (our family has it in three rooms). It states clearly and concisely the Church's doctrine on the family. It serves the Church globally, as the principles stated within it are universal.

One page for the Latter-day Saint plan for the family, and sixty-four pages for the Catholic plan. In so many ways and on so many topics this kind of difference appears between the two churches. Simplicity, plainness, and concise statements on one hand; complexity, inaccessibility, and weighty scholarship on the other. For Marilyn and me, this difference was a compelling one and felt so much like the Restoration that we were being taught from the very first day of our investigation. We needed tools we could use and, perhaps more important, tools that were *in use* by those around us. We found such tools in The Church of Jesus Christ of Latter-day Saints.

Supporting the Family Proclamation is the family home evening program, instituted in 1915 where families were asked to designate one night a week for teaching and sharing time as family. In 1970 Joseph F. Smith designed Monday night as the official night for Family Home Evening. Oddly enough it was the same year when ABC began airing regular Monday Night Football telecasts (Satan has his ways!).

Church leaders constantly exhort families to pray and read the scriptures together daily. There are scores of songs that have been written by the Church to reinforce the family theme, and they are sung frequently in church meetings and at church-related activities. The focus on family is not just words; it is a continuous campaign.

This kind of practical application of doctrine greatly impressed Marilyn and me during our investigation, rejuvenating the focus on our own family and the families of those around us. While we knew as Catholics that family should be important, there was no sustainable campaign to make that happen at the local level. Therefore, we naturally found that next level for strengthening our family in The Church of Jesus Christ of Latter-day Saints and went in that direction.

Temples

The word *temple* conjures up a variety of images and definitions across different cultures and religions around the world. Temples are typically defined as edifices or places which are dedicated to the service or worship of a deity or deities. Temples have existed since the earliest days of man—including the periods before, during, and after Christ—and are generally regarded as holy places by those who build or maintain them.

Temples are central to The Church of Jesus Christ of Latter-day Saints for a number of reasons, mainly revolving around the eternal nature of families. This section will consider the views of both churches and how temples came to be a key component in our conversion.

CATHOLIC DOCTRINE

The Catholic Church has parish, diocese, seminary, convent, administrative, and other building sites worldwide, none of which are considered temples. Temples are considered a place where the people of God in earlier times went to be educated, pray, offer sacrifices, and participate in ordinances and rituals that magnified worship of God. There have been abuses and excesses associated with temples, both ancient and modern. Ritual in some cases became an obsession. The attitude of Jesus toward the Jewish temple and its spiritual evolution is encapsulated in the following passage: "Jesus venerated the Temple by going up to it for the Jewish feasts of pilgrimage, and with a jealous love he loved this dwelling of God among men. The Temple prefigures his own mystery. When he announces its destruction, it is as a manifestation of his own execution and of the entry into a new age in the history of salvation, when his Body would be the definitive Temple" (Catechism 593).

Worship of God is not linked to any one particular place, and thus there is no need for a temple, as there was in times of old. Today the

Church is the temple of the Holy Spirit, and the Holy Spirit is "the temple of the living God" (2 Corinthians 6:16 and Ephesians 2:21). This cascades down to each individual being a temple of the Holy Spirit on which the Church is built. In this way the temple is not a place, but rather a symbolic corridor which the Holy Spirit occupies in the lives of the Church and its members.

See Catechism 593, 797, 809, 1179, 1197, 2581, and glossary.

Latter-day Saint Doctrine

The Church of Jesus Christ of Latter-day Saints defines temples as the following:

> In the temples, members of the Church who make themselves eligible can participate in the most exalted of the redeeming ordinances that have been revealed to mankind. There, in a sacred ceremony, an individual may be washed and anointed and instructed and endowed and sealed. And when we have received these blessings for ourselves, we may officiate for those who have died without having had the same opportunity. In the temples sacred ordinances are performed for the living and for the dead alike.[4]

As houses of the Lord, temples are places for learning and participating in the sacred ordinances that will allow us to return and live with our Heavenly Father in the eternities. All that the Church does points to the hallowed ordinances that are performed in the holy temples of the world.

Because of the sacredness of the temple, it is required that all individuals be found worthy before entering—adults and youth. For adults, worthiness is determined through two brief interviews: one with a member of the individual's bishopric or branch president, and a second with a member of the individual's stake presidency or a mission president. These interviews are not interrogations. Members are asked simple questions about basic moral conduct, obedience to the commandments, and adherence to their covenants. If there are no major transgressions, a temple recommend is granted. A temple recommend, which is based upon personal worthiness, lasts two years for adults and one year for youth and is required to enter the temple.

For youth ages twelve to eighteen or adult new members of less than one year, a temporary recommend may be granted to participate in baptismal and confirmation ordinances. The questions asked are similar to those asked for a two-year recommend.

The sacred nature of the ordinances performed in the temple makes it inappropriate for members to discuss the details of these ordinances outside the temple. This is true also of personal experiences had in the temple that relate to ordinances themselves.

The temple is respite from the world. It is the experience of Walden Pond without Thoreau's account of it. The temple is, if nothing else, a wondrous experience—all the more wondrous because it must be earned through personal worthiness through our faith in Jesus Christ.

Regarding the ordinances and this principle of sacredness, Church members are provided the following counsel: "They are kept confidential lest they be given to those who are unprepared. Curiosity is not a preparation. Deep interest itself is not a preparation. Preparation for the ordinances includes preliminary steps: faith, repentance, baptism, confirmation, worthiness, a maturity and dignity worthy of one who comes invited as a guest into the house of the Lord."[5]

The ordinances performed in the temple include baptisms, confirmations, initiatories, priesthood ordinations, endowments, and sealings. While baptisms and confirmations are always done for those who have passed on, initiatories, ordinations, endowments, and sealings can be done for the living and the dead.

Temple baptisms and confirmations are performed for ancestors of Church members who while on the earth were either not baptized at all, or who were not baptized by the proper authority. Jesus taught that baptism was essential for an individual to enter into the kingdom of God (John 3:5). While this principle remains in force, God in his infinite mercy has prepared a way for those who have died without being baptized to be baptized and confirmed by proxy in the temple. Church members can go to the temple and "stand in" for those who are deceased and be baptized and confirmed—thus offering them this ordinance and blessing. Because agency is an eternal principle, the deceased are completely free in the spirit world to accept or reject a baptism and confirmation that was performed on their behalf.

The initiatory is an ordinance that can be likened to a washing and anointing. This ordinance is done in preparation for the endowment and includes the bestowing of the Melchizedek Priesthood for male recipients. After completing an initiatory for oneself, an individual can complete by proxy initiatories for those who are deceased.

The endowment is an ordinance which enriches the recipient as the name would suggest—something of great worth being bestowed. Brigham Young described the endowment in this way: "Your endowment is, to receive all those ordinances in the House of the Lord, which are necessary for you, after you have departed this life, to enable you to walk back to the presence of the Father, passing the angels who stand as sentinels, being able to give them the key words, the signs and tokens, pertaining to the holy Priesthood, and gain your eternal exaltation in spite of earth and hell."[6]

Regarding the covenants that are made by those receiving their endowment (living or deceased), Elder James E. Talmage wrote that individuals covenant to

> . . . observe the law of strict virtue and chastity, to be charitable, benevolent, tolerant and pure; to devote both talent and material means to the spread of truth and the uplifting of the race; to maintain devotion to the cause of truth; and to seek in every way to contribute to the great preparation that the earth may be made ready to receive her King—the Lord Jesus Christ. With the taking of each covenant and the assuming of each obligation a promised blessing is pronounced, contingent upon the faithful observance of the conditions.[7]

Endowed members are given the blessing of wearing the temple garment (underclothing) for the remainder of their lives (provided they retain their membership). The garment, which is worn according to specific instructions, provides a constant reminder of the covenants made in the temple, gives protection against the adversary, and serves as an outward expression of a member's inward commitment to follow Jesus Christ.

The crowning ordinance of the temple is celestial marriage, where a husband and wife make sacred covenants and are sealed together for time and all eternity. In cases where a husband and wife have children (alive or deceased), those children are also sealed to the parents. Where additional children are born after the sealing, those children are automatically sealed to the parents as being "born under the covenant." It is through this sealing ordinance that families can be together forever.

The temple is rich with symbolism of the gospel of Jesus Christ. It is a place where we will make the most sacred covenants of our eternal lives. We are urged to keep and obey every covenant that we make in the holy temple so that the blessings upon us "shall be of full force when they are out of the world; and they shall pass by the angels, and the gods, which are set there, to their exaltation and glory in all things, as hath been sealed upon their heads, which glory shall be a fulness and a continuation of the seeds forever and ever" (D&C 132:19).

While the temple is a place that allows us to participate in sacred priesthood ordinances, it is also a place of prayer, peace, and revelation. In the temple we can receive inspiration and guidance on matters that we take before the Lord. Adding to the peace and tranquility of the temple are the many individuals around us who are dressed in white to symbolize the purity and consecrated nature of heaven—especially in the Celestial Room of each temple.

See *Gospel Principles*, 245; and James E. Talmage, *The House of the Lord*.

Thoughts and Commentary

In our conversion story, I write of a trip to California that Marilyn and I made with our infant son Jason where we visited the Oakland Temple. I spoke of the peace, tranquility, and love we felt on the temple grounds, as well as from those whom we met at the visitors' center.

After being baptized Latter-day Saints, and before going to the temple, we studied more about why a temple is necessary to our spiritual lives. Up until that time, our understanding was more aligned along the lines of Catholic doctrine of there no longer being a need for temples. During our study of the temple we came across the following scripture from Isaiah 2:2–3: "And it shall come to pass in the last days, that the mountain of the Lord's house shall be established in the top of the mountains, and shall be exalted above the hills; and all nations shall flow unto it. And many people shall go and say, Come ye, and let us ago up to the mountain of the Lord, to the house of the God of Jacob; and he will teach us of his ways, and we will walk in his paths: for out of Zion shall go forth the law and the word of the Lord from Jerusalem."

This scripture is surprisingly clear that in the last days the Lord's house would be established and all nations would flow to it to be taught the ways of the Lord. In direct fulfillment of this scripture, in 2007 there were nearly 140 temples operating throughout the world, with additional temples being planned. Millions of people are coming to these temples on a regular basis to be taught and to participate in sacred ordinances.

The above scripture from Isaiah is repeated nearly verbatim in Micah

4:1. Micah was a prophet in and around the time of Isaiah. Rarely do scriptures from the Bible repeat themselves in such exact ways, giving further importance to the passage. We found other references in the New and Old Testaments regarding the temple that helped convince us of the scriptural foundation on which the doctrine of the temple stood—including the fact that Jesus Christ recognized the temple and did not make mention that they would go away forever. When studying modern-day scriptures the necessity for the temple became extremely clear.

We were quite overwhelmed when we first went to the temple to receive our own endowments and to be sealed. We were reminded of the scripture from Isaiah 55:8: "For my thoughts are not your thoughts, neither are your ways my ways, saith the Lord." Nowhere in the Latter-day Saint faith can one find more symbolism than is exhibited in the temple. As Catholics we were accustomed to symbolism and therefore were comfortable with the symbolism of the temple; however, what we learned in the temple went far beyond what we expected. We came to fully understand why we are counseled not to discuss what happens in the temple outside of the temple with others—even with other members. Paul put it perfectly when he counseled the disciples of Christ to seek milk before meat (Hebrews 5:12–14), or when Christ told Nicodemus that he cannot understand heavenly things until he understands earthly things (John 3:12).

The wearing of the temple garment was something that gave us a little concern, at first. However, after only a short while we developed a strong testimony of why the garment is such a powerful component in the gospel of Jesus Christ. One can find numerous references to the armor of God and the outward and inward signs of faith to give scriptural context to the temple garment. When we heard it called the garment of the holy priesthood (its proper name), we later thought of the vestments of a Catholic priest and how such vestments are worn as an outward and inward sign of faith, or the roman collar that symbolizes the covenants priests make. In the same tradition, as a Melchizedek priesthood holder, it made sense that I would wear such a garment and Marilyn, like other women who share in the spiritual blessings of the priesthood of their husbands, would wear a similar garment.

Beyond the spiritual nature and symbolism of the temple garment, Marilyn and I found wearing the garment brought unexpected blessings to our marriage in terms of modesty and the sacredness of our union. This is difficult to explain, but simple in application. It didn't take long for us to comprehend the significant value the garment of the holy priesthood would have in our lives. It was another simple, plain, and practical tool for becoming stronger in our faith and more diligent in the keeping of our covenants. We are physical beings influenced by physical things. The influence of the garment, the quiet and comfortable reminder that it is—this we cherish deeply.

Almost nineteen years of temple attendance and service, we continue to grasp the spiritual significance of the temple. However, the most important aspects of the temple are the ordinances that happen within. We don't believe in the temple just because of what we have read or experienced, we believe in the temple because we believe in the ordinances that seal families together for time and all eternity and make it possible for those who have passed on before us to have the essential ordinances they need in the eternities. Without the temple we know that these ordinances are not possible, and that the Lord has provided a way for us to have these blessings by coming to the house of the Lord, learning of his ways, and partaking of his goodness.

Marilyn and I have been to many temples throughout the world, and each time our feelings and experiences have been very much the same in revealing to us the ways of the Lord in these sacred ordinances. The temple is the "House of the Lord." The Lord's presence is truly felt by those who attend. It is a place where Marilyn and I, together and separately, have received significant counsel from the Lord. We're thankful for the restoration of temples in these latter days where we can go to receive these sacred blessings.

Eternal Families

The section on earthly families dealt with the family that we have here on earth during our time in mortality. But what will happen after the Second Coming of Jesus Christ and the final judgment? Will we still be a part of a family in the eternities?

As seen in the previous section, a central doctrine in The Church of Jesus Christ of Latter-day Saints is the principle that families can be together forever. Although not as explicit, the doctrine of eternal families from a Catholic doctrinal perspective may surprise you. This section tackles these questions about eternal families and compares the answers from a Catholic and Latter-day Saint doctrinal point of view, while sharing our own thoughts and insights on this exceptionally important subject.

CATHOLIC DOCTRINE

There is no Catholic doctrine on the sealing of families for time and all eternity; however, the Catechism of the Catholic Church includes the following statement on the possibility of a "reunion" in the afterlife:

> A farewell to the deceased is his final "commendation to God" by the Church. It is "the last farewell by which the Christian community greets one of its members before his body is brought to its tomb." The Byzantine tradition expresses this by the kiss of farewell to the deceased: By this final greeting "we sing for his departure from this life and separation from us, but also because there is a communion and a reunion. For even dead, we are not at all separated from one another, because we all run the same course and we will find one another again in the same place. We shall never be separated, for we live for Christ, and now we are united with Christ as we go toward him . . . we shall all be together in Christ" (Catechism 1690).

Although this statement is not explicit in any way about the heavenly gathering of families in the eternities, it does imply that some kind of gathering of loved ones does take place, laying the foundation of hope for the faithful.

LATTER-DAY SAINT DOCTRINE

By the authority of the Melchizedek Priesthood, which has the power in the holy temple to bind on earth and in heaven (Matthew 16:19), families can be sealed together for time and all eternity. Death cannot separate those who remain faithful to the covenants they make in the temple. Mothers, fathers, children, and ancestors will be together forever in the eternities in the holy mansions of God the Father.

THOUGHTS AND COMMENTARY

As Catholics we often imagined going to heaven and seeing loved ones who had passed away, even becoming familiar with ancestors we never knew. Certainly Catholic doctrine provides an avenue, although ambiguous, by which such reunions can take place in the afterlife. Marilyn and I placed our own hopes on this possibility as we strongly desired to be together in the eternities, going as far as to write into our marriage vows in the Catholic Church that we would be together forever.

When we learned during our investigation that families can be sealed for time and all eternity through the authority of the priesthood, we wanted to have such a blessing. The opportunity to be together forever went from being a vague possibility in the Catholic Church, to a covenant that could be made that would guarantee such a reunion after death in The Church of Jesus Christ of Latter-day Saints. We wanted our family to be together forever and therefore desired to do all we could to make this happen. It became abundantly clear that to be together forever we would need to embrace the restored gospel of Jesus Christ, become members of The Church of Jesus Christ of Latter-day Saints, enter into the covenant of eternal marriage, and partake of the sealing powers of the priesthood in the holy temple.

For Marilyn and me, it simply made all of the difference in the world to have this blessing in the lives of our family. It is the fulfillment of our most intimate spiritual desires, long before we ever found The Church of Jesus Christ of Latter-day Saints.

Redeeming the Dead

Before the resurrection and final judgment, is there an opportunity for individuals who have died to be redeemed or to improve their eternal opportunities? In an earlier chapter, we discussed the post-mortal states of purgatory (Catholic), and the spirit world (Latter-day Saint). But what can be done for these individuals once they are in a post-mortal condition? And who can do it?

In this chapter, where we are discussing earthly and eternal families, the subject of redeeming the dead is an important and critical one. Each of us has scores of ancestors who have died hundreds, even thousands of years before us and exist in a post-mortal state awaiting the resurrection and final judgment. One of those individuals is my brother Robert who tragically took his own life several years ago.

This section will examine the doctrines of both churches pertaining to redeeming the dead in order to understand how those in the afterlife will fair and what those on earth can do to help their cause.

Catholic Doctrine

As part of the final phase of the mission of Jesus Christ on earth, he descended into hell, so "the gospel was preached even to the dead" (1 Peter 4:6). In doing so the message of redemption was shared with all men, regardless of their time and place on earth before their death, making available salvation to all. This great act of love was described by the apostle John as "the dead will hear the voice of the Son of God, and those who hear will live" (John 5:25).

The Catholic Church today honors the memory of the dead in purgatory and offers prayers on their behalf. These prayers have the power to help those beyond the grave in "loos[ing them] from their sins," while "making their intercession for us effective" (Catechism 958). This practice of praying and making atonement for the dead is mentioned in the second book of Maccabees. These prayers and suffrage, along with the Eucharistic sacrifice, almsgiving, indulgences, and works of penance are offered so that the dead may be purified and led to the opportunity to realize the beatific vision of God.

Ultimately the dead are in the hands of God to render mercy as he sees fit to bestow. The prayers and offerings of the faithful on behalf of the dead are given to seek God's mercy for the souls in purgatory.

The Catholic Church rejects all forms of "divination" with respect to the dead, including appeals to Satan, illusions of bringing back the dead, and fortune telling. Such admonition to turn away from that which disrespects the power and love of God extends to astrology, palm reading, horoscopes, and so forth.

Consulting horoscopes, astrology, palm reading, interpretation of omens and lots, the phenomena of clairvoyance, and recourse to mediums all conceal a desire for power over time, history, and, in the last analysis, other human beings, as well as a wish to conciliate hidden powers. They each contradict the honor, respect, and loving fear that we owe to God alone.

See Catechism 634, 958, 962, 1032, 1055, 1498, and 2116.

LATTER-DAY SAINT DOCTRINE

The scriptures make clear that Christ himself visited the spirit world and commenced the preaching of the gospel to the dead. John 5:25 states, "Verily, verily, I say unto you, The hour is coming, and now is, when the dead shall hear the voice of the Son of God: and they that hear shall live." 1 Peter 3:18–9 states, "For Christ also hath once suffered for sins, the just for the unjust, that he might bring us to God, being put to death in the flesh, but quickened by the Spirit: By which also he went and preached unto the spirits in prison." Doctrine and Covenants 138 records a vision given to President Joseph F. Smith on the preaching of the gospel to those in the spirit world. In that vision President Smith saw Jesus Christ "went not in person among the wicked and the disobedient who had rejected the truth to teach them" (D&C 138:29), but rather he chose spirits "from among the righteous" and thus "organized his forces and appointed messengers, clothed with power and authority, and commissioned them to go forth and carry the light of the gospel to them that were in darkness" (D&C 138:30).

The vision goes on to describe the work being done in the spirit world: These spirits "were taught faith in God, repentance from sin, vicarious baptism for the remission of sins, [and] the gift of the Holy Ghost by the laying on of hands" (D&C 138:33).

This great work of preaching the gospel in the spirit world, more specifically to those in spirit prison, is on-going and will continue until the Second Resurrection. These efforts are essential and demonstrate the great mercy of our Heavenly Father in not wanting to lose one soul in the eternities. Just as many of the righteous spirits are given the opportunity to preach the gospel in the spirit world, we are given the opportunity to take part in the work of redeeming the dead through vicarious ordinances performed on earth in the holy temple. This principle of vicarious work for the dead was given to the Prophet Joseph Smith by the Lord through revelation.

Although the concept of vicarious work may seem foreign to some Christians, President Gordon B. Hinckley offers the following: "I think that vicarious work for the dead more nearly approaches the vicarious sacrifice of the Savior Himself than any other work of which I know. It is given with love, without hope of compensation, or repayment or anything of the kind. What a glorious principle."[8]

When work is performed for the dead there isn't an automatic change, nor does such work usurp one's agency. These ordinances are performed and available for acceptance by the spirits in prison for their benefit in the same way that the Atonement of Christ is available to everyone who chooses to have faith in him and repent. Nothing is compelled. At every stage of this life and after it, one is free to choose.

The motivation behind this vicarious work in the temple is a combination of love of the individuals for whom the work is being performed and a firm and relentless testimony of the Savior. D. Todd Christofferson of the Presidency of the Seventy explains the nature of this testimony of Christ in relation to temple work:

Our anxiety to redeem the dead, and the time and resources we put behind that commitment, are, above all, an expression of our witness concerning Jesus Christ. It constitutes as powerful a statement as we can make concerning His divine character and mission. It testifies, first, of Christ's Resurrection; second, of the infinite reach of His Atonement; third, that He is the sole source of salvation; fourth, that He has established the conditions for salvation; and, fifth, that He will come again.[9]

Latter-day Saints are encouraged to be diligent about completing family history to identify ancestors who are in need of temple ordinances for their eternal progression. In performing these labors of love, the latter generations are turning their hearts towards the earlier generations, fulfilling the prophecy from the Lord: "Behold, I will send you Elijah the prophet before the coming of the great and dreadful day of the Lord: And he shall turn the heart of the fathers to the children, and the heart of the children to their fathers, lest I come and smite the earth with a curse" (Malachi 4:5–6).

Latter-day Saints are encouraged to frequently attend the temple to perform the needed ordinances for their ancestors and others—an act of on-going service that brings love and inspiration into both the living and the dead. Each ordinance is done in the spirit and name of Jesus Christ who said, "I am the resurrection, and the life: he that believeth in me, though he were dead, yet shall he live" (John 11:25). There is a deep belief that Christ "died for all" (2 Corinthians 5:15) and that "He is the propitiation for our sins: and not for ours only, but also for the sins of the whole world" (1 John 2:2).

The work of redeeming the dead, a work commenced by the Savior himself, is a devoted demonstration of the Latter-day Saint passion and belief that Christ will come again in his glory and majesty upon the earth. This work is in preparation of the Second Coming for both ourselves, and those who have passed on before us. The Church knows with a surety that "His grace and promises reach even those who in life do not find Him. Because of Him, the prisoners shall indeed go free."[10]

See D&C 124, 128, 132; *The Personal Writings of Joseph Smith*, ed. Dean C. Jessee (1984), 486; *The Words of Joseph Smith*, ed. Andrew F. Ehat and Lyndon W. Cook (1991), 49; Ben Fenton, "Mormons Use Secret British War Files 'to Save Souls," *The Telegraph* (London), 15 Feb. 1999; Greg Stott, "Ancestral Passion," *Equinox*, April/May 1998, 45.

THOUGHTS AND COMMENTARY

Each Sunday during Mass, Catholics pray for the dead as part of the liturgical celebration. I distinctly remember on many occasions praying for my deceased relatives by name, as well as selected friends who crossed my memory during the moment. I regularly prayed for these individuals because I knew they were alive in the afterlife and likely being purified in purgatory.

As we investigated The Church of Jesus Christ of Latter-day Saints, we realized that the Church took this concept of praying for the dead to an entirely new level through temple ordinances. We were astounded at the faith rendered by Latter-day Saints on behalf of those who were caught up in the spirit world.

At first glance this concept of actively doing service in the temple for the dead was foreign to us. Praying for the dead was one thing, but being vicariously baptized and confirmed for the dead was an entirely different matter altogether. However, when we took the time to ponder and reflect on it, we realized that if we were willing to pray for the dead as Catholics every Sunday, why wouldn't we be willing to do more if more could be done to help these loved ones?

We thought if God would allow us to pray for those who were dead, wouldn't he allow us to intercede more fully by doing work on their behalf as proxies, much like what Christ had done for us? We studied, prayed, and received a confirmations about such scriptures as Obadiah 21 in the Old Testament which states, "saviours shall come up on mount Zion," and Hebrews 11:40 which states, "God having provided some better thing for us, that they without us should not be made perfect."

We then enlarged our own vision of this concept by understanding that many would leave this life without having been baptized at all—many through no choice of their own. In the Catholic Church, we knew that those who had not been baptized where left in an unpredictable state before the resurrection. We came to realize that such doctrine was not consistent with the justice and mercy of God. If someone died without knowledge of the gospel, or the opportunity to be baptized, would God leave their salvation up in the air?

Since Marilyn and I felt the answer to this question was a resounding *no*, we then had to reconcile the following scripture, "Except a man be born of water and of the Spirit, he cannot enter into the kingdom of God" (John 3:5). If someone dies and no longer has a body, how could they be baptized? If they can't be baptized, they cannot enter into the kingdom of God. Applying the Catholic doctrine to this scripture would lead one to believe that those not baptized will not enter into the kingdom of God, because Catholicism does not provide a way for baptism after death.

We then made across the scripture from 1 Corinthians 15:29 which reads, "Else what shall they do which are baptized for the dead, if the dead rise not at all? why are they then baptized for the dead?" This scripture stopped us clean in our tracks!

Were there baptisms for the dead performed during the time of Paul? We had no way of knowing, but the scripture left open that possibility. Perhaps baptism for the dead was yet another restored truth in the Latter-day Saint doctrinal system.

We came across the scripture from 1 Timothy 2:5 which reads, "There is one God, and one mediator between God and men, the man Christ Jesus." Jesus Christ is the great mediator between God and men; therefore, the gospel of Jesus Christ can provide a way for those who have left the earth without an opportunity to participate in the required ordinances to have them done by proxy—just as Jesus did for us.

Marilyn and I have been participating in ordinances for the dead in the temple for many years now and have come to understand the significance and sanctity of these ordinances. We have built enduring testimonies on the redemption of the dead through Jesus Christ. We have found it wonderful not just to pray for those who have died, but to actively join in the work started by the Savior and to participate in helping them enter the kingdom of God, if that is their choice. There are few doctrines that exemplify more than this one the love, mercy, and justice of God.

NOTES

1. *Gaudium Et Spes* 47 § 1, Promulgated by Pope Paul VI, December 7, 1965.
2. *Pathways to Happiness*, comp. Llewelyn R. McKay (1957), 116.
3. *Gospel Principles*, 236.
4. "Preparing to Enter the Holy Temple," *Preparing to Enter the Holy Temple*, 1, www.LDS.org, accessed 27 Oct. 2007.
5. Ibid.
6. *Discourses of Brigham Young*, comp. John A. Widtsoe (Salt Lake City: Deseret Book, 1971, 416.
7. James E. Talmage, *The House of the Lord* (Salt Lake City: Bookcraft, 1962).

8. Gordon B. Hinckley, "Excerpts from Recent Addresses of President Gordon B. Hinckley," *Ensign*, Jan. 1998, 72.

9. D. Todd Christofferson "The Redemption of the Dead and the Testimony of Jesus," *Liahona,*, Jan. 2001, 10–13.

10. Ibid.

16

By Their Fruits Ye Shall Know Them

DURING his public ministry, Jesus taught many things that angered Jewish leaders. New ideas, new doctrines, and a new way of thinking challenged the Pharisees and others. They were required to consider their beliefs in ways that were uncomfortable. Jesus knew this process and challenge would continue long after his Ascension. To make sure all of God's children would now the truth, he gave some very simple counsel: "Wherefore by their fruits ye shall know them." (Matthew 7:20).

Because it's much harder to "walk the walk" than to "talk the talk," Jesus Christ offers this counsel to look at the fruits of the individual to really know them—whether they be prophets or individuals. The works and life examples of a person are likened to grapes (fruit) that grows naturally from the grape vine. Look to the fruit He warns, to know the *source* of that fruit.

Christ's counsel is useful in considering a church, including the doctrines and people that make up that church. What are the fruits of that church and its people? If the works and examples of Christian people in a particular church are positive, then, preliminarily at least, the Christian church itself can be considered positive.

This chapter compares the fruits of both the Catholic Church and those of The Church of Jesus Christ of Latter-day Saints to better understand how each church is doing in leading God's children on earth. What kind of a tree has each church built? If "by their fruits ye shall know them," then such a comparison can perhaps reveal, or at least suggest, the effectiveness of doctrines, practices, principles, culture, and leadership of each church.

Identifying fruits for comparison is challenging. Any comparison needs to be as much "apples-to-apples" as possible, using meaningful spiritual metrics—if one can conceive of such a thing. Complicating this search is the fact that faith and religion are spiritually qualitative in their essence, thus applying quantitative measures must be done so with great care.

Acknowledging these serious limitations, but lacking any better tools, I will seek to apply available quantitative data in a way that might yield, or at least suggest, some qualitative answers. Having confidence in the Lord's counsel, by observing its fruits, we can know something of the tree.

Comparison of Youth Fruits

The youth, ages thirteen to seventeen years, make up the future generation of adults who will be the forthcoming leaders of the church. Understanding the attitudes and behaviors of a church's youth will provide a glimpse into what the future may hold for that church.

The book, *Soul Searching,* by Christian Smith with Melinda Lundquist Denton, provides an illuminating glimpse into the religious and spiritual lives of American teenagers. In reading the book, I became familiar with a remarkable study called the National Study of Youth and Religion (NSYR), the results of which constitute an excellent data set for the comparison of Catholic and Latter-day Saint youth. The following are only a few of the points that stand out from the study in comparing Latter-day Saint (LDS) youth, with the youth of the Catholic Church. "More likely" indicates 10 to 20 percentage points, and "far more likely" indicates more than 20 percentage points:

- LDS youth are far more active in regularly attending church services
- LDS youth are far more likely to believe that their religion is important
- LDS youth are more likely to view God as a real and personal being
- LDS youth are more likely to believe in miracles and life after death

- LDS youth are far more likely to believe in the existence of evil
- LDS youth are far more likely to have had spiritual experiences
- LDS youth are far more likely to believe they receive answers to prayers
- LDS youth are far more likely to participate in their religion
- LDS youth are far more likely to have ever had an experience of spiritual worship that was very moving and powerful
- LDS youth are far more likely to be a part of and participate in their youth group
- LDS youth are far more likely to participate in religious education
- LDS youth are far more likely to discuss spiritual matters with their family
- LDS youth are far more likely to pray with their family
- LDS youth are more likely to have adults in their congregation, other than their parents, who support them and they can talk to
- LDS youth are far more likely to have a welcoming religious environment
- LDS youth are far more likely to have a congregation that helps them understand and maintain moral standards

While numbers from the NSYR reveal significantly more positive results for the Latter-day Saint youth as compared to the Catholic youth, equally revealing was the weakness of the Catholic numbers in comparison with the national average. Marilyn and I are not at all surprised by these numbers and are able to associate numerous experiences from our Catholic past that fully explain the weak Catholic youth numbers.

If, as Jesus said, we can know Christian youth by their fruits, I submit that the data from the NSYR study reveals an abundance of fruit appearing on the tree of The Church of Jesus Christ of Latter-day Saints in the form of solid religious attitudes and behaviors from the church's youth.

Comparison of Adult Fruits

There are several results from the NSYR that reveal a strong and involved adult Latter-day Saint population. Though these numbers are revealing, they are not comprehensive as to adults. Fortunately, we were able to identify an excellent study conducted by The Barna Research Group, Ltd., an independent marketing research company located in southern California. The study was conducted from January 2000 to June 2001 and included telephone interviews with a nationwide random sample of 6,038 adults.

The following are only a few of the notable results from the study, where "more likely" indicates 10 to 20 percentage points, and "far more likely" indicates more than 20 percentage points:

- LDS adults are far more likely than Catholic adults to believe that their religious faith is important
- LDS adults are over three times more likely than Catholic adults to believe that Satan is real and that there is an existence of evil in the world
- LDS adults are over twice as likely as Catholic adults to believe that Jesus Christ was sinless while on the earth
- LDS adults are more likely than Catholic adults to believe that God is all powerful and all knowing

Beyond these important facts are a number of additional attributes that are important to both the Catholic Church and The Church of Jesus Christ of Latter-day Saints. Using the state of Utah as a proxy to The Church of Jesus Christ of Latter-day Saints the following statistics for the state of Utah can be considered as fruit:

- Lowest Nationwide Abortion and Teen Pregnancy Rate: Data from the U.S. Census Bureau lists Utah as the state with the lowest teen pregnancy and abortion rate in the United States.[1]
- Fewer Children out of Wedlock: The latest federal health figures from 1997 rank Utah as having the fewest births to unwed mothers.[2]
- Lowest Divorce Rate: National demographic studies indicate that couples in which both partners are Latter-day Saints (and who marry in the temple) have the lowest divorce rate among all U.S. social and religious groups studied.[3]
- Dramatically Fewer Suicides: The national suicide rate among 20- to 34-year-old males was 2.5 to 3 times higher than among active Latter-day Saints of the same age. Suicide risk was also 3 to 6 times higher among non-Latter-day saints in comparison to active Latter-day Saints.[4]
- Child Friendly Environment: Utah was ranked as one of the top

ten states in which to raise children in the 1996 rankings by the Children's Right's Council.[5]

- Most Charitable: Citizens of Utah rank first among all U.S. states in the proportion of income given to charity by the wealthy (households with annual gross income of more than $200,000).[6]
- Dedicated to Education: Utah has one of the highest high school graduation rates in the nation.[7] Utah "spends a larger percentage of state dollars on education" than any other state.[8]
- Most Self-reliant: Utah spends much less of its budget on public welfare than the other states according to the US Bureau of Census data released April 2000. "On average, other states spend 22.4 percent of their budgets on public welfare . . . Utah spends 14 percent."
- Healthiest: James E. Enstrom of the UCLA medical school, following a large study of Latter-day Saint adults, reports that Latter-day Saints have a much lower rate of mortality than other Americans for all cancers, all cardiovascular diseases, and for all causes of death. The National Institute of Mental Health ranked Utah as the second-lowest U.S. state in new inpatient admissions to state mental hospitals and ranked Utah as having the lowest per-capita alcohol consumption.[9] In 2000 *Self* magazine ranked Provo, Utah, as the healthiest city in the United States for women.

Whether we are considering youth or adults, the aforementioned data and statistics provide a solid view of Latter-day Saints as being dedicated Christians who are bearing good fruit in a number of ways, thus glorifying God as bringing strength of the body of Christ.

Life is not a contest but rather a short time in our eternal journey where we are tested and are able to gain experiences. The Lord's Church was meant to be a guiding force in the children of God's lives to point the way down a narrow path and provide support in staying the course. This comparison of Latter-day Saint and Catholic data is an exercise that was meant to visually validate the counsel given by Jesus Christ of knowing a people by their fruits. Jesus Christ told his disciples, "A good tree cannot bring forth evil fruit, neither can a corrupt tree bring forth good fruit" (Matthew 7:18). One can only conclude from this exercise that the tree represented by The Church of Jesus Christ of Latter-day Saints is not a corrupt tree, but rather a good tree that helps its members reap a harvest of spiritual fruit.

NOTES

1. *Statistical Abstract of the United States 1997: National Data Book* (Washington, D.C.: Census Bureau, U.S. Dept. of Commerce, 1997).

2. U.S. Department of Health and Human Services, October 13, 2005, http://www.ksl.com/?nid=148&sid=118054.

3. Daniel K. Judd. *Religion, Mental Health and the Latter-day Saint* (Bookcraft, 1999).

4. *American Journal of Epidemiology,* 2002; 155:413–19, cited in Charnicia E. Huggins, "High Religious Commitment Linked to Less Suicide," (Reuters Health), *Daily News,* 6 March 2002.

5. "Testimony of Cynthia L. Ewing," Senior Policy Analyst, Children's Rights Council before the U.S. House of Representatives Committee on Ways and Means, February 6, 1995; http://www.peak.org/~jedwards/crc.htm.

6. Kent Allen, "Philanthropy: Give and Take—Individual Potential in Relative Terms" in *Washington Post,* 3 January 1999, A17.

7. U.S. Bureau of Census data, released April 2000.

8. Graduation Rates in the United States, National Center for Education Statistics.

9. Mayrav Saar, "Many faith-based dietary restrictions can benefit body, spirit," *Orange County Register,* 27 July 2001.

17

What's Really Important

ARE you a Catholic? Have you considered taking the same journey Marilyn and I did. If so, this chapter is especially for you.

To be Catholic is to participate in the world's largest and enduring Christian denomination. Catholicism is a rich tradition, an identity, and for many it is a way of life. The thought of joining another church can be frightening—even unthinkable. That is how we felt when we set out on our journey of conversion.

We suggest you ask yourself four key questions. The answers will help determine your course.

1. Do you want more spirituality in your life?

Do you desire a richer and more robust spiritual life for you and your family?

We have met scores of Catholics who are happy with their spiritual lives and are not looking for anything more for themselves or their families. They appreciate being part of the Catholic culture and feel their knowledge of Jesus Christ is adequate. They read the scriptures occasionally but do not find particular pleasure in studying them; they pray occasionally; feel they have the tools to raise their children successfully; and don't want to make a change that might disrupt their family balance. If you are one of these people, the demands inherent in an investigation of and membership in The Church of Jesus Christ of Latter-day Saints may not be for you.

We can tell you that we found these demands to be trivial compared to the rewards; however, this finding is deeply personal. It is one you will have to arrive at on your own. If you want a more robust spiritual life, let's go on to the next question.

2. Are you willing to do what it takes?

If, on the other hand, you are seeking a more robust spiritual life, are you willing to put the effort into making that a reality in your life, and in the lives of your family?

There are many who want more from their relationship with Heavenly Father and Jesus Christ. They want more joy and happiness for their family but don't really want to put forth the effort it takes to make that happen—regardless of the religion they profess. We can tell them it is worth the effort, but our assertions are empty if they do not test them.

We're not talking about quitting your job. We are talking about putting in a significant effort. When Jesus said, "If any man will come after me, let him deny himself, and take up his cross, and follow me, and whosoever will lose his life for my sake shall find it" (Matthew 16:24 and Luke 9:23), he was talking about the children of God taking a more active role in their spiritual lives. This is done through study, service, and sacrifice so that the kingdom of God can be built on earth. Edmund Burke is quoted as saying, "All that is necessary for the triumph of evil is that good men do nothing." Taking yourself and your family into a closer relationship with your Heavenly Father and Jesus is not something you can do in your spare time; it's a way of life that requires active participation.

It is hard work, but at the end of the day, it doesn't feel like work at all. Like rendering an act of service—sometimes reluctant—to someone in need, the reward in joy and happiness you feel at the end of it erases the memory of the reluctance and the hardships.

If you want a more robust spiritual life and are willing to spend a little extra effort to get there, let's go on to the next question.

3. Do you believe the Catholic Church has lost its way?

Since you want a more robust spiritual life and are willing to spend a little extra effort to get there, you have to decide if the Catholic Church can provide you the means to achieve your goal. This means asking an uncomfortable question: Has the Catholic Church fallen away from the fulness of true Christian doctrine, and, if it has, how can it enable you and your family reach their spiritual potential?

We believe that centuries ago the Catholic Church fell away from teaching the fulness of the doctrines and principles of Jesus Christ, lost the authority of the priesthood, and ceased to receive direct revelation from God. What remains today is good, some of it very rich and uplifting, but it no longer advances the fulness of the gospel of Jesus Christ, and therefore, it falls short in its effectiveness to shepherd the children of God back to our Heavenly Father.

Perhaps this was inevitable. The Roman Catholic Church has a long history and has come through deeply troubling times—some of those times marked by conclusive evidence of a falling away. Recent problems involving Catholic clergy and the tentative handling of those problems by Church's leadership add to the growing body of evidence of this decline. A simple question emerges: Does the Catholic Church have the capacity to satisfy the needs of God's children in these troubled times?

We sought at first to meet our spiritual goals by sticking with the Catholic Church and fully utilizing its resources. We tried this for years and ran into chronic shortages of priests, inconsistencies of counsel, a lack of religious education, questionable doctrines, disappointments in leadership, questions left unanswered, and the absence of role models for our children. All of this reinforced our belief that something was wrong, and when we learned about the apostasy, we immediately understood it. We took no delight in this understanding, and it was not delivered to us in that manner—but it explained so much that had before simply mystified us.

If you want a more robust spiritual life, are willing to spend a little extra effort to get there, and feel the Catholic Church has lost its way, let's go on to the last question.

4. Do you want a church that is organized as Jesus Christ organized his church while on earth and has the fulness of the gospel?

Since you want a more robust spiritual life; are willing to spend a little extra effort to find and live such a life; and you do not find the tools you need in the Catholic Church . . . what's next?

You need to find a church that can help you and your family reach the spiritual goals to which you are committed. Dozens of Christian churches would be delighted to have you as a member, but are they organized in the same way that Jesus Christ organized his Church on earth during his public ministry and has the fulness of the gospel? Is this important to you, as it was to us?

If you are interested in finding out more about the restored Church of Jesus Christ on the earth, if you are seeking the spiritual tools and authority necessary to help you and your family reach the full potential for joy and happiness in this life and the next, then you owe it to yourself to take a look at The Church of Jesus Christ of Latter-day Saints . . . a hard look!

Come Find Out for Yourself

If you are where we were so many years ago, it may take you weeks, months, or even years to arrive at the decision that we arrived at so long ago. It was a decision that started with a desire for more, and led to the Church of Jesus Christ and the fulfillment of his promise that "I am come that they might have life, and that they might have it more abundantly" (John 10:10).

We offer our most sincere prayers and encouragement on your behalf. We invite you to do as Jesus Christ implored us to do—to become as little children—and open your heart to the news of the restored gospel of Jesus Christ and allow the Holy Ghost to bear witness to you of its truthfulness. We encourage you to respond to the challenge of Moroni in the Book of Mormon to seek out the truth and allow God the Father to tell you through the Holy Ghost of these things.

The decision to take a hard look at The Church of Jesus Christ of Latter-day Saints will be one of the most important decisions of your life. It was for us, and we have never ceased to thank the Lord for leading us to his church. But whatever your decision, we wish you all of the joy and happiness that our Heavenly Father has to offer through his son Jesus Christ.

Our Heavenly Father loves us, and he would have us love one another.

We love you, dear reader, and pray that your path back to our Heavenly Father is a clear one—full of love, joy, and happiness in this life and the next.

Selected Bibliography

Athanasian Creed DS 75; ND 16.

Ballard, M. Russel. "Let Our Voices Be Heard." *Ensign*, Nov. 2003.

Benedict XII, Benedictus Deus (1336): DS 1000; cf. LG 49.

The Church of Jesus Christ of Latter-day Saints. *Bulletin,* No. 31. Salt Lake City: The Church of Jesus Christ of Latter-day Saints. September 1986.

Catechism of the Catholic Church, Second Edition. 1994.

Catholic Answers. *Pillar of Fire, Pillar of Truth.* El Cajon, 1996.

Challenges for the Year Ahead (pamphlet, 1974). Reprinted in "Things They're Saying." *New Era*, Feb. 1974.

Clark, James R. *Messages of the First Presidency.* Salt Lake City: Bookcraft, 1965–75. 3:112–13.

Clement. *Miscellanies, Book III,* quoted in Colm Luibheid (translator), *Eusebius, The Essential Eusebius.* New York and Toronto: New American Library. 1966.

Code of Canon Law. Libreria Editrice Vaticana. 1983.

Conference Report, Apr. 1971, 18; or *Ensign*, June 1971, 33.

———, Apr., 1937.

———, Oct. 1942.

———, Oct. 1968.

———, Oct. 1998; or *Ensign*, Nov. 1998.

Cullimore, James A. "Q&A: Questions and Answers." *New Era*, Dec., 1975.

D&C and Church History Gospel Doctrine Teacher's Manual. Salt Lake City: The Church of Jesus Christ of Latter-day Saints.

Dahl, Larry E. "I Have a Question." *Ensign*, Mar., 1988.

Ehat, Andrew F., and Cook, Lyndon W. *The Words of Joseph Smith.* 1980.

Elwell, Walter. *Evangelical Dictionary of biblical Theology.* Baker Publishing Group, 1996.

Epistle of Ignatius to the Ephesians.

Eusebius, Eccles. *Hist., Book III,* chap. 32.

Family Guidebook. Salt Lake City: The Church of Jesus Christ of Latter-day Saints, 2002.

Faust, James E. "Born Again." *Liahona*, Jul. 2001.

Fenton, Ben. "Mormons Use Secret British War Files 'to Save Souls'. London." *Telegraph,* Feb. 1999.

First Presidency letter, 14 Nov. 1991.

For the Strength of Youth. Salt Lake City: The Church of Jesus Christ of Latter-day Saints, 2001.

Gaudium Et Spes 47 § 1, Promulgated by Pope Paul VI, December 7, 1965.

General Handbook of Instructions. Salt Lake City: The Church of Jesus Christ of Latter-day Saints, 1989.

Gospel Fundamentals. Salt Lake City: The Church of Jesus Christ of Latter-day Saints, 2002.

Grant, Heber J. *Gospel Standards.* Comp. G. Homer Durham. 1941.

Hales, Robert D. "Gifts of the Spirit." *Ensign*, Feb. 2002.

Hansen P., *Vita Mirabilis.* Louvain, 1668.

Hinckley, Gordon B. "The Symbol of Our Faith." *Ensign*, Apr. 2005.

———, "True to the Faith." *Ensign*, Jun. 1996.

Humanae Vitae 11.

Irenaeus, *Against the Heresies, Book I,* quoted in *Luibheid*, 135–46.

Jessee, Dean C. *The Personal Writings of Joseph Smith.* Salt Lake City: Deseret Book, 1984.

Kimball, Edward L. *The Teachings of Spencer W. Kimball,* 1982.

Kimball, Spencer W. "Small Acts of Service." *Ensign*, Dec. 1974.

———. "When the World Will Be Converted." *Ensign*, Oct. 1974.

———. *The Miracle of Forgiveness*. Barnes and Noble, 2002.

Kirsch, J.P. *The Catholic Encyclopedia*, Volume X. Published 1911. New York: Robert Appleton Company. Nihil Obstat, October 1, 1911. Remy Lafort, S.T.D., Censor. Imprimatur. John Cardinal Farley, Archbishop of New York.

Lectures on Faith. Salt Lake City: Deseret Book, 1985.

McBrien, Richard P. *Encyclopedia of Catholicism*. San Francisco: HarperCollins, 1995.

McConkie, Bruce R. *Doctrines of Salvation*. 1954–56.

———. "The Lord God of the Restoration." *Ensign*, November, 1980.

———. *Mormon Doctrine*. Salt Lake City: Bookcraft, 1958.

———. *A New Witness for the Articles of Faith*, Salt Lake City: Deseret Book, 1985.

McKay, Lewelyn R. *Pathways to Happiness*, 1957.

"Message of the First Presidency." *Improvement Era*, Nov. 1942.

Monson, Thomas S. "An Invitation to Exaltation." *Liahona*, Sept. 1986.

———. "Our Sacred Priesthood Trust." *Ensign*, May 2006.

Nelson, Russell M. "Computerized Scriptures Now Available." *Ensign*, Apr. 1988.

New Revised Standard Version of the Bible, Division of Christian Education of the National Council of the Churches of Christ in the United States of America, 1989.

Occupational Outlook Handbook, 1998-99, UM-St. Louis Libraries Edition. Derived and modified by Raleigh Muns April 14, 1998.

Office of Vocations, Diocese of Providence, http://www.catholicpriest.com/faqs.htm#FAQ1.

Packer, Boyd K. *For All Time and Eternity; Marriage and Family Relations*. Salt Lake City: The Church of Jesus Christ of Latter-day Saints, 2000.

———. *The Holy Temple*. 2001.

Peterson, Donl H. "I Have a Question." *Ensign*, Apr. 1986.

"Protestants, Catholics, and Mormons Reflect Diverse Levels of Religious Activity." Barna Research Group. Ventura. January 2000 to June 2001.

"Religious Beliefs Vary Widely by Denomination." Barna Research Group. Ventura. Jan. 2000 to June 2001.

Revised Standard Version of the Bible, Division of Christian Education of the National Council of the Churches of Christ in the United States of America 1946, 1952, 1971.

Robinson, Stephen E. "Background for the Testaments." *Ensign*, Dec. 1982.

Sacrosanctum Concilium 112.

"Sed Contra Crisis," Zogby International, originally published in *USA Today*. January, 2002.

Smith, Christian with Denton, Melinda Lundquist. *Soul Searching*. Oxford University Press, 2005.

Smith, Joseph F. *Gospel Doctrine*. Deseret Books, 1978, 1999.

Smith, Joseph. *Lectures on Faith*.

Snyder, Walter. "Holy Spirit or Holy Ghost? A Spirited Comparison." http://www.adishakti.org/_/holy_spirit_or_holy_ghost.htm.

St. Augustine, Conf. 9, 6, 14: PL 32, 769-770.

St. John Chrysostom, *De incomprehensibili* 3, 6: PG 48, 725.

———. *Hom. in Lazaro* 2, 5: PG 48, 992?.

St. John Damascene, De fide orth. 3, 24: PG 94, 1089C.

St. John of the Cross, *The Ascent of Mount Carmel*.

St. Justin, *Apol.* 1, 67: PG 6, 429.

Stott, Greg. "Ancestral Passion." *Equinox*, April/May 1998.

Teachings of Presidents of the Church: Spencer W. Kimball. Salt Lake City: The Church of Jesus Christ of Latter-day Saints, 2006.

Teachings of the Prophet Joseph Smith, ed. Joseph Fielding Smith. Salt Lake City: Deseret Book, 1938.

The Catholic Encyclopedia, vol I. Robert Appleton Company, 1907; online edition by K. Knight, 2003;

The Donum Vitae, Instruction on Respect for Human Life in Its Origin and on the Dignity of Procreation. February, 1987.

The National Survey of Youth and Religion (NSYR). University of North Carolina at Chapel Hill, 2002-2003 .

True to the Faith. Salt Lake City: The Church of Jesus Christ of Latter-day Saints, 2004.

Vennari, John. "Limbo to be Cast into the Outer Darkness?" http://www.cfnews. org/Limbo.htm .

Wells, Robert E. "We are Christians Because . . ." *Ensign*, Jan. 1984.

Wesley, John. *John Wesley's Works*, vol. VII.

Youngreen, Buddy. "From the Prophet's Life: A Photo Essay." *Ensign*, Jan. 1984.

About the Author

Eric Shuster is the fifth of six children born to George and Patricia Shuster. He is a graduate of Saint Lawrence Catholic College Preparatory School and earned a Bachelor of Science degree from San Jose State University and a Masters of Science degree from the University of Phoenix. He is a veteran of the information technology industry and the President and CEO of IntelliClear Inc., a Colorado-based market research firm (www.intelliclear.com). Eric is also the Founder and Executive Director of the Foundation for Christian Studies (www.studychristianity.org), a non-profit organization dedicated to the study, teaching, and practice of Christianity. Eric was born into the Catholic faith and was an active member for twenty-seven years. During this time, he served in a variety of lay leadership roles relating to music, youth ministry, and young adult ministry.

Eric's wife, Marilyn, is the third of eight children born to Bruce and Bettie Williams. She is a graduate of Nathan Hale High School and earned a Bachelor of Arts degree from the University of Saint Thomas (magna cum laude). Like Eric, she was born into the Catholic faith and was an active member for thirty-four years. During this time, she served in a variety of lay leadership roles, including certified Catholic youth minister, and Franciscan nun.

In 1989 Marilyn and Eric converted to The Church of Jesus Christ of Latter-day Saints. They have been active Latter-day Saints ever since. They have served in a many ward and stake leadership roles.

The Shusters have three children and make their home in Colorado Springs, Colorado.